The United States and Mexico

The United States in the World:
Foreign Perspectives
Akira Iriye, Series Editor

Already published:

The United States and Britain
H. G. Nicholas

France and the United States:
From the Beginnings to the Present
Jean-Baptiste Duroselle
Translated by *Derek Coltman*

Russia and the United States
Nikolai V. Sivachev and *Nikolai N. Yakovlev*
Translated by *Olga Adler Titelbaum*

Josefina Zoraida Vázquez and Lorenzo Meyer

The United States and Mexico

The University of Chicago Press
Chicago and London

The University of Chicago Press, Chicago 60637
The University of Chicago Press, Ltd., London

94 93 92 91 90 89 88 87 86 85   5 4 3 2 1

Library of Congress Cataloging in Publication Data

Vázquez, Josefina Zoraida.
   The United States and Mexico.

   (The United States and the world, foreign perspectives
   Bibliography: p.
   Includes index.
   1. United States—Foreign relations—Mexico.
2. Mexico—Foreign relations—United States.
I. Meyer, Lorenzo. II. Title. III. Series.
E183.8.M6V39   1985   327.73072   85-1061
ISBN 0-226-85023-4

JOSEFINA ZORAIDA VÁZQUEZ is director
of the Center for Historical Studies at
El Colegio de México.

LORENZO MEYER is professor at the
Center for International Studies at
El Colegio de México.

To the memory of Daniel Cosío Villegas, founder of El Colegio de México, who cared so deeply about Mexico and who was one of the first to understand the importance of a systematic study of the United States.

Contents

List of Maps

Foreword

This book is a volume in the series The United States and the World: Foreign Perspectives. As that title indicates, the series aims at examining American relations with other countries from a perspective that lies outside the United States. International relations obviously involve more than one government and one people, and yet American foreign affairs have tended to be treated as functions of purely domestic politics, opinions, and interests. Such a uninational outlook is not adequate for understanding the complex forces that have shaped the interactions between Americans and other peoples. Today, more than ever before, it is imperative to recognize the elementary fact that the traditions, aspirations, and interests of other countries have played an equally important role in determining where the United States stands in the world. As with individuals, a country's destiny is in part shaped by how other countries perceive it and react to it. A good way to discover how foreigners view and deal with the United States is to turn to a non-American scholar of distinction for a discussion of his country's relations with America.

The authors of this volume are well-known historians who have written extensively on Mexican history, American history, and Mexican-American relations. They have made frequent trips to the United States to do research and to teach. Most of their writings, however, have remained inaccessible to English-language readers, and therefore this book is a particularly welcome addition to the series.

Professors Vàzquez and Meyer describe how the politics, economic interests, and ideologies of the two countries have interacted, and they present a judicious treatment of controversies that have arisen between the United States and Mexico since the Mexican War. Today, when American relations with Mexico are of critical importance because of such issues as Mexican immigrant labor in the United

States, economic and financial instability in Mexico, and American concern with revolutionary activities in Central America, it is more than ever important to transcend a narrowly parochial outlook and to gain an understanding of the Mexican perspectives on the history of those relations. It is to be hoped that this book will be widely read and discussed by officials and citizens in the two countries and elsewhere who are concerned with the peace and welfare of the Western Hemisphere.

AKIRA IRIYE
Series Editor

Preface

The history of Mexican-U.S. relations is a subject that, notwithstanding its importance to both countries, has not produced much general literature, although there are monographs on specific subjects. United as the two countries are by geography, their cultural backgrounds are so different and their interrelations have been so difficult that their interlocking history is not easy to recount.

Authors in the United States seem not to understand to what degree the conquest of half of Mexico's territory in 1848 determined the feelings of resentment and mistrust that have prevailed since that time in the relations between the two countries. These historians surely intend to be objective, but they often omit details that are essential to an understanding of Mexican reactions. Others unwittingly use different criteria by which to judge similar phenomena. For example, almost all U.S. writers emphasize Mexico's stubborn refusal to accept the independence of Texas, but the same writers justify as natural Lincoln's decision not to permit the secession of their own South.

The authors of this book do not claim to clarify all the problems involved in the relations between Mexico and the United States. Our purpose is much more modest: we intend to explore, from today's perspective, the historical space in which the complex and difficult texture of the relations between Mexico and the United States arose and developed. Of course, we have tried to be objective, but we do not claim impartiality, although we have tried to include all the main issues. We are offering the Mexican perspective.

In writing this book, we consulted the available published literature as well as unpublished primary research into certain aspects of Mexican-U.S. relations during the nineteenth and twentieth centu-

ries. We have appended a basic bibliography as a guide to further
reading or analysis.

We would like to clarify the criteria used in defining historical
periods. Following a brief introduction to the history in Chapter 1,
each of the authors has addressed the period with which she or he was
more familiar; Josefina Z. Vázquez has written about the nineteenth
century in Part 1 and Lorenzo Meyer has treated of the twentieth
century in Part 2.

The second chapter provides the minimum necessary background;
that is, the colonization of New England and the first reactions of the
new United States to the Spanish empire in general and to New Spain
in particular. The third chapter deals with one of the most difficult
stages in Mexican-U.S. relations, the period between 1821 and 1848.
This covers the armed confrontation between the two countries that
ended with the loss of half of Mexico's territory. The third chapter
analyzes what we consider a stage of transition, 1848 to 1867, in
which both countries were engaged in their own civil wars. The
discussion of the nineteenth century closes with the period from 1867
to 1898, which began and ended in a relatively cordial atmosphere,
despite serious disputes about the border between the countries. It
was during this period that the United States was industrialized, a
crucial development for Mexico because of the substantial commerce
between both countries and the influx into Mexico of capital from the
United States.

The second part of this book begins with the sixth chapter, a brief
examination of the problems and consequences of the opening of the
Mexican economy to U.S. capital. The seventh chapter is dedicated to
a single decade in which relations between the nations became intense
and extremely strained owing to the negative effect of the Mexican
Revolution of 1910–20 on U.S. economic and political interests. The
eighth chapter continues the analysis of this same problem from 1920
to 1940, when the civil war in Mexico ended and the period of
reconstruction and institutional reforms began; during this period the
United States, which had already become a major world power,
transformed the old-style imperialism into the New Deal. The ninth
chapter deals with the most important aspects of the relations between Mexico and the United States during and following the Second
World War. During that war, Mexico and the United States were
allies. After the war, new bilateral issues—trade, Mexican workers in
the United States, and inter-American politics—began to emerge.
Such differences of interest reveal that the coexistence of countries so

different in power and tradition is not easy. The final chapter is an analysis of the causes and result of the increase of Mexico's activities in the international arena since the seventies. It was precisely in this period that it became necessary to acknowledge and manage the disagreements and incompatibilities that currently characterize Mexican-U.S. relations.

This book was originally presented in a series of seminars in which many of our colleagues at the Center of International Studies and of Historical Studies of El Colegio de México participated. Their careful reading and their comments enriched this book; of particular importance were the contributions of Professor Mario Ojeda. We owe the English version to our translators Gloria Benuzillo and Magda Antebi, as well as to Monica Mansour and Stanley Watson, who not only corrected style but also helped us with many comments that resulted in a clearer text. We also thank Ana Josefa Sanchez and Norma Zepeda M, for their conscientious typing of the manuscript.

Josefina Zoraida Vázquez
Lorenzo Meyer

1

Present Disparities

The contrast between the United States and its neighbor to the south is a striking one. The border between the United States and Mexico marks not only a political division; it divides two very different economies and two cultures. The dramatic difference between cities as close as San Diego and Tijuana makes clear to even the most casual observer the difference between development and underdevelopment, between riches and poverty, between the post-industrial world of the north and the semi-industrial world of the south.

This was not always so. While the United States and Mexico were from the very beginning two different cultures and societies separated by large, almost uninhabited hinterlands, their material differences were not as dramatic. At the beginning of the nineteenth century, per-capita income in the Kingdom of New Spain (Mexico) was only slightly less than half that in the new republic of the United States of America. The population of New Spain in 1810 was 6.1 million, only a million fewer than that of the United States, and Mexico City was an urban center larger than any to the north.

Mexico's long war for independence (1810–21), a bitter civil struggle that ruined the mining industry and affected other vital economic activities, also destroyed the political fabric of the old Spanish colony. The creation of a new and viable political arrangement that followed took more than a half-century and was as destructive of cultural and economic wealth as the war against Spain had been. When peace was finally regained in the 1870s and economic development started anew, the gap between Mexico and the United States had widened so far that it was almost impossible to close:

per-capita income in the United States was almost seven times that of Mexico, and U.S. national income was thirty-five times greater.

The differences, while less acute than a century ago, are still there. At the beginning of the 1980s, per-capita income was four-and-a-half times greater in the United States than in Mexico and gross domestic product about fifteen times as great. In the international arena, economic differences are translated into power differences, and that is exactly what has happened. Both countries are now linked through countless transactions across a two-thousand mile border, but the end-product of such a complex wave of exchanges is perceived differently.

Viewed from the north of the Rio Grande, the relationship between Mexico and the United States is one of interdependence. But viewed from the south of the same river—Mexicans call it Río Bravo—the relationship with the United States is one of dependency. One of the most conventional kind of exchanges among countries—trade—illustrates these differences in the perception of the same phenomenon. In 1980, Mexican exports to the United States comprised 63 percent of all Mexican exports but only 5 percent of all goods imported by the United States. The same year, the United States exported to Mexico 6.7 percent of all goods and services it sold in the international market and these same goods and services comprised 66 percent of all Mexican imports. What was of vital importance to Mexico was of marginal importance to the United States. The picture remains almost the same if for trade is substituted investment, technology, loans, tourism, or almost any other transaction, with the exception of immigration.

It is obvious that the United States is the single most important factor in shaping Mexico's relations with the outside world and that the contrary is not true. Lack of symmetry is the basic characteristic of contemporary United States–Mexico relations. Asymmetry is present even in the way each country views the history of their relationship. From the Mexican perspective, the long history of conflict between the two countries is an integral part of any dealings with the United States. The trauma of the Mexican–U.S. War of the last century, known in Mexico as the American Intervention, for example, is still very much alive. However, from the point of view of the United States, this same historical event is as dead and as irrelevant to the present as the French and Indian war of the mid-eighteenth century. History still shapes Mexican responses to U.S. actions, but not the other way around.

The difference in outlook between Mexico and the United States bears heavily on their approach to common problems. It would be relatively unimportant if the problems that have to be solved by common action were fewer or less important, but that is not so, especially for Mexico. The agenda of U.S.–Mexican relations as the twentieth century draws to a close have become more and more complex; trade imbalances, trade barriers, the impact of sudden changes in one's economy on the other's, foreign investment, transfer of technology, foreign debt, fishing rights, the use of common rivers, undocumented Mexican workers in the United States, problems of environment along the border, so-called in-bond industries in the same area, and tourism.*

Last but not least are the political problems arising from the different perception of revolutionary change in the Caribbean and Central America. If the many problems in these and other parts of the universe of U.S.–Mexican relations are to be solved, or at least managed, the differences in the national interests and international views of both countries have to be understood. A knowledge of the history of such interests and outlooks is a first step toward the attainment of so desirable a goal.

The Earliest Problems

The origin of many ideas and prejudices can be traced back at least to the Anglo-Spanish military confrontations in the New World during the sixteenth century, the establishment of competing and hostile religious structures in areas under their differing control a bit later, and probably to Spanish-English quarrels on the continent of Europe much earlier. And New Spain was known to be rich, a fact that excited greed and envy in New England, although London's mercantilist policies inhibited the New Englanders from exploring the matter further.

Without a doubt, the English colonists were prejudiced against their southern neighbors; evidence of this is the effort exerted by Cotton Mather, who learned Spanish in order to write a small treatise entitled *La Fe del Christian Ambiada a los españoles* (*The Christian Faith Sent to Spanairds*), published in Boston in 1699, for the spiritual

---

*The term *in-bond industries* refers to assembly plants on the Mexican side of the border, in which Mexican workers assemble parts made in the United States; the assemblies are then sent across the border, subject only to a value-added tax.

regeneration of the inhabitants of New Spain. This early Anglo-American missionary work was followed by less idealistic exports: contraband, for instance. In the eyes of the colonists, the kingdom to the south was the owner of riches jealously guarded, promising markets, and lands populated by half-breeds and fanatic papists who were totally lacking in liberty.

Ruling circles in New Spain did not worry too much about their northern neighbors, thinking of them as heretics in the far north, but friction on the borders of Florida and Louisiana in the eighteenth century (Spanish at that time, and so of some concern in Mexico) drew their attention to these areas. When the British colonies attained their independence, Madrid immediately saw the danger to its empire and New Spain slowly became aware of the possible threat to its own position. The only partially formulated objectives of both countries began to take shape at that time: well-informed Mexicans saw room for growth in their vast territories to the north, and the former British colonists were always pressing south and west. While the supposed colossus of the South was becoming weaker, the country in the north grew stronger. Offenses and pretexts made relations more difficult and pushed both countries into events that inevitably led to the Mexican–U.S. War of 1846.

Independence and War

Ever since the beginning of the nineteenth century, when Mexico first became a sovereign state, its relations with the United States have been vitally important. Even Mexico's continued independence rested, in large part, on the outcome of the clash between its effort to defend its territory and the violent territorial and economic expansion of the United States.

In the midst of this unremitting pressure from the north, Mexico strove to instill valid social and cultural institutions into the republic which had supplanted the viceroyalty of New Spain. The problem was to transform a Spanish colony into a nation, a difficult problem because, although its territory seemed to contain almost unlimited natural resources, its population was sparse and in no way homogeneous. Socially, racially, and linguistically, Mexico was badly fragmented, and large areas—especially in its north, where the threat from the United States was most immediate—were almost unpopulated.

The durability of all the countries that emerged from the dismemberment of the Spanish empire in the New World was tested from the first moment; some countries broke up and others have not yet managed to become true national states. New Spain passed the test, and it still seems exceptional that it was the only viceroyalty with two *audiencias*—Mexico and New Galicia to its north—that remained united. However, twice it was on the verge of division: once when the short-lived independent Mexican empire failed in 1823, and again at the end of the war with the United States in 1848.

Geographical proximity to the United States made the Mexican experience unique. Other Latin American countries, with the exception of Paraguay, did not face as many external dangers. The notion that it was the "manifest destiny" of the United States to press west and south was not the only problem from abroad faced by the young Mexican republic: the Spanish tried to reconquer the country, the French attempted two invasions, adventurers as well as Indians attacked. The United States was the main problem, however: its actions left the strongest mark on Mexico's perception of the external world and the deepest imprint on the national consciousness.

The territorial consolidation of the United States reached its climax about the middle of the nineteenth century. The purchase of Alaska; its annexation of the Philippines, Puerto Rico, and the Virgin Islands; the virtual protectorate it established in the Caribbean; and its military action in Mexico during the Revolution of 1910 all confirmed the Mexican view that the expansionist United States was an active threat to its territorial integrity during the first part of the twentieth century.

Economic Change

Following the latter years of the nineteenth century, as a result of the Mexican government's liberal policies and the growing economic strength of the United States, relations between the two countries centered more and more on economic affairs. But their overall relationship between the two countries did not improve as a result; the two economies were so far out of balance that what had been a simple inequality became an unbridgeable gap. By the time of the Mexican Revolution in 1910, U.S. investments in Mexico had become very large, that country's largest financial commitment in any Latin American state. From Mexico's point of view, the United States was the largest foreign investor in the country, more important than any of the European countries which had formerly been the principal foreign investors.

The problem was that the defense of U.S. interests (railroads, mines, oils, plantations) and the reaffirmation of its political predominance in what the United States considered its natural sphere of influence—Mexico, Central America, and the Caribbean—led many administrations in Washington to oppose some of the most significant economic and social changes sought by revolutionary Mexicans and their successors. This conflict, open or disguised but always present, added as it was to the tragic legacy of the nineteenth century, produced a strong nationalistic feeling in Mexico that occasionally became xenophobic but which was usually predominantly and specifically anti-United States. The continuing confrontation with the United States between 1910 and 1940— with its government, entrepreneurs, diplomats, bankers, clergy, and journalists, indeed with every member of the complex U.S. community in Mexico—resulted in the formation of contemporary Mexican nationalist feeling.

The Second World War and the Postwar Period

The Second World War brought about a change in this point of view, since the great jolt suffered by the international power structure led the two countries to quick agreement on all pending matters. This allowed them to cooperate in the great alliance against the Axis countries and in defense of democratic values. The Mexican military contribution to the antifascist effort was symbolic, but its economic contribution to U.S. military commitments was, within its capabilities, considerable.

Beginning in the thirties and especially during the Second World War, the strategic needs of the U.S. government required it to modify its politics vis-à-vis Latin America in general and Mexico in particular. Mexico's authorities were already committed to the process of transforming its economy, primarily dependent on mining and farming, to a more balanced one with much more stress on industry and manufacturing. The advantages of closer collaboration with the United States were obvious: commerce would increase, foreign investment would bring about the needed transfer of technology and an end to undercapitalization, and new industries—such as tourism—would help to exorcise the ghosts of invasion and military threats from north of the border. During this period, Mexican and U.S. national interests seemed to be convergent and mutually supportive.

During the postwar period and cold war between the United States and the Soviet Union, however, it became clear that the apparent coincidence of interests and attitudes between Mexico and its powerful neighbor was ephemeral.

The United States vis-à-vis Latin America

Mexico slowly discovered that Washington's global interests after 1945 left little time to transform the wartime alliance into a permanent and close collaboration, as some Mexican authorities had hoped. For quite some time, Mexico's leaders had assumed that an inter-American alliance would be useful in the transformation of Latin America from an underdeveloped area into a reasonably prosperous and modern region, fostering self-sustaining growth and sociopolitical structures that would lift all of Latin America out of the banana republic stage. From this point of view, the prosperity of all the hemisphere's countries was the best political guarantee of continental security against the external threats that had obsessed the United States since Monroe promulgated his doctrine.

Reality proved different. Latin America interested the United States mainly as the country's authorities perceived a danger from the Soviet Union—as it did in Guatemala, Cuba, Brazil, and Chile. While U.S. reaction to left-wing movements in Latin America contributed very little to the democratization of the area, it was decisive in consolidating an authoritarian mode of development, supporting dictatorships very similar to those which, during the forties, had been the United States' main enemies.

The U.S. government decided, during the postwar period, that when Latin American countries needed U.S. capital and technology, these would be channeled through private enterprises and not made available by loans and by transfers between governmental organizations, as they had been, although briefly and exceptionally, during the war. It thus remained Latin America's responsibility to build up and maintain an atmosphere favorable to foreign investment. According to Mexican nationalists—represented throughout the country's social spectrum, although not with the same intensity—this U.S. policy was a renewal of the past economic and cultural penetration which had undermined Mexico's capacity for independent action.

The dilemma persists. How can a country bordering the United States, one concerned with maintaining its national identity, also develop into a strong and modern capitalist economy?

Josefina Zoraida Vázquez

Part One

2

The English Settlements in America

The English settlements along the North American coast were established more than a century later than the Spanish empire in America, and their humble character made it difficult to imagine that some day they would surpass proud New Spain in power. The lands colonized by the English did not possess the mining resources of the two great Spanish viceroyalties—Peru and the Kingdom of New Spain. However, this lack became an advantage because it allowed the English colonies to develop without interference from the home country; within a century, these settlements had become prosperous agricultural or commercial provinces.

Indeed, the northern lands, disdained by sixteenth-century explorers, constituted splendid shelters for those fleeing religious persecution or bypassed by the economic transformation of England. Puritans, Catholics, Quakers, and other minority groups obtained large allocations of land and turned them into colonies in which to welcome their coreligionists. The royal grants of huge tracts of land also promised an improved standard of living while, at the same time, they created an ever-present temptation to search further for even better land. The American West always seemed to offer something more, and once people adjusted to living in the solitude of new places it became easier to risk exploring the unknown; they could profitably sell their possessions to the newly arrived and go farther inland. This simple operation was the first pattern of Anglo-American expansionism.

The English colonies tended to reproduce the society they had left behind, but their experience in the New World changed habits and institutions, creating new relationships among people and their institutions. Social hierarchies became more flexible and the ownership of land reduced social differences. In other words, a revolutionary society arose, unaware of its character.

But there were important differences among the English colonies. The southern colonies developed prosperous plantations exploited by slave labor imported from Africa, and in those colonies a society developed in which some people enjoyed exceptional privileges while others lacked any rights at all and were bought and sold as merchandise. Nonetheless, before the War of Independence, a set of privileges or rights commonly held by free white males allowed these settlers to identify themselves with each other. They were distinguished from Europeans by the possession of rights which were merely a goal, even during the eighteenth century, in the most enlightened European countries.

In 1763, at the end of the Seven Years War in Europe, the Treaty of Paris bestowed total victory on Great Britain. The colonial possessions of France and Spain were traded away. France lost Canada and its possessions in India, as well as some islands in the West Indies. Spain lost Cuba, conquered by the English during the war, although it was later traded back for the Floridas. France, to compensate its ally, yielded Louisiana to Spain.

The Treaty of Paris greatly affected European equilibrium, since it made Great Britain a real empire despite its financial impoverishment during the war. Britain's colonies were until then considered too inconsequential to merit a specific administrative department within the British government, but the extent of the new acquisitions created the need for organized and systematic political, financial, and military relations with its lands overseas. As a result of this unexpected situation, the British colonies in America were placed under stricter supervision. The Crown designated governors, and the autonomy of the colonies was weakened. Since they all had representative bodies to control important affairs and approve taxes, they soon felt that their relative independence of the Crown was being threatened.

It is thus not difficult to understand why the colonists resisted the belated attention visited upon them and why a long struggle over commercial practices and political philosophy arose. Hostilities erupted in 1775; and, on 4 July 1776, the thirteen colonies declared their independence and established a Confederation of States.

The United States of American and Spain

It was one thing for the British colonies to declare their independence, another to win it. Independence could be won only when the British authorities were expelled from their lands, thus the colonists turned, for help, to France, so recently England's victim. By 1778, France was sufficiently convinced of the feasibility of the revolutionists' victory to sign a treaty of friendship and commercial relations with them. Spain was invited to join France but delayed, fearing that support of a rebellion in North America would set a dangerous example for the Spanish possessions to the south. Spain finally agreed in April 1779, in hope of recovering Gibraltar and Minorca, lost in the Treaty of Utrecht in 1713. French diplomats triumphed not only over Spanish scruples, but also persuaded Holland to cooperate. Russia organized the League of Armed Neutrality, to which nearly all of the maritime states of Europe eventually acceded, leaving England diplomatically isolated.

By the end of 1782, the British government finally accepted the independence of the Confederation of the United States of America. On 3 September 1783 a new treaty was signed in Paris, by the terms of which Great Britain yielded Senegal and Tobago to France and Minorca and the Floridas to Spain. In fact, the treaty made Spain the owner of all the littorals of the Gulf of Mexico for the first time. Although Spain did not recognize the United States as a sovereign country, it exchanged diplomatic representatives who were soon elevated to the rank of plenipotentiaries.

Great Britain set generous boundaries for its thirteen newly independent colonies. The southern border was the thirty-first parallel, the northern one was more or less the present border with Canada, and the western one was the east bank of the Mississippi River. Thus, the United States shared its borders with two great European naval powers: to the south and west with Spain, and to the north and northwest with Great Britain. Map 1 shows the political situation in America following the Treaty of Paris of 1783.

Luck favored the new nation. Events between 1789 and 1815 kept the European powers so busy that the United States, born a pigmy according to Charles III's minister, the Count of Aranda, had time to consolidate its organization and to expand. The wisdom and pragmatism of its founders played an important role: they persuaded the separate colonies to yield a substantial portion of their political and economic autonomy and to the new federal government.

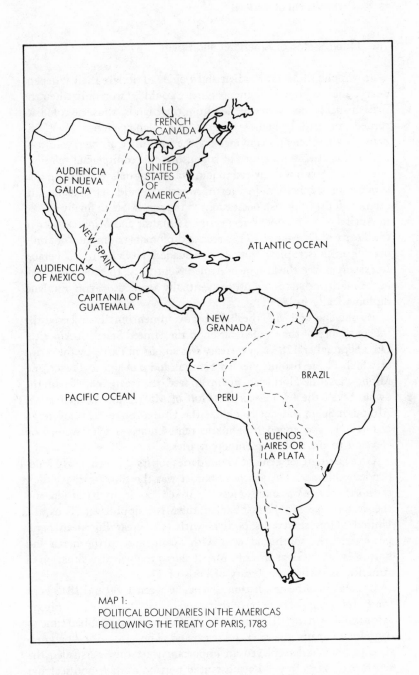

MAP 1:
POLITICAL BOUNDARIES IN THE AMERICAS
FOLLOWING THE TREATY OF PARIS, 1783

Spain soon became aware of the danger the new nation presented to her American possessions and proceeded to encourage settlements, to establish *presidios* (garrisons), and to fortify the borders of New Spain. But after 1789, events took an adverse course for Spain. The French Revolution, which affected European life in general, weakened Spain particularly, since it marked the end of the Family Compact between the ruling houses of France and Spain which had allowed for the close coordination of national policies between the two countries. An incident in Nookta, Vancouver, forced Spain to acknowledge Great Britain's rights in the Pacific Coast of Upper California. Spain's position became more and more precarious; alternately an ally or an enemy to the successive French revolutionary governments, Spain lost political strength, a circumstance ruthlessly exploited by the new country. In 1793, the French, with help from the United States, encouraged civil disorder in Louisiana. Even though the plan did not prosper, Spain appeased the United States by signing the Treaty of San Lorenzo. This agreement gave the United States the right to navigate the Mississippi River, and recognized as its all the territory north of the thirty-first parallel. The treaty was an error, since it included in U.S. territory the forts that protected Spanish ports of New Orleans and Mobile. Spain also committed itself to preventing Indians from raiding American territories, an obligation it was unable to fulfill and which engendered many problems, including the loss of the Floridas.

By 1796, Spain had again drawn closer to France, but with the rise of Napoleon Bonaparte and the greatly enhanced military strength of that country, it slipped into the role of a client state. Later, in 1805, Spain lost the greater part of its effective fleet in joint operations with the French at Tragalgar.

Even earlier, in 1800, Spain signed the secret Treaty of San Ildefonso by which it was forced to return Louisiana to France. This treaty stated that if a further transfer should take place, Spain would have the option of re-acquiring the territory. In 1803, however, Napoleon offered to sell it to the United States for $15 million, not even taking Spain into account. Owing to the magnitude of Napoleon's power, Spain could offer only a feeble protest. This transaction became the source of many problems, both for Spain and for Mexico, since the borders of the Louisiana Territory were never specified. The United States took advantage of this fact to claim Texas as part of Louisiana, although Texas had always been Spanish and had been clearly defined in the maps of the time as a separate province.

Despite their alliance, and even after Napoleon had forced the king of Spain to yield his crown to him, Napoleon's troops invaded Spain in 1808. Some of the Spanish colonies in America took advantage of this situation and declared themselves independent. The United States—quick to seize an opportunity—advanced on western Florida and occupied it in 1810.

As part of its struggle against the Napoleonic occupation, Spain became an ally of Great Britain. Thus, in 1812, when the United States declared war against England, it also announced the annexation of western Florida. By then, the Spanish had convened in Cádiz to establish a constitutional monarchy, but the new government was precarious. In consequence, Louis de Onís, Spain's agent in the United States, was not granted recognition as such until 1815.

Once he was able to present his credentials as representative of Ferdinand VII, who had by then recovered his crown, Onís hastened to bring up with the Department of State a number of issues concerning Florida and, of course, the question of the boundary between Texas and the Louisiana Territory. After a long diplomatic give-and-take, the United States agreed to talk. John Quincy Adams, who represented the United States, insisted that the Rio Grande be the border between the United States and the Spanish empire. Onís, assisted by documents and evidence, insisted that it should be the Sabine River, which today serves as the boundary between Louisiana and eastern Texas. The disagreement was settled only by a new invasion of eastern Florida, led by General Andrew Jackson in 1818, which convinced Spain to sell the disputed territory if, in exchange, the United States would recognize a satisfactory border between New Spain and the United States.

The agreement, known as the Transcontinental Treaty or the Adams-Onís Treaty, was not signed until 22 February 1819. The border was set from the outlet of the Sabine River, along its course to the thirty-second parallel, from there in a straight line east to the Red River, and along it until it reached the Arkansas River. It then proceeded in a straight line to the forty-second parallel, the northern border, and thence to the Pacific. The boundary established by Spain and the United States in 1819 is shown on map 2.

This treaty was a stunning victory for the United States, which thus obtained an outlet to the Pacific. Moreover, the United States established a pattern of seizing a territory by force and paying for it later on. Spain was to be paid $5 million for Florida, but the United States kept the money to cover various claims. Spain was never paid.

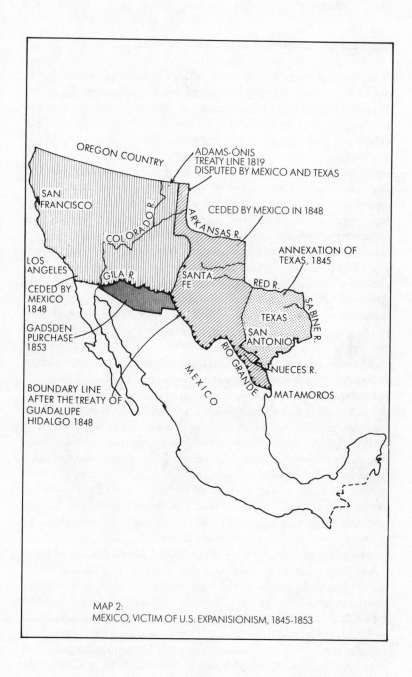

MAP 2:
MEXICO, VICTIM OF U.S. EXPANISIONISM, 1845-1853

The Spanish Settlements in Southern America

In most of Spanish-colonized America, Indian settlements were not exterminated but were conquered and Christianized. Thus, the Spanish founded their society upon those already existing; following previous patterns of conquest elsewhere in the world, they simply carved out for themselves a privileged status.

The Spanish thus created a mixed society in which many Indian institutions persisted. And, as there were also slaves imported from Africa, the society that resulted was a complex one. Legally, the society was divided into estates, in which each group had a more-or-less defined status. In reality, marriages among the different racial groups were so common that only the whites could recognize each other easily. The wide range of castes (people of mixed parentage) made it difficult to discern the difference between them and Indians and even blacks. Languages, as well as race, were heterogeneous. Although the whites and Indians enjoyed various privileges, tribute was exacted from the Indians and power and wealth were concentrated in the conquering Spanish group, a situation which was resented by the rest of the population.

The unifying forces were Christianization and the subjection of the Indians to the power of the Spanish Crown: the racial mix, along with the recognition by the Catholic Church and the Spanish Crown of the essential equality of all human beings regardless of race, formed the basis for relatively liberal Spanish legislation. There was less fear of racial vengeance in New Spain, a benefit deriving from the intermingling of the different races. And when, in 1829, slavery was abolished by an independent Mexican government, it was a relatively simple matter, perhaps because slaves were not at the base of the economic system, or perhaps because the North European Calvinist concept of predestination, which provided a theological foundation for existence of slavery, had no place in Spanish thought.

The portion of the Spanish empire that had boundaries with the young North American republic to the west was, in 1804, the richest of the Spanish kingdoms in the eighteenth century. Its vast territory extended, after 1819, from the forty-second parallel to the Captaincy General of Guatemala. Its mining, agriculture, and commerce yielded considerable sums of money that Spain used, in part, to help support other colonies. This siphoning off of revenue did not sit well with the criollos, those of Spanish ancestry, who sponsored the independentist ideas that arose at the end of the eighteenth century. The criollos were also influenced by the enlightened despotism that was pervading Europe, including Spain, and by the French Revolution. The Bourbon monarchy's reforms, intended to secularize and modernize Spanish institutions, created additional resentment in New Spain. The establishment of intendencies and the direct collection of taxes by the Spanish government deprived the more influential colonial groups of some of their privileges. The expulsion of the Jesuits left the criollos without their schools, and the decree of 1804 that disentailed the properties of the Catholic Church deprived them of part of the capital of the Juzgado de Capellanías y Obras Pías, which in practice acted as central bank of New Spain. And the revolution to the north provided an example of what could be done.

The Movement for Independence in New Spain

By the beginning of the nineteenth century, political dissatisfaction in the Spanish colonies had become an insurgent movement. When Napoleon usurped the Spanish throne in 1808, the people of New Spain seized their opportunity. The numerous criollos and Spaniards who enrolled in this movement were, however, violently and successfully opposed by a reactionary group which abruptly ended their reach for independence, leaving them no alternative but to conspire and struggle. In 1810, a Creole priest, Miguel Hidalgo, started a fleeting movement that inflamed the entire nation and mortally wounded the viceroyalty. Unlike the autonomist criollo movement that occurred throughout Spanish America, the movements led by Hidalgo and his successor, José María Morelos, mobilized other social groups and led a wider social revolution whose goals were to impose a more just social order through the abolition of slavery and the exacting of tribute from the Indians, and by redistributing the land.

The attempt in 1812 to establish a more liberal government in Spain afforded the colonists their first opportunity for representation in the Spanish Cortes. The new constitution made Spain a parliamentary monarchy and guaranteed the liberties sought by the enlightenment: the equality of all Spanish subjects and the abolition of the American-Indian tributes. However, when Ferdinand VII reoccupied the Spanish throne in 1814, he abolished the constitution and restored absolute monarchy.

By 1815, the authorities in New Spain had succeeded in restoring peace to much of the country, but the central area had suffered great losses of life and property, and order had not been totally imposed. The voluntary and compulsory loans demanded by Spain, and the struggle for independence itself, triggered a flight of capital from New Spain. Once absolutism had been safely restored in Madrid, a number of rich businessmen transferred their money and themselves back to the home country.

Toward the end of the decade, as we have seen, events in Spain again offered an opportunity for military action to reinstate the Constitution of 1812. In New Spain the time was ripe; most socially conscious groups desired autonomy. The representatives of New Spain at the Spanish Court struggled for a restoration of the Constitution in order to permit at least limited autonomy within the empire. Within New Spain, a criollo officer, Agustín de Iturbide, commander of the royalist troops, joined forces with the only rebel who had maintained the insurgent struggle in the south, Vicente Guerrero.

In February 1821, a plan for the independence of Mexico was proposed by these various allies. It called for the union of all racial groups, the establishment of the Catholic religion as the only religion within New Spain, and the seating on the throne of the newly independent country of one of the princes of the Spanish Bourbons, the ruling house of Spain. On 27 September, thanks to the cooperation of the last *jefe político*, Juan O'Donojú, this independence was declared.* New Spain became the Mexican Empire, Iturbide was enthroned, and the Central American territories decided to join the new state.

The optimism of the criollos was uncontainable, but the basis of their new government was weak. The constant outflow of money since 1804 had impoverished the country. The economy was bankrupt: mining and agricultural activities had been drastically curtailed, and trade and industry were seriously damaged. The debt had reached over seventy-six million pesos, for the new nation had agreed to pay the debts created by Spain in the long struggle against independence. In addition, the Spanish Court, fortified by the Holy Alliance, did not recognize Mexico's independence and it was necessary for the new nation to go further into debt to defend itself. The new nation was also threatened by British, U.S., and French ambitions, as well as by domestic dissension. The omens were not favorable.

*A *jefe político* was a governor with executive, military, and judicial powers.

Relations between the Two New Countries

During their struggle for independence, the people of New Spain turned to their northern neighbors, considering them a natural partner, and tried to gain their cooperation. However, things were not as they thought: the United States saw in every neighboring territory, to the north, south, east, or west, an area for possible expansion. As Thomas Jefferson told his friend Archibald Stuart, a prominent Virginia legislator, in 1786: "Our Confederacy must be viewed as the nest from which all America, North and South, must be peopled." These ambitions were freely expressed in speeches, and expeditions of filibusters into Spanish territories multiplied.* Later, when Jefferson was president of the United States, he was visited by Baron Alexander Von Humboldt, who stopped in Washington on his return trip to Europe from a South American tour and made a copy of Von Humboldt's map of the Kingdom of New Spain, based on the information gathered for him by students at the College of Mining in Mexico City. The map of course contained what was then known about the Louisiana Territory, and one has to wonder whether Jefferson had in mind the Lewis and Clark expedition into that area which followed shortly.

On the other hand, the U.S. government followed the same cautious policy set by its first president: it avoided involvement in European or Latin American affairs. But weapons were sold and independence was encouraged by informal agents who brought along propaganda and distributed copies of U.S. Constitution.

While U.S. concern for its southern neighbors centered on preventing their seizure by some European power, the leaders of the movement for Mexican independence turned to the north for help and for a model to follow. The first Mexican agents, Pascacio Ortiz de Letona and Bernardo Gutiérrez de Lara, were commissioned in 1810 by Hidalgo and by Ignacio Allende, an army captain who had become a revolutionary leader, to create a defensive and commercial alliance. Ortiz de Letona was arrested before embarking. Bernardo Gutiérrez de Lara managed to interview James Monroe, then U.S. secretary of state, and immediately became aware of the young nation's intention of profiting from the situation. He renounced any further diplomatic

---

*Filibusters, prominent in the U.S. expansionist era, were men who took part in private expeditions organized to seize control of territories and set up local governments that would then apply to the United States for annexation.

efforts and organized an expedition to make Texas independent of Spain. The abundance of U.S. adventurers interested in joining his foray into that territory created problems for the Spanish authorities.

Morelos, in his turn, also appointed some agents, including two men from the United States, but they succeeded only as purchasers of weapons. The Congress of Apatzingán—elected in the territory dominated by Morelos to draw up a constitution for the newly independent nation—then appointed José Manuel Herrera. He left for the United States with a plaintive letter written by Morelos: "we had faith . . . in the powerful aid from the United States, who with their example, had almost been our guide . . ." It was all useless. No treaties were drawn, no help was offered, and there was no recognition. The situation became even more desperate after Ferdinand VII recovered the Spanish throne in 1814, for the United States then banned all shipments of arms to the former Spanish colonies.

Before the declaration of Mexico's independence, one U.S. agent, James S. Wilcox, who had come to Mexico some time before, wrote to Johnn Quincy Adams, by then secretary of state, urging him to recognize the new nation. Later on, he was the bearer of a letter from Foreign Minister Juan Manuel Herrera, in which the establishment of the Mexican empire was formally announced. Adams replied in February 1822. He promised to appoint a minister to Mexico; however, Joel R. Poinsett, a rich South-Carolina planter, was sent only in the capacity of U.S. agent, without diplomatic status. Poinsett was nonetheless a true republican, spoke good Spanish, and had lived in Chile.

Despite the uncertainty of recognition in the United States, Iturbide, after he was declared emperor, sent José Manuel Zozaya to Washington as minister pleni-potentiary. Zozaya arrived on 20 December 1822 with extensive instructions: draw treaties, negotiate a loan, secure help in case of a war with Spain, obtain information on U.S. intentions about the border with Louisiana, and look for settlers for the territories in the northern, almost uninhabited, parts of the Empire.

Poinsett returned from Mexico satisfied with his trip. This clever U.S. agent had performed his mission well. He achieved some agreement about the settlement of Texas (as we shall see in the following chapter). And, aware of the threat of the republican movement to Iturbide's Mexican monarchy and its imminent downfall, he advised his country to delay recognition. But the pressure of some groups that sympathized with Latin American independence were such that

Adams decided to draw up an official statement of recognition of the Mexican Empire on 27 January 1823. No minister was sent until 1825 because of the hesitancy of the young republic to interfere in international problems and because various candidates declined the post.

In March 1823, Iturbide abdicated, the Mexican empire collapsed, and it seemed as though its enormous territory would be broken up. Central America and Chiapas seceded and many Mexican states declared themselves free and sovereign. There was no authority other than the National Congress, but it took effective action to maintain the union. Its new republican formula proved attractive and, except for Central America, the rest of the former empire decided to become part of the federation of the United States of Mexico.

However, the new and the untried federal institutions were established just as the troops of the Holy Alliance were restoring absolutism to Spain. Observers both in and outside Mexico anticipated that an absolutist Spain would make every effort to reestablish its authority in Mexico, and there was understandably great concern in Mexico City and in European capitals.

This fear of possible war moved Great Britain to invite the United States to declare jointly that the independence of the former Spanish colonies was a fact, that they trusted that an agreement between Spain and her ex-colonies would be reached, and that it was admissible that the colonies be transferred to the rule of any other power. The possibility of dividing America among the powers of the Holy Alliance existed, particularly since Alexander I's ukase of 1821, assuming Russia's rights over the northwestern coast of America, from the fifty-first to the seventy-first parallel. Great Britain exchanged notes with France and was reassured to learn that the Holy Alliance would not back Spain in restoring its authority in the New World; therefore, the joint declaration was left pending. However, the United States government felt threatened and acted on its own behalf. On 2 December 1823 President James Monroe, in his annual message, proclaimed the doctrine that has been given his name and that contained the warning that his country would not tolerate any further European colonization or intervention in the Americas. Although the young republic had very little chance of carrying out its threat, the declaration clearly demonstrated that U.S. politicians considered the entire continent a natural zone of influence.

For Mexico, still suffering the presence of a Spanish garrison in San Juan de Ulúa, just across from Veracruz, it was important to obtain

British recognition and a loan with which to buy arms and ships that would enable the country to expel this last Spanish bastion. Britain's Prime Minister Canning sympathized with Mexico, and at the news of Iturbide's final failure and his execution, which demonstrated the new Mexican Republic's resolve and stability, Canning granted it recognition on 31 December 1824. Before this, two loans had been negotiated. They were to become a problem later, but for the time being they enabled the country to buy arms and ships, push out the Spaniards, and recover San Juan de Ulúa in 1825.

Following British recognition of the new nation, the United States hastened to appoint a minister plenipotentiary. Joel R. Poinsett, the former U.S. agent, was designated and accredited. His arrival marked the beginning of a difficult period of relations between two neighboring countries with such different pasts.

3

The Most Difficult Decades: 1824–1848

The United States: Model and Menace

Mexico's attitude toward the United States continued to be a combination of admiration and distrust. The northern neighbor, after barely a half-century of existence, had succeeded in establishing itself as a stable nation enjoying material advancement that was evident to all observers. Still, despite its own colonial experience, it had acted very warily toward movements for independence in Latin America. Some Mexican politicians, such as its first foreign minister, José Manuel Herrera, who served as agent of the Congress of Apatzingán to the United States in 1814, were aware of the desire of the United States to absorb Mexican territory. They were nevertheless, impressed by the miracles of free trade, free settlement, and free enterprise and decided to use similar practices in Mexico in order to attain the same results.

The liberties they yearned for, however, did not produce the results they expected: instead, from a political dependence on Spain, Mexico advanced only to an economic dependence on the new imperialists. In the absence of native capital and manufactured goods, the opening of Mexican borders to commerce and investment only helped foreigners gain control of most of the trade and the mines, while the importation of finished goods only set back the incipient textile industry. The result of freely admitting new settlers to relatively unpopulated areas was even worse.

In 1821, the Mexican's reaction against the mercantilist restrictions of the Spanish empire had been only natural. True, after the late-eighteenth century, the Bourbons had loosened those restrictions somewhat; later, the Napoleonic invasion of Spain in 1808 and its subsequent war for independence had provided Mexico with the opportunity for greater contact with foreign countries, both legal and illegal. It was thus no surprise to find foreigners firmly settled in New Spain after it achieved its own independence. With the establishment of the new nation, a sharply increased flow of emigrants turned from the United States toward Texas, and a constant flow of people and merchandise streamed through the ports and the road south to Santa Fe.

Mexico's initial policy of opening its doors to settlement had one severe limitation: only Catholics were allowed to immigrate, for religion was the only common denominator of a population so heterogeneous in language, mores, and racial mixture. The new Federal Republic, established in 1823, delegated to the state governments the task of coordinating and administering this colonization. Thus, after 1824, Texan concessions were negotiated in Saltillo, the capital of Coahuila, and not in Mexico City. Lucas Alamán, a young man who distrusted the United States and who was a fervent advocate of Latin American solidarity, was in charge of foreign affairs at the center.

The new U.S. minister, Joel R. Poinsett, had previous experience in Latin America; he had been to Chile and had acted as the U.S. agent in Mexico. His instructions were clear: to negotiate a treaty of friendship and a commercial agreement giving preferential treatment to his country; to counteract British activity; and to halt Mexican–Columbian plans to emancipate Cuba, making it clear that, if necessary, the United States would annex that island because of its geographic position. He also had some propositions to make. The first was the joint construction of a commercial road from Missouri to Santa Fe; the second was the relocation of Mexico's western border from the Sabine River to the Rio Grande, on the ground that the Mexicans would thereby be spared the problem of fighting the belligerent Indians of the area. He was also to remind the Mexicans of his country's early recognition of their independence and of how grateful they were for having the U.S. Constitution to use as a model for their own in 1824. He was instructed to be constantly ready to explain the operation of the U.S. Constitution.

By the time Poinsett presented his credentials to President Guadalupe Victoria, Victoria had already received the British minister plenipotentiary. This act symbolized the executive's determination to seek equilibrium with help from England, which had already signed a trade agreement with Mexico. Poinsett decided that he, too, should look for allies. He found them among the radical members of the national legislature, attained great influence over them, and helped them to negotiate the authority to found in Mexico a York Masonic Lodge subordinated to the Grand Lodge of Pennsylvania.

A confrontation between Poinsett and Foreign Minister Alamán could be foreseen. Ever since their first meeting, Alamán had been firmly against the expansionism of the United States. He never admitted to any doubts about the border, inasmuch as Mexico had inherited the clauses of the Transcontinental Treaty signed by Spain with the United States. In response to the U.S. hopes for acquiring most-favored nation status through a commercial treaty, Alamán made it clear that Mexico wished to reserve that status for other Latin American countries. In regard to the proposed road to Santa Fe, he said that it should first be determined what articles could be traded and by whom. The foreign minister also objected to the proposal to have the U.S. flag cover the merchandise; not even Great Britain had asked this.

Alamán's bold attitude bothered Poinsett, who did not hesitate to use the influence he had gained within the radical group to force Alamán out of the cabinet. By September 1825, Alamán was replaced by Manuel Gómez Pedraza who, in turn, was replaced by Sebastián Camacho. These changes did not modify Mexico's policies, though they did weaken Latin American solidarity, which Alamán had declared the basis of Mexican foreign policy, and they did lead to the failure of the Inter-American Congress in Panama. During the preparations for that meeting, both Victoria and Grand Columbia's president, Francisco de Paula Santander, insisted on having the United States participate even though that country showed no interest in continental unity. The agreements that were discussed in Panama were not approved, and only a few countries participated in the second meeting, which was held in Tacubaya, Mexico. Disorganization and bankruptcy had forced the new Latin American countries to concentrate on their own problems and made them incapable of working together to make Bolivar's dream of a united Hispanic America come true.

Poinsett achieved great influence in Mexican politics. While he was very careful not to raise international issues that could hurt Mexican sensibilities, he was not as careful in domestic political affairs. His alliance with the radicals enraged the traditionalists and those who feared that a foreign ambassador's intervention could jeopardize the country's sovereignty.

The U.S. minister realized that the questions of the border and of the future purchase of Texas, which he had proposed as U.S. agent to

Francisco Azcárate in 1822 and then to Alamán in 1825, were very delicate subjects. He therefore never tried to insist on these despite Secretary of State Henry Clay's desire for progress in these matters. It was only after Hayden Edwards', a would-be colonist, organized an uprising in Anáhuac (later Galveston) to emancipate Texas that Poinsett again suggested relocation as a solution. Even then, however, the Mexicans agreed among themselves not to discuss this issue further, and Poinsett advised his government to wait for the time when the steady American colonization of Texas would bear fruit. Mexico's position on this matter has always been criticized by U.S. politicians and analysts; they cannot understand the stubborn refusal of the Mexican government—badly in need of money—to sell land that was almost uninhabited. The United States had long been able to purchase land from the British Crown, the Indians, France, and Spain, but the Mexicans had received their territory as an inheritance. The difference in the two countries' point of view was irreconcilable.

In 1827, Secretary of State Henry Clay urged Poinsett to offer $1 million as compensation for the territory up to the Rio Grande, and in 1829 Secretary of State Martin Van Buren took advantage of Mexico's difficult situation when the Spanish attempted to reconquer the country, and again tried to consummate the transaction. This time the offer was either for purchase or mortgage. The offer was doubly painful to the Mexicans: besides having to deal with the U.S. ambitions, they were made aware of the very limited meaning of the Monroe Doctrine, for the Spanish soldiers reached Mexican coasts in U.S. merchant vessels.

Despite his ability to penetrate influential circles in Mexico City, Poinsett's diplomatic negotiations were a failure; none of his initiatives prospered. The only treaty that was signed was one of limits and, in fact, one which confirmed the Transcontinental Treaty and thus the failure of the attempt to move the border toward the west. This treaty was not ratified until 1836, after Texas had declared its independence, an event which, in practice, invalidated it.

Neither did Poinsett succeed in drawing up a commercial treaty, for the following reasons: religious tolerance was demanded for U.S. citizens; no agreement about the borders was reached; and there was the problem of returning fugititve U.S. slaves who had escaped to Mexico. With great effort, Poinsett succeeded in overcoming most of these difficulties and, by 1828, had managed to stipulate that "perfect reciprocity" obtain and even in having an agreement ratified by the U.S. Senate. But the Mexican Senate did not ratify the treaty, being unable to agree to commit itself to the restitution of fugitive slaves. The aversion provoked by the minister's intrusions into domestic politics also played an important role: his own friend, President Vicente Guerrero, Grand Master of the York Lodge, felt compelled to ask for his recall. Thus, on 23 December 1829, Poinsett requested his passports in a letter expressing his regrets and his belief that the friendship between the two countries should be above party passions. The new, traditionalist government led by Anastasio Bustamante ignored this comment. Poinsett left on 2 January 1830.

Meanwhile, in Washington, Anthony Butler was appointed the new minister to Mexico. He had been in Mexico since late 1829, on a business trip connected with land speculation in Texas. Butler was Jackson's personal friend, and although he was also from the South, he differed from Poinsett, who had been polite and courtly. Butler was a rough man, a heavy drinker, and violent in argument. No sooner had he occupied his post when the newspapers reported that his main mission was to purchase Texas. In fact, among other instructions, he was to move the border as far west as possible; prevent Lorenzo de Zavala, a Mexican who had purchased property in Texas, from obtaining permission to settle near the border between Texas and the United States; and to notify the Mexicans that not until they signed a trade agreement would the treaty concerning the limits be ratified. He was also asked to question the ill-treatment to which Minister Poinsett had been subjected.

President Bustamante reinstated Lucas Alamán as foreign minister, and Butler found no support for his cunning arguments about the convenience of setting the border in the desert between the Rio Grande and the Nueces River. According to his obscure interpretation, it was the Sabine Lake and not the Sabine River that the Transcontinental Treaty mentioned. In order to support his arguments, he spread rumors that the northern Mexican states were seceding from the country and insisted on the incapacity of Mexicans to govern themselves. Alamán, who by then had reports from Manuel Mier y Terán, the special envoy to the northern Mexican provinces, was convinced more than ever of the danger that the United States presented, not only to Mexico but to all of Latin America. On 13 March 1831, in an effort to obtain help from other Latin American countries, Alamán sent them a circular and two commissioners, Díez de Bonilla and Juan de Dios Cañedo, explaining the threat and appealing to solidarity in order to defend Latin American independence and integrity. This initiative, known as the Family Pact, was a failure; U.S. dynamism won an easy victory over Latin American stagnation.

Butler also made no progress regarding the border; finally, convinced that the Mexicans would never sell, he agreed to the Adams-Onís line. An exchange of signatures took place in 1832; however, the agreement did not take effect because the members of the commissions in charge of recording the border in maps and on the ground were not appointed. After several deadlines had expired, a new one was set in April 1835: the agreement was to be ratified on 30 April 1836 and was to become effective within one year from that date. The United States nevertheless again offered $1 million in exchange for moving the border from the forty-second to the thirty-seventh parallel, to enable it to acquire the Port of San Francisco.

Butler, however, had more success than Poinsett, for in 1832 he succeeded in having the Trade Treaty signed and it stayed in force for a half-century. Butler withdrew the clause requiring the return of fugitive slaves, introduced an article regulating trade with Santa Fe, and added a series of agreements on control of Indian raids on the border zone. The most-favored nation clause to which Alamán had been so opposed in 1825 was finally accepted. Butler's great victory was to turn a series of individual claims from U.S. citizens into an instrument of pressure on the Mexican government. By September 1833, Butler, without classifying the claims that had been submitted to his legation, presented them to the Mexican government: most of them concern compulsory loans of cash or services during the revolts or the Spanish invasion of 1829. Some of the claims were fair in principle, but the damages were exaggerated.

Neither Butler nor the U.S. government worried about the validity of the claims; they simply used them to place pressure on Mexico at a very difficult time, during a terrible plague of cholera and when liberal political reforms were being initiated.

The Mexican government treated the claims lightly, inviting the interested parties to present themselves before the Ministry of Finance, which was to consider each case individually according to Mexican law. The following year, the U.S. government asked Butler to follow up those claims which merited attention and not to allow U.S. citizens to appear before Mexican courts, which was interpreted as an improper exercise of Mexican authority over them. From that year until the war between the two nations, the United States pressed the claims sporadically, and President James Polk even cited them as the main issue between the countries in the U.S. declaration of war.

Butler's negotiations were stained with lies; not wanting to admit that he had failed to change Mexico's attitude position about the border, he led his government to believe that there was hope of inducing the Mexican government to sell Texas, and he even assured Washington that imminent agreement depended only on the offer of sufficiently large bribes. Members of President Andrew Jackson's cabinet pressed for his retirement, but the president allowed him to return to Mexico: Butler had promised that the confessor of one of General Antonio López de Santa Anna's sisters would help him obtain Texas. On his way back to Mexico, however, Butler became involved in the Texan revolt and Mexico complained to Washington. On 1 December 1835, he was finally dismissed; for a while he stayed on anyway, creating a series of problems. After he insulted Mexican authorities, they forbade him to cross into Texas on his return trip.

The new American minister, Powhatan Ellis, arrived on 11 May 1836 and made his debut by trying to mitigate some of the problems that his predecessor had created. Ellis dispatched home Butler's scandalous correspondence with the Mexican government and received orders to apologize to the Mexican authorities. In a letter dated 16 November, U.S. Secretary of State Forsyth wrote Ellis as follows:

The president directs that you will make known to the Mexican government that Mr. Butler's conduct in writing those letters is altogether disapproved by him and express his hope that it will not be permitted to disturb the friendly disposition which he has always endeavored to preserve between the two countries.

Texas: A Generous Error?

The northern territory of New Spain remained virtually unsettled until the nineteenth century. The apprehension generated by the independence of the British colonies induced Spain—at the end of the eighteenth century—to try to populate Texas and to establish *presidios* there, but with little success. The U.S. purchase of Louisiana in 1804 and of Florida in 1819 made populating the province more imperative; in addition, Texas was under constant attack by filibusterers.

The signing of the Adams-Onís Treaty, which established a clear border and set to rest the U.S. claim that Texas was part of Louisiana, calmed the Spanish authorities somewhat. Having been forced to sell Florida, the Spanish were worried about the Spanish subjects who still lived there and authorized its ex-subjects to move to other parts of the empire. Moses Austin, a former Spanish subject, took advantage of this opportunity and asked to be transferred to Texas along with a few other families. The grant he received was a generous one: it authorized the settlement of 300 families. They were given 640 acres for each family head, 320 for each wife, 100 for each child, and 80 for each slave. Tax exemptions were granted for a period of seven years, and permission to import freely whatever the settlers felt was needed. Before he could move, however, Moses Austin died, and his son Stephen decided to make use of the concession. But since New Spain had already declared its independence, he had to travel to the capital of the new Mexican empire to have the offer revalidated.

The Spanish Colonization Act, which had given the lands for free, granted tax exemptions, and allowed free importation of goods, had also restricted foreign colonization to Catholics, and had forbidden settlement on the coast or near the border. The new Imperial Act, like the previous one, permitted the importation of slaves but prohibited their sale and declared that their children would be born free. Austin was granted his permit within this law. Austin himself was put in charge of the civil, judicial, and military administration of his colony.

It is important to realize that the authorization came from a central monarchical government, because Austin later contended that Mexico's political change from federalism to centralism was his reason for seeking the independence of Texas. From the outset, the restrictions regarding religion and slavery were not respected by the U.S. colonists, and no one actually insisted on their fulfillment.

When the Federal Republic was established in 1823, the administration of the settlements was left to the states and, in consequence, a new law was promulgated on 18 August 1824 by the state of Coahuila and Texas. In 1825, new permits were issued: to Robert Leftwich for 200 families, to Hayden Edwards for 800, to Green Dewitt for 300, to Martín de León for 150. Other permits were granted in the following years, and the town of Saltillo became the administrative center of foreign activity. There U.S. colonists and speculators obtained their concessions. Many in the United States began to view Texas as a good place to do business, and U.S. companies and banks began selling the permits that the Mexican government had granted for free. Some Mexicans, among them Lorenzo de Zavala, Ramos Arizpe, and Vicente Filisola, procured some of these concessions for themselves.

Mexican politicians began to worry about the situation in Texas, particularly in view of the open support for expansion in the U.S.

press and the repeated offers of purchase by ministers Poinsett and Butler. Their fears were confirmed in 1826, when Hayden Edwards seized Nacogdoches and proclaimed the Republic of Fredonia. On this occasion, Stephen Austin behaved like a loyal Mexican subject and cooperated in the reestablishment of order; as a reward, he was allowed to colonize near the coastline.

In 1827, General Manuel Mier y Terán was commissioned to study the problem of the Texan border as well as the general situation. The report he tendered in 1829 was most alarming. He informed the Mexican government that the United States was preparing an army of fifty thousand men to invade Texas and that resistance would be difficult because the foreign population was eight times the size of the Mexican population; furthermore, the few Mexican soldiers stationed there were scattered all over the province and were without horses or other resources for combat. In addition, some of the Mexican towns were dominated by belligerent Indian tribes who frequently demanded tribute. Of the numerous foreign colonies, only those of De Witt and Austin appeared to be legal; others were peopled by adventurers who had entered without authorization. Mier's advice was to establish more *presidios* to represent the Mexican authorities, to colonize the area with Mexicans and Europeans, and to establish customhouses, as the early exemptions from customs had already expired.

For their part, the colonists in Texas were becoming increasingly impatient with the restrictions on slavery. As mentioned earlier, the Imperial Act had permitted the introduction of slaves but had prohibited their resale. A later federal law of 1824 freed all the slaves previously introduced into the country, and a state law of Coahuila and Texas had prohibited the entrance of new slaves. Finally, on 15 September 1829, all slavery was abolished throughout the Republic. According to the decree, "All those who up to now had been considered slaves are free," and "when the national financial circumstances will permit it, the owners of slaves will be indemnified." The colonists' protest was so violent that the government was forced to allow existing slaves to remain in slavery; however, it sustained the prohibition of the entrance of new slaves. This prohibition was easily evaded by signing fictitious working contracts in U.S. border towns.

In accordance with Mier y Terán's recommendation, Lucas Alamán promulgated, on 6 April 1930, a new colonization law. The law placed all matters concerning colonization under the direct control of the Federal Republic and prohibited the entrance of new U.S. settlers. An attempt was made to establish in Texas a contingent of about three thousand men from the militias of the Mexican states neighboring Texas, but they refused to cooperate. Alamán and Mier y Terán promoted Mexican colonization in Texas by asking the governors of all the states to send poor and honest families there and committed his government to help them settle.

Austin complained bitterly to Mier y Terán about the new law and Téran, in turn, assured Austin that all previous agreements would be respected. Téran's efforts to promote calm were vain. Toward the end of 1831, a widespread rumor that all previous concessions were to be cancelled led to an incident. When a customshouse was established in Anáhuac (now Galveston) in 1831, a crowd of foreign settlers gave their support to the U.S. schooners *Tyson, Nelson,* and *Sabina* so they would not have to comply with the instruction of the Mexican authorities. The Mexican detachments were powerless; the schooners fired and moved on down the channel.

The Mexican insurrection that overthrew President Bustamante in 1832 dampened the Texans' enthusiasm for secession, for most of the settlers supported the anti-Bustamantists. Nevertheless, a movement to separate Texas from Coahuila was taking shape. The vast territory had, at that time, 24,700 inhabitants and only 3,400 were Mexican.

At the end of 1832, a convention of settlers was organized in San Felipe. Mexicans were excluded. Austin, who presided, suggested that all future settlers should be invited Mexican or U.S. citizens. The settlers drew up a list of "petitions" to the Mexican government: the shutting down of the customhouses, a three-year extension of tax exemptions, the issuance of titles to property to the"illegal" settlers, and the establishment of Texas as a separate state. It was a list of favors requested rather than of grievances needing redress, since the settlers had received their land free of charge, had never paid taxes to Mexico, and were not numerous enough to meet the minimum population requirements set by the Mexican Constitution of 1824 for a separate state. There were few who supported annexation to the United States, a country less liberal with its land than Mexico.

In January 1833, a second convention of U.S. settlers met in San Felipe, drew up a constitution for a state of Texas, and delegated Austin to travel to Mexico City to present the petition to the Mexican government. The Texan arrived at a bad moment: a wave of cholera was devastating the population and the authorities were preoccupied with new laws reforming the church and the army. Realizing the difficulty of accomplishing anything, Austin wrote to Texas advising his colleagues there to proceed with the organization of city councils without bothering further about the Mexican government. His letter was intercepted in Saltillo and, when he stopped there on his return trip, he was apprehended by the authorities of Coahuila and sent back to Mexico City. He was freed during a general amnesty granted by Santa Anna in 1834. The president himself explained to Austin that Texas could not become a state because it had not yet attained the minimum population of sixty thousand required by law. Austin returned to Texas via New Orleans, where he picked up a shipment of arms. He had new plans.

A new law, enacted in 1835, prohibited the sale of lands granted to colonists by concession—in order, it was said, to stop speculation. The colonists did not agree. After the first encounters between the Mexican General Perfecto Cos and the rebel colonists, in which the would-be colonists were forced to surrender, volunteers were recruited in New Orleans, New York, and other parts of the United States to go to Texas. These people marched, incited not only by their country's "manifest destiny" to expand to the Pacific Ocean, but also by the Texan leaders promise of 1,000 hectares of land to each volunteer. The U.S. authorities supported this Texan action so openly that the schooner *El Correo Mexicano* was illegally detained and forced to proceed to New Orleans; when it was released, it had been damaged and could not sail. Mexico claimed damages and demanded that the neutrality laws of 1818, under which U.S. citizens were not allowed to interfere in foreign wars, be respected, but without result. The Mexican government decreed that "foreigners who disembark in any port of the Republic, or penetrate by land, armed and with the purpose of attacking our territory, shall be treated and punished as pirates." The decree was transmitted to Washington.

In Texas, another U.S. citizen, William B. Travis had seized the *presidio* of Anáhuac on June 30 and had been elected governor. Austin temporarily assumed command on his return, but by then, Samuel Houston, an ex-governor of Mississippi, a friend of President Jackson's, and the leader of the anti-Mexican party, had become the principal figure. In December 1835, San Antonio Béjar—the most important Mexican city in Texas—surrendered to Houston's army.

The suspension of federalism in Mexico provided the rebels with an ideological justification. As was noted earlier, the first settlers had received their permits from a centralist monarchical government. Still, the conventions of November 1835, held in Washington-on-the-Brazos and in San Felipe, declared Texas independent on the pretext that in 1835, when Santa Anna established a centralised Mexican republic, the social pact between Texas and the rest of the country was dissolved. Texas's formal Declaration of Independence was dated 1 March 1836. David L. Burnett, a self-appointed colonist, was named president and the Mexican, Lorenzo de Zavala, vice president.

The new central government had already been greeted by an uprising in the State of Zacatecas, which was crushed by Santa Anna's army. The Mexican president therefore decided to gather an army of six thousand men to subdue the Texans, but it was an inexperienced conscript army with little equipment. This recently created army had a difficult march but was able to reconquer Béjar and to seize El Álamo and El Encinal del Perdido. At El Álamo, Travis demanded "victory or death"; the Mexican position was that the decree of 1835 allowed no foreigner to enter the country bearing arms, precisely what the majority of the defenders of El Álamo had done. Had the victory been Mexico's, the historians' verdict would have been different. Texan troops surprised Santa Anna's army in San Jacinto, 21 March 1836 became a symbol of Mexican cruelty, and the penury of the Mexican state turned the incident into an important defeat. Since the Texans had the popular and the semi-official support of the United States and had received aid in arms, money, and volunteers, the Texan struggle cannot be considered a civil war. It was almost an international struggle.

The support given by the U.S. government can be deduced from the facts themselves. As soon as U.S. Minister Powhatan Ellis arrived in Mexico in May 1836, he received instructions to press the claims of U.S. nationals against the Mexicans. The United States knew that Mexico had no money and thought that, unable to satisfy these claims, it would have to compromise on the question of Texas. By October, Ellis was threatening to leave if he was not paid immediately, and he did leave by the end of the year.

During the same year, Manuel Eduardo de Gorostiza—the Mexican representative to Washington from March to October 1836—witnessed the support given by President Jackson to the Texan rebels when he ordered General Gaines to advance to Nacogdoches: in other words, to enter Mexican territory (ironically, at the same time the treaty setting the Sabine river as the border was ratified). As in Florida, the pretext for this movement of U.S. troops was provided by the Indians: Gaines had been ordered to avoid "any violation on the part of the Mexicans, Texans, or Indians." Jackson asked Congress for funds to reinforce the defense of the Southwest with volunteers. In September, when Gorostiza learned of the violation of the Mexican territory, he protested and demanded the withdrawal of the troops. When the Mexican minister realized that the order had come from Jackson himself, he decided to leave, but before doing so, he published some of the notes he had exchanged with the U.S. government. This was considered an offense in Washington. At the end of the year, when Mexico gave Ellis his passports, the Mexican government announced its decision to close its legation in Washington. Jackson tried to persuade Congress to authorize a fleet to be sent to Mexico to demand indemnity for the insults and claims, but Congress simply decided to send a new representative to the Mexican government.

Although Jackson did not succeed in annexing Texas at that time, the subsequent Mexican defeat at San Jacinto and General Filisola's withdrawal made the loss of Texas final. Santa Anna, taken prisoner, accepted the Treaties of Velasco, whereby the end of hostilities was declared and the Mexican general agreed to withdraw his troops to the other side of the Rio Grande and to pay for all Texan property or services that had been used. In an additional secret text, Santa Anna also committed himself to obtain the recognition of Texan independence by the Mexican government and to arrange for it to receive a Texan diplomatic mission. To top his unpatriotic deed, Santa Anna, fearing for his life, contacted Jackson and asked him to mediate between him and the Texans who considered him responsible for many deaths and, instead of returning directly to his country, traveled via Washington. Publicly and officially, Mexico condemned Santa Anna and even prosecuted General Filisola for having obeyed his order to withdraw. Santa Anna's public career appeared to be over, but he recovered his popularity after losing a leg during an attack he led against the French in the war of 1838.

Claims and U.S. Expansionism

Powhatan Ellis left Mexico and Gorostiza left Washington in 1836. Hence, in 1837, the countries had broken diplomatic ties and the annexation of Texas had not been consummated. The respected expansionist idealist, John Quincy Adams, accused his government of aggression against Mexico. The only step the United States took was to recognize the Republic of Texas.

The political instability and lack of funds that prevented Mexico from attempting to reconquer Texas also hindered the payment of its many foreign debts. The lack of financial resources, combined with the hope of pitting Great Britain against the United States, led Mariano Michelena, Mexico's minister of war, to concoct a plan to exchange the bonds of the British debtholders—which in 1837 amounted to $50 million—for large parcels of Texan land. Later, an attempt was made to carry out this plan, adding to it the proviso that the granted lands be from Texas, Chihuahua, Sonora, and California.

From the Mexican point of view, the foreign claims were questionable and exaggerated, since no one had justified or verified them. Both the U.S. and French claims continued to accumulate in the legations and were presented indiscriminately. Most of them related to loans exacted by the Mexican government from foreigners residing in the country or to the use of their boats or other transportation. Some of them sought compensation for insults to consuls or damages caused to private property during riots. There were also several questionable cases: one concerned the *Topaz* vessel, whose sailors had mutinied against their U.S. captain because he had not given them money entrusted to him by the Mexican government and who had thrown him overboard. Mexican soldiers put down the mutiny, but the U.S. legation characterized the act as an invasion of U.S. property. Claimants from the United States had been the most insistent, using their grievances as a platform for urging the sale or cession of Texas, but the Mexican government remained firm in its stand that proof had to be presented before Mexican tribunals.

In 1838, however, in the midst of a distressing financial crisis in Mexico, France decided to use its claims as a pretext for war. Fortunately for Mexico, U.S. Secretary of State John Forsyth proposed that the his country's claims be submitted for arbitration by an international convention headed by the king of Prussia. The king declined, but agreed to name a representative in 1839. The court consisted of two Mexicans, two U.S. citizens, and the arbiter. Of the claims presented to it—a total of 8,788.221 pesos—the court awarded damages equivalent to 1,386,745 pesos. Mexico accepted the finding and began paying in installments in 1840; it continued to do so until the fall of Bustamante's government a year-and-a-half later.

The interruption of payments was not really a decisive factor in the war with the United States that led to the loss of half of Mexico's territory. Sentiment in the United States for territorial expansion had increased—independently of the claims—at all levels, from the president down, and had even acquired a messianic nature. Both the president and the U.S. political parties viewed expansionism as the road to popularity. The groups who opposed expansionism on moral, political, or racist grounds were rather small and found no support among the majority who longed for the benefits that the lands of the West would bring: among others, free trade with Santa Fe; access to San Francisco, the key port for trading with Asia; and cotton-producing lands. The right to occupy lightly populated or tyrannically governed lands was publicly defended.

Incessant westward travel increased the desire to obtain not only Texas, but Oregon, California, and Canada. What had originally been a spontaneous movement had become a doctrine that took its name from journalist John O'Sullivan's famous phrase that the West was the United States' "manifest destiny." In its original form, this doctrine opposed the use of violence. It was simply an argument that any group of people could settle in unoccupied land, organize its government by social contract, and ask to be admitted to the Union. Spanish Americans could be admitted into such a community but would have to purge themselves of allegiance to their tyrannical governments. Some expansionists, of course, pointed out that it would be convenient to limit admissions from Latin America to the Sierra Madre ranges so that the United States would not have to absorb "mongrel races."

The Texans, certainly not immune to the expansionist fever, soon claimed that New Mexico and California were an integral part of their territory. In 1842, they attempted to seize Santa Fe and block Mexico's gulf ports. But the Texan movement was itself part of a larger one which already had important supporters in the U.S. government. A U.S. fleet had been stationed on the Pacific Coast since 1840, although the United States possessed no land bordering that ocean. In 1842, thinking that the two countries were at war, U.S. Commodore Thomas apCatesby Jones seized the port of Monterrey in California. When he realized his mistake, he apologized. However, his act clearly indicated what the U.S. objectives were and the rapidity with which its forces could be mobilized in California.

Meanwhile, Powhatan Ellis had returned to his post in Mexico City and diplomatic relations between the two countries had been renewed. But they were darkened by the expansionist sentiment of the United States and by Mexico's resentment of the independence of Texas. In 1842, Waddy Thompson, a new U.S. envoy, arrived in

Mexico. The first thing he did was visit the Texans who had been captured by the Mexican garrisons during the assault on Santa Fe, and he insisted that they be released. They were, as part of a general amnesty that was declared on Santa Anna's birthday, but Thompson considered it a personal victory.

Agitation for the annexation of Texas and Oregon became so popular throughout the United States that the politicians in power, as well as the candidates who wanted to succeed them, supported the movement. That is why, even though his secretary of state preferred to buy it, President John Tyler openly supported the annexation of Texas. Still, the Mexican minister in Washington was confident that Congress would block any attempt at annexation: those opposed to expansionism were powerful, particularly John Quincy Adams. Even in Texas, Sam Houston doubted the desirability of being annexed, and Anson Jones, who had succeeded Mirabeau B. Lamar as president of the Republic of Texas, was totally opposed to it. European leaders, who approved of further U.S. expansionism, favored the autonomy of Texas. Great Britain, for example, insisted that the Mexican government recognize Texan independence in exchange for a commitment that it would not join the United States. This solution was unacceptable in Mexico; although many Mexican politicians privately thought that the idea was sound, no one was prepared to risk supporting so unpopular a proposal.

The first attempt at annexation promoted by Tyler's administration in 1844 failed because it was not supported in the U.S. Senate. During his presidential campaign, the Democrat, James K. Polk, declared himself in favor of the annexation of Texas and Oregon. The first time the proposal went to Congress, it was treated as a foreign-relations matter and, as such, had needed the Senate's approval by a two-thirds vote; the second time, it was offered as a resolution in the House of Representatives that required approval by only a simple majority of both houses. The joint resolution was passed on 27 February 1845; and on 1 March, Tyler signed a decree annexing Texas to the United States. The Mexican minister in Washington, Almonte, in accordance with his country's warnings that annexation would be considered an act of aggression, asked for his passports.

In the meantime, the moderate government of General José Joaquín Herrera, who had been inaugurated in December 1844, when Santa Anna fell, had slowly begun to consider the British suggestion. It was too late. The Mexican document recognizing Texan independence was handed to the British representative in Texas at almost the same moment as the U.S. offer of annexation. President Jones, responding to popular feeling in Texas, organized a special convention to decide his country's fate and annexation was approved on 21 July 1845.

Expansionism and War

With an expansionist like James K. Polk in the White House, future events took on a predictable, even inevitable, cast. His cabinet included three true believers: Secretary of State James Buchanan, Treasury Secretary Robert J. Walker, and Secretary of the Navy George Bancroft. Polk was bent on provoking a war between Texas and Mexico so the United States would be forced to interfere and he ordered General Zachary Taylor to "defend" the Texan frontier. Commodore David E. Conner, in charge of the U.S. fleet in the Gulf of Mexico, was ordered to keep the gulf ports under surveillance, and Commodore John D. Sloat was to take San Francisco in case of war. These preparations were made to counteract a Mexican attack, a highly improbable event since the border was garrisoned by only twelve or thirteen hundred Mexican soldiers who were virtually unarmed. Even U.S. reports indicated that the Mexican army almost did not deserve the name, resembling more a ghost comprised of untrained conscripts who deserted as soon as the opportunity presented itself, and led by officers who devoted themselves to politics. The cavalry and the artillery, which had acquired a certain fame, had declined owing to the lack of funds and failure to maintain proper levels of enlistment.

Herrera's government, fully aware of the difficulty of the situation, tried to obtain the cooperation of the various provincial administrations in order to strengthen the northern border and thus avoid war. His prudent attitude was so unpopular that it caused his fall at the end of 1845. When Almonte left Washington, the U.S. government withdrew its minister from Mexico and replaced him with a U.S. agent. The man appointed was one of the claimants against the Mexican government.

Mexico's internal situation was extremely weak, and the country lacked outside support. Although U.S. authorities were suspicious of the British and the French, in reality Mexico could expect very little from them. France had just broken diplomatic relations with Mexico over an incident provoked by its imprudent representative, Alleye Cyprey.* But Great Britain had shown its good will toward the Mexicans and had frequently acted as a intermediary in the Texas affair. This made Mexicans confident they would obtain some help from the English; even though Tomás Murphy, the Mexican agent in Great Britain, had warned that no help would be offered. Moreover, the British had their own problems with the United States because of Oregon, and they faced a difficult situation in Europe. The Spanish, who might have been helpful, were at that time conspiring to place members of the royal family in Mexico, a plot to which both France and Great Britain consented.

By September 1845, Polk had a plan of action in case of war, but he wanted to avoid unnecessary expense as well as the political conflicts a war would inspire. Hence, the U.S. government asked the Mexican Foreign Relations Ministry if it would welcome a special commissioner and, upon receiving an affirmative answer, appointed John Slidell. Nevertheless, Zachary Taylor's army, stationed in southwest Texas, was ordered to mobilize "as near to the Rio Grande as circumstances permit" and to prepare either a defense in the event of a Mexican attack or an offensive march to the river. At the same time, Robert Stockton, an active expansionist, was sent to the Pacific Coast with orders for Commodore Sloat and for Robert Larkin, the consul in California. The orders repeated those that had been sent earlier: to incite a local uprising for the independence of California and to disembark as soon as war started.

A special commissioner, which Mexico said it would welcome, was a diplomat with instructions to repair the grievances caused by the breaking of relations. But Slidell, the man appointed, had no such instructions. Instead, he presented an offer of up to $40 million for the territory between the Nueces River and the Rio Grande, plus the northern part of New Mexico and California. He had been appointed minister plenipotentiary, that is, one with full diplomatic powers,

---

*When he presented himself to complain about a misunderstanding between his coachman and the people in charge of Las Delicias Spa, the Baron de Cyprey, who had a terrible temper, ended up screaming and insulting the Mexicans, precipitating a mob attack. Cyprey demanded an official apology and all types of reparations; when he did not obtain all he demanded, he broke off diplomatic relations. Matters worsened when, a few months later at the opera, Cyprey spat in the face of a journalist who had criticized him. The government asked him to leave Mexico for his own safety.

and he arrived when Herrera's government was at its weakest. Since welcoming him would have been political suicide, Foreign Relations Secretary Peña y Peña refused to receive him.

The United States pronounced itself aggrieved. President Polk's annual message was replete with threats against Mexico and Great Britain. The expansionist movement was reaching its peak. John O'Sullivan wrote, in a December issue of the *Democratic Review*, that Oregon had to be obtained in order to fulfill "the right of our Manifest Destiny to overspread and to possess the whole continent, which Providence has given us for the development of the great experiment of Liberty and federated self-government entrusted to us."

In the midst of these developments, General Paredes y Arrillaga, who had been named commander in chief of the Mexican Army Reserves, revolted against the government. Disobeying the orders he had received in December 1845 to march to the border, he moved instead toward the capital to seize power. He justified his action by promising that his new government would take a firmer stand against the United States and that he would eliminate corruption. And from January 1846 till June, when he was in power, he did indeed strive for reform, nor did he receive Slidell, who had remained in Mexico. He soon discovered what every politician knew: the Mexican situation was desperate.

The Mexican–U.S. War

On 13 January 1846, President Polk ordered General Taylor to march to the Rio Grande, and began to write his declaration of war on Mexico. By March, Taylor had established himself on the river's northern bank and had begun to construct Fort Brown, near the river's mouth. The inhabitants of Matamoros protested in vain. When Mexico's General Ampudia arrived, he threatened the U.S. Army and demanded its withdrawal to the border; in response, Conner's fleet blocked the mouth of the river. Some U.S. observers evaluated the situation perceptively. Ethan Hitchcock, a U.S. Army colonel, wrote: "We do not have a particle of right to be here . . . it looks as if the government sent a small force on purpose to bring on a war, as to have a pretext to take California."

The awaited and dreaded incident took place on 25 April, when Mexican soldiers who were keeping watch over the river fired on U.S. soldiers. A laconic message from Taylor arrived in Washington on

9 May: "hostilities may now be considered as commenced." By then, he had asked the local governments of Texas and Louisiana for eight regiments with which to attack Mexico.

The message Polk had previously written justified the war by reviewing the insults and grievances the United States had suffered. Only one sentence was added: "American blood has been shed on American soil." Even though there a faction of Congress was opposed to the war, Polk had little problem securing its approval to recruit volunteers or obtaining the funds necessary in the two long years that the invasion of Mexico would last. Polk wanted a small war, sufficient to obtain a peace treaty. It was well known that Mexico could not pay any indemnities, therefore, the Polk administration expected to demand territory in exchange. Among the first orders issued were Secretary of War William L. Marcy's instructions to General Stephen Kearny, who was stationed in Missouri, to march with troops furnished by that state to Santa Fe and California. Bancroft reminded Commodore Sloat that the fleet on the Pacific Coast was to seize Monterrey and San Francisco and, if possible, Guaymas and Mazatlán. Commander Conner, in the gulf, received orders to blockade the ports and to favor any attempt at secession that might develop. There was no doubt that this was a war of conquest and not one merely to satisfy grievances or to collect debts.

General Winfield Scott was named commander in chief of the expeditionary forces. Scott took time to train his volunteers and to gather information about the country before beginning his mission of invading Mexico by the key route of access—from Veracruz to Mexico City, the capital of the Republic. Meanwhile, General Taylor carried his own invasion down to Monterrey; in February 1847, was facing the Mexican troops formerly commanded by General Santa Anna in the lost battle of Angostura. But the swiftest and steadiest movements were carried out by Kearny's troops. They entered the northwest—the most uninhabited and desolate area of the country—and by January 1847, had completed the conquest of California.

Even so great an invasion on so many fronts did not stop political change in Mexico. In mid-1846, a federalist group snatched power from Paredes y Arrillaga, the general in command of the Mexican Army Reserves in the north, and by August the seemingly irreplaceable General Santa Anna had re-assumed the presidency. Exiled to Havana, he had there entered into secret negotiations with the U.S. government which, in return, permitted him to penetrate the naval blockade and return to his country. Polk's agent had explored the possibility of buying Santa Anna's cooperation in order to shorten the war and curtail its political and material costs. Santa Anna appeared to accept the offer, but his purpose was only to be enabled to slip through the blockade. His subsequent conduct confirms that, while he may have disappointed some U.S. agents, he was not a traitor to Mexico. Nevertheless, the fact that he was authorized to pass through aroused suspicions that weakened Mexican morale.

Polk also dispatched Moses Beach, a prominent U.S. Catholic, to obtain the cooperation of important Mexican ecclesiasts. His plan was not far-fetched. The church was known to be dissatisfied with the Mexican government, and since it was the only institution that had property and credit, the government from time to time forced it to lend money to the state.

Gómez Farías was elected vice president and when Santa Anna became president, and he remained in charge of the government, while the general left to take charge of the army. Gómez Farías—a radical liberal—could not resist the opportunity to strike at the church; besides, it was the only source of money to finance the war. In January 1847, Congress approved a decree authorizing the government to sell property that belonged to the clergy up to the amount of 15 million pesos, needed for defense.* The reaction was immediate and adverse, and in February the clergy sponsored an uprising in the capital while Santa Anna was fighting at Angostura and Scott was getting ready to occupy Veracruz.

The president left the northern battlefront for Mexico City to resolve this dispute, which he did by revoking the decree in exchange for the church's financial cooperation in prosecuting the war. This done, he left again to organize the defense of the east. Such large movements of the army, plus its lack of funds and supplies, help to explain its disasters. The U.S. forces—disciplined and well-equipped—faced numerous but improvised troops with almost no weapons.

Scott, as already noted, moved slowly because he was reluctant to penetrate the country before the ports had been secured. Thus, in June, he was in Jalapa, where Nicholas P. Trist—appointed by the United States to discuss peace terms—joined him. Trist was authorized to offer several alternatives comprised of territorial absorption

---

*During the nineteenth century, the dollar and the peso were equivalent in value. After 1890, the price of silver fell, affecting the peso, which by 1905 was valued at fifty cents.

and compensation up to the amount of $30 million. He was instructed to negotiate a perpetual right of transit across the Isthmus of Tehuantepec and the cession of Baja California, but these were not among the necessary conditions. The acquisition of Upper California and New Mexico were. After he arrived in Mexico, Trist was also instructed to obtain the Gila Valley, necessary to the construction of a railroad.

Trist announced his presence in Puebla to Santa Anna's government through the British representative. There a new attempt was made to bribe the chief executive and the Mexican troops. Everything seems to indicate that Santa Anna's initial acceptance was intended to delay any further action by the U.S. army while the defense of the capital was being organized, but when the negotiations were made public, he was again accused of treason and the Mexican ranks were again divided.

Scott began to advance again in August. On the twentieth he reached Mexico City and the commanders in chief of both armies agreed to an armistice. Hostilities ceased within a radius of 30 leagues from Mexico City and prisoners were exchanged. The armies remained in their positions but without receiving reinforcements and without interfering with the incoming supply of provisions.

The Treaty of Guadalupe

Before signing the armistice, Santa Anna called a meeting of the Mexican Congress to discuss the possible signing of a peace treaty, since Trist's proposals were going to be heard. The Congress did not in fact meet, but the government still named its commissioners, who met with Trist from 27 August to 6 September 1847.

The position of the Mexican commissioners (José Joaquin Herrera, Bernado Couto, and Ignacio Mora and Villamil) was a difficult one, since Santa Anna, owning to the his fear of a lack of support in Congress, had delegated to them very limited powers; moreover, the U.S. terms were very harsh. The Mexicans unrealistically insisted on the Nueces River as the border, as well as on a neutral strip 20 leagues wide abutting it. They did not agree to a territorial cession, nor to the right of transit through Tehuantepec—only to the establishment of an agency in San Francisco. After protracted debate, they agreed to cede territory down to the thirty-second parallel, retaining the Nueces River as a border, and demanded that no slavery be established on territory from Mexico. Trist insisted on the thirty-second parallel but consented to consult his government about the Nueces. On 6 September, no agreement having had been reached, Trist declared the talks broken off and the United States resumed its offensive. On 15 September, despite heroic resistance from the capital's inhabitants, the stars and stripes waved over the National Palace and the Mexican government removed to Querétaro. Santa Anna had resigned and the presidency was assumed by Manuel de la Peña y Peña who, as president of the Supreme Court of Justice, was designated by law to act as temporary president.

Meanwhile, victory had created in the United States a movement to absorb all of Mexico. President Polk himself felt that Trist's instructions had fallen short of what could be accomplished, and ordered him to return to Washington in October. However, Trist had already entered into negotiations with Luis de la Rosa, the foreign relations secretary, who had agreed to name new commissioners on 31 October and the Mexican government urged Trist to stay to negotiate an agreement based on his original instructions.

Trist, fearful that prolongation of the war would provoke the total annexation of Mexico, which he considered undesirable for his own country, decided to stay and assumed total responsibility. In his message to Congress, on 7 December, Polk warned that Mexican stubbornness would only bring about a bigger territorial loss.

On 2 January 1848, Trist met with the Mexican commissioners—Bernardo Couto, Luis G. Cuevas, and Luis Atristáin—who proposed a cession from the Nueces to the Gila rivers and a line in the Pacific marked "north of San Diego." Trist adhered to his instructions and demanded that territory to the Rio Grande and a border in California extending north to the thirty-second parallel and including San Diego, be the cession. He offered a maximum indemnity of 15 million pesos and did not agree to the exclusion of slavery from the ceded territories.

The Mexicans achieved as much as they could, considering their position as representatives of an occupied country: they saved Baja California and were able to have it linked by land to Sonora. The treaty was signed on 2 February in Villa de Guadalupe. The enormous territory lost by Mexico was compensated for by $15 million plus the cancellation of the claims unpaid prior to the signing of the treaty. (It is interesting that, once the U.S. government assumed responsibility for those claims, they were substantially reduced.)

Articles 3 and 4 of the treaty referred to troop withdrawals and the return of all occupied installations. Article 5 established the border and specified that the map of the United States published there by J. Disturnell in 1847 would serve as a basis for its physical demarcation. The boundary agreed upon in article 5 of the Treaty of Guadalupe Hidalgo is shown on map 2.

The Mexican government was particularly concerned about the future of the Mexicans who would remain in the ceded territories and about the protection of their rights and property. To that end, Article 7 read:

> . . . those who shall prefer to remain in the said territories may either retain the title and rights of Mexican citizens, or acquire those of citizens of the United States . . . In the said territories property of every kind, now belonging to Mexicans, now established there, shall be inviolably respected.

Article 9 specified that the Mexicans would enjoy

> all of the rights of the citizens of the United States according to the principles of the Constitution, and in the meantime shall be maintained and protected in the free enjoyment of their liberty and property and secured in the free exercise of their religion without restriction.

Article 11 was advantageous to Mexico, since the northern regions had suffered for years from continual incursions of belligerent Indians. It read:

> Considering that a great part of the territories which, by the present Treaty, are to be comprehended for the future within the limits of the U.S., is now occupied by savage tribes, who will hereafter be under the exclusive control of the Government of the U.S. and whose incursions within the territory of Mexico would be prejudicial in the extreme; it is solemnly agreed that all such incursions shall be forcibly restrained by the Government of the U.S., *whensoever* this may be necessary and that when they cannot be prevented, they shall be punished by the said Government, and satisfaction for the same shall be exacted: all in the same way, and with equal diligence and energy, as if the same incursions were mediated or committed within its own territory against its own citizens.

Article 14 read:

The U.S. do furthermore discharge the Mexican Republic from
all claims of citizens of the U.S., not heretofore decided against
the Mexican Government . . . which discharge shall be final and
perpetual, whether the said claims be reported or be allowed by
the Board of Commissioners provided for in the following Article
and whatever shall be the total amount of those allowed.

The document also renewed the Treaty of Friendship and Trade,
established the procedure by which both governments would solve
future differences, and set forth the rules of war, should there be a new
one.

Trist sent the treaty to Polk, and in Mexico a convention comprised of two Mexican and two U.S. representatives agreed to a
cease-fire and a suspension of hostilities beginning in March 1848.
They also agreed on the collection of war taxes. The treaty reached
Washington in March. Polk was unhappy. New Mexico and California were annexed already, and the Treaty did not provide for the
annexation of Baja California and the right of transit through Tehuantepec or the reduction of the indemnity to be paid to Mexico.
However, since the presidential election had already begun, Polk
decided to submit it to the Senate without a recommendation. The
Senate considered rejecting it, but approved it with a few corrections
on 10 March 1848.

A treaty so punitive had to create great discontent in Mexico.
Paredes y Arrillaga and other politicians attempted to revolt and some
Indian groups in different parts of the country took advantage of the
confusion of 1848 to rebel. But the Treaty was ratified by the Mexican
Congress and on 30 May the signed copies were exchanged.

The Treaty of Guadalupe Hidalgo disappointed the believers in the
manifest destiny of the United States. Some groups tried to get
around it by organizing filibusters; others, in important political
positions, urged several subsequent administrations to exert pressure
on Mexico to force it to sell more territory. These efforts persisted
until the twentieth century; even then, Baja California continued to
arouse the aspirations of many in the United States.

The terms of the Treaty of Guadalupe are among the harshest
imposed by a winner upon a loser in the history of the world. Mexico,
which as New Spain had been the first country in the Americas, was

reduced to half its original territory and had become subject to all types of imperialist attacks. The fact that it survived a war in which there were nothing but disadvantages seems, even today, almost a miracle. The U.S. invasion increased the divisions within Mexico, and at times the country was on the verge of being hopelessly fragmented. On the other hand, the moral shock of the war stimulated national cohesion and strengthened the political groups concerned with reforming the country.

The United States, with the addition of its conquered territory, became a continental power which finally looked out on the Pacific. Despite complaints about the enormous cost of the war, which amounted to $100 million and fifteen thousand lives, the price seems very low for what was obtained in return.*

---

*Battle deaths were 1,733; the others died of tropical sicknesses or disappeared.

The Transition Stage: 1848–1867

Postwar Rebellion

The two decades following the U.S. invasion of Mexico were crucial for both countries. Both countries endured civil war, and Mexico, in addition, suffered foreign invasion. Many of the obsolete structures that had survived the changes brought about by independence were altered, and the changes helped to consolidate both nations internally to promote their economic development.

In the United States, this period was a transition between fulfilling the ambitious dream of extending the national territory to the Pacific Coast and entering fully into the Industrial Revolution. It was a difficult stage because it was necessary to eliminate slavery, the pillar of the southern way of life and one of the most important obstacles to the socioeconomic and political unification of the country. Newly conquered Mexican territory sowed the seeds of discord. The forty-niners who flocked to California's goldfields populated it so rapidly that, by 1850, the territory was eligible for statehood. It was admitted into the Union as a free state, demonstrating to the slaveholding states that they were destined to be a minority.

Mexico's condition when the invading U.S. troops left in the middle of 1848 was depressed, not only because of the ravages of war and occupation; in addition to the demoralizing defeat, there were uprisings, riots, and attacks from belligerent Indians from the U.S. side of the border.

Some of these uprisings, such as the Caste War in Yucatan, occurred before the war and were not related to the United States: they were caused by the modernization of agriculture that slowly displaced the Maya Indians and their maize crops. After centuries of exploitation, the Mayas rose up against the criollos who owned the lands, killing the men and enslaving the women and children. In this cruel war, the criollos, who had lost thousands of friends and relatives or seen them enslaved, retaliated with extreme measures. The ruling group in Yucatan, unable to obtain help from Mexico City—because of the distance and because the federal government was bankrupt—finally decided on annexing themselves to the United States during the Mexican–U.S. War. They commissioned Justo Sierra O'Reilly, a Yucatan criollo, to petition the U.S. authorities, but succeeded only in arranging for the withdrawal from Ciudad del Carmen of the U.S. troops who were occupying the area; in return the criollos pledged neutrality in the war. Even this much was regarded as aid to the criollos, since it allowed them to import arms more easily: arms for the Mayan rebels were believed to be coming from abroad through Belize, and the criollos needed to be reinforced as best they could be. Other uprisings, such as in Xichu (Guanajuato), and in Huasteca and Misantla (both near Veracruz) also had old roots, but it was suspected that some had been instigated by the United States.

Other political uprisings were directly linked to the Treaty of Guadalupe. Some people believed the treaty to be traitorous, and others—directly linked to the landlord class—feared that the departure of the U.S. troops would spread the Caste War throughout the country. Some prominent families went as far as to offer the government of Mexico to General Winfield Scott, and U.S. citizens were pushing a secessionist movement in the area adjacent to Texas, where the former Texan, José María Carvajal, was suspected of wanting to establish a Republic of the Sierra Madre with the help of some U.S. citizens. In view of the plethora of problems, it is surprising that Mexico maintained its integrity.

After 1847, the moderates were in power. President José Joaquín de Herrera reorganized the treasury and the army and spent part of the indemnity Mexico had received from the United States to meet some of the immediate problems of the country. The army was reorganized and equipped to provide a more efficient defense of the northern border, where militias and *presidios* were created in order to quell the attacks from filibusterers and belligerent Indians who for some time had been causing substantial damage. Mexican troops were finally sent to Yucatan to smother the Indian rebellion there, and the region was reintegrated into the country. The interest on the debt to Great Britain was paid, and a new rate and schedule of payments, favorable to Mexico, was negotiated.

Troubles on the Border

The United States exerted considerable pressure on the Mexican border for a long time, despite its vast conquest. Some expansionists, who desired all of Mexico or at least its northern states, continued to promote their ideas, alarming the Mexican government. President James Polk was himself one of the disappointed. He had hoped to annex Yucatan and to buy Cuba, but both enterprises failed. Yucatan, as noted in the previous paragraph, was reincorporated into Mexico, and Spain did not accept the tempting offer of $100 million for Cuba, even though that island was politically unstable and an economic liability. This did not end all aspirations to obtain Cuba, however. In 1851, a filibuster expedition was organized to conquer the island; its members were captured and shot.

Article 9 of the Treaty of Guadalupe placed a burden on the United States: it obligated the victors to halt any attacks on Mexico from the Indians who inhabited the ceded territory and made them responsible for any losses that might occur. The United States promised to prevent the kidnapping of Mexicans by raiding tribes from the United States and to restore the property of those who had been attacked. The U.S. Senate accepted these provisions partly because Polk's justification of the annexation of the Territory of New Mexico had been that Mexico was too weak in the border areas to control the movements of these tribes.

There were approximately two hundred thousand Indians in the recently acquired territories. Many had come there from the East, whence they had been forced to emigrate by the expansion of the white settlers who continually pushed them westward in order to occupy their lands. This caused great instability among the people of the tribes, who resorted to a violent way of life. Texas went to the extreme of denying the Indians any rights, to force them to move to other regions, and the nearest place was Mexico. Some Indians crossed the border and settled peacefully in the north of Mexico, but the majority only made incursions, usually to steal cattle, since the prohibition against selling them in the United States was never enforced. The U.S. authorities did not try to stop these incursions, partly because the Department of Indian Affairs had no money.

In 1851, the United States started to press, through its representatives, for the dropping of this clause in the treaty in exchange for a monetary payment. The northern states of Mexico, for their part, asked the national government to negotiate with Washington an agreement that would permit their forces to pursue the transgressors on the other side of the border—as the only way to teach them a lesson. In 1852, a band of U.S. citizens led by one Frederich Matthews was very active; in this instance Mexico again failed to obtain an indemnity for its claims. The problem acquired such magnitude that those affected formed an association to defend themselves. Cattle stealing had become a profitable business, practiced not only by Indians but by U.S. citizens as well. Fred Rippy assures us, however, in his classic *The United States and Mexico*, that something was attempted in this respect and that, by 1853, four treaties were concluded with Indian tribes to ensure their peaceful behavior.

The border was plagued not only by cattle rustlers. Large-scale smuggling had become the favorite business of merchants on both sides; it helps to account for the rapid growth of the Mexican city of Monterrey. All the measures taken by the national government to combat smuggling failed, and the U.S. Civil War made it a way of life in that area. It remains a big business to this very day.

Filibustering, which reached its height during that period, affected not only Mexico, which was so accessible, but the Caribbean countries and Central America as well. Baja California, Sonora, and some of the other northern Mexican states were the most common targets of the filibusters. They were usually organized in California, at that time a home for adventurers from many parts of the world, but the United States refused to enforce the Law of Neutrality of 1818, which clearly established

That any person shall, within the territory of jurisdiction of the United States, begin or set on foot, or provide or prepare the means for, any military expedition or enterprise to be carried on from thence against the territory or dominion of any foreign prince or state, colony, district, or people with whom the United States are at peace, every such person so offending, shall be declared guilty of a high misdemeanor and shall be fined not exceeding three thousand dollars, and imprisoned not more than three years.

The expansionist spirit was still very strong, and the local and national U.S. authorities, who were often sympathetic to those who wanted to expand U.S. territory, did nothing to stop the expeditions openly organized in the United States. There were many types of filibusters from small groups of cutthroats who were satisfied with raiding and stealing to those whose goal was to conquer territory. One Colonel White, who had served as mercenary in Yucatan, succeeded in 1849 in recruiting 540 men to conquer a region in the Sierra Madre, Yucatan, or Cuba. Other expeditions, led by men who were ready to risk anything, had more specific plans.

The most notorious filibuster of this period was the French Count Gaston Raousett de Boulbon, whose ambition led him to exploit the restlessness of the French adventurers, who were not being treated very well in California. Intending to establish an independent regime in Sonora, Raousset took advantage of a Mexican concession to reopen old mines and brought 150 men to the country in 1852. His small army seized Hermosillo, the state capital, but he was soon defeated and returned to San Francisco. This failure did not discourage him. By 1853, he was dreaming of a realm which would include Sonora, Chihuahua, Sinaloa, and Durango. He returned to Mexican territory in 1854 to carry out his mission, but this time he was even less fortunate. After roving about in search of plunder for a few months, he was captured and shot.

An expedition led by William Walker was even more threatening because he was a U.S. citizen and very popular in California. Santa Anna, always imaginative, even toyed with the idea of trying to use the French count to stop him. Walker had two alternative plans: to provoke a war with Mexico which would end in a further annexation or to establish a new and independent republic which would later be annexed to the Union. In 1853, he headed toward Baja California and, after threatening to strike some of the small villages in the south of the Peninsula, declared the establishment of a republic. Eventually he was expelled. Failure fired Walker's ambition also. A year later, he returned and declared the foundation of a Republic of Sonora, with little luck. He managed to escape and repeated his attempt in Nicaragua, where he was quite successful for two years.

The filibusters were stopped rather quickly. Nevertheless, they caused damage, and forced Mexico to spend part of its limited financial resources on defense, which could have been avoided had the famous decree of neutrality been enforced. Some U.S. authorities apparently took pleasure in watching the ships that sailed to attack Mexican territory; in San Diego, Walker was officially received as president of the Republic of Sonora. To add insult to injury, subsequent U.S. claims included amounts for damages suffered by some of the filibusters.

Compliance with Article 5 and Expansionism

The U.S. negotiator of the Treaty of Guadalupe, Nicholas Trist, had insisted that the border be carefully defined and had even enclosed with the treaty an official U.S. map in order to make it as clear as possible. But such a long line was bound to have some built-in problems, especially since most of the area was uninhabited and unknown. The first section of the border was marked by the Rio Grande in its deepest part and then

westwardly, along the whole southern boundary of New Mexico (which runs north of the town called Paso) to its western termination; thence, northward, along the western line of New Mexico, until it intersects the first branch of the river Gila; (or if it should not intersect any branch of that river, then to the point on the said line nearest to such branch, and thence in a direct line to the same; thence down the middle of the said river; until it empties into the Rio Colorado; thence across the Rio Colorado, following the division line between Upper and Lower California, to the Pacific Ocean.

The southern and western limits of New Mexico, mentioned in this article are those laid down in the map entitled *"Map of the United States, as organized and defined by various acts of the Congress of said Republic, and constructed according to the best authorities.* Revised edition. Published at New York, in 1847 by J. Disturnell."

There were indeed a number of doubts—potential problems—from which expansionist U.S. groups tried to benefit; in addition, the task of defining the line on maps and with boundary monuments also created political problems between the Whigs and the Democrats. It was not until July 1849—just before the deadline in the treaty expired—that the joint commission met in San Diego. In October, after many delays caused by the U.S. commissioners, the commission agreed on a first point and a document written in both languages was buried inside a bottle at the spot where the border monument was being built. Work continued slowly, but by January 1850 the border between the two Californias was marked out from San Diego to the point where the Colorado and the Gila rivers converge.

The commission postponed some of its meetings and agreed to meet again in June at El Paso, the border between Texas and the Territory of New Mexico, on the north, and between Chihuahua and

Sonora on the south, but the U.S. representation was changed and the meeting was not held until December. The discovery of an error in Disturnell's map created an immediate problem: El Paso had been placed northeast of its actual location. After much debate, the joint commission reached a compromise, but it was never ratified by the U.S. Senate. Underlying the issue was the desire of U.S. representatives to find an excuse for acquiring yet more Mexican territory; they argued that the southern line of the transcontinental railroad had to traverse the Mesilla Valley.

The Mesilla Valley is a fertile plateau where Mexicans from the ceded territories had settled and which had attracted many North Americans as well. The problem of whose authorities would be respected soon emerged: the Mexicans supported the authority of the governor of Chihuahua, but the settlers from the United States refused to recognize the line that the commissioners had agreed upon and requested the intervention of the governor of New Mexico.

The weakness of the Mexican central government encouraged the northern emigrants to the extent that by 1853 the U.S. governor of the Territory of New Mexico threatened to occupy the disputed area by force. Fortunately, the military commander of the region did not second his motion, which was later disallowed by U.S. federal authorities, but the situation was so critical that, in July, the U.S. government named James Gadsden, a railroad contractor, to represent it in talks with the Mexican government, partially for the purpose of finding a solution to the problem of the Mesilla plateau.

The Gadsden Treaty

By the summer of 1853, when James Gadsden was appointed to negotiate with the Mexicans, many claims had accumulated south of the border. Several articles of the Treaty of Guadalupe had not been enforced and numerous incidents had occurred as the U.S. troops left: among them were the U.S. failure to return the money collected in Mexican customhouses between the time Mexico was scheduled to resume their administration and the actual day they were returned to the Mexican authorities; and the thefts of objects and valuable documents from the National Palace, the Parish of Veracruz, and other buildings that had been used by the invading troops. There was an accumulation of claims under Articles 8 and 9 concerning the rights of Mexicans who had remained in the ceded territories and the property rights of Mexicans who were not residents of that area.

Article 8 stated that Mexicans who had decided to stay in ceded territory were guaranteed the right to retain their nationality

or to acquire the title and rights of United States citizens. However, the choice of citizenship must be made within one year beginning on the date when ratifications of this Treaty will be exchanged. Those who will remain in the said territories after the year has passed, without declaring their intentions of retaining their Mexican nationality, will be considered as having chosen to be citizens of the United States . . .

Article 8 also expressly guaranteed that all titles to property held by Mexicans would be respected. Article 9 concerned the political rights of the residents of the ceded territories.

Disputed cases falling within these articles increased in number, especially those regarding real estate. In 1851, the U.S. Congress organized a commission to pronounce judgment on the validity of titles to property, although U.S. agents had already rendered a decision that practically all of them were valid and that the fraudulent ones were easily detectable. The new commission delayed its decisions; some landowners, forced into long lawsuits before several authorities, were ruined. Another complaint arose from the discrimination suffered by Mexicans in California. The gold rush attracted enormous numbers of people from all over the world and the authorities began to require that foreigners obtain a special permit to work in the goldfields. This was also required of the Mexicans, despite the Treaty of Guadalupe and the fact that most of them, the year stipulated in the treaty having expired, had automatically become U.S. citizens.

The Mexican government presented its grievances in Washington and ordered its consuls, especially the one in San Francisco, to insist on protection for Mexicans. The discrimination and abusive treatment, however, induced many Mexicans to decide to repatriate—so frequently in the Territory of New Mexico that, fearing a labor shortage, the U.S. authorities there began to obstruct the Mexican government agents who travelled there to expedite the repatriation. The last important instance of friction concerned the Tehuantepec railroad, which was not mentioned in the Treaty of Guadalupe. Owing to a series of transfers from the original concession, the case finally involved U.S. citizens. In 1842, the Mexican government had granted an ample concession to one José de Garay, a Mexican, to build a railroad across the Isthmus of Tehuantepec, a concession which included 10 leagues of land on each side of the proposed railway. Garay was not able to fulfill his part of the agreement on time, but he did renew the concession. In 1846, before it expired, it was transferred to the British firm of Manning and Makintosh. They, in turn, were not able to construct the railway and, in 1848, sold the concession to Hargous Brothers of New York. The whole operation was questionable, but it involved a U.S. company and the U.S. government felt it could press the matter. The Mexican government, on the other hand, held that Garay's concession had expired in 1848 and that its subsequent transfers were invalid. Since the Tehuantepec Railroad Company of New Orleans had been formed in 1850 with Garay himself as one of its shareholders, the U.S. government felt correct in ordering its minister to Mexico City, Robert P. Letchee, to negotiate an agreement that would protect the rights of the constructors and allow the trans-isthmus line to be built.

The Mexican government, concerned about maintaining its sovereignty, moved to prevent any work at the Isthmus of Tehuantepec but was nevertheless willing to make a new concession and signed the Treaty of Tehuantepec in 1851. This treaty granted privileges to the holders of the concession and to the U.S. builders. Mexico accepted the U.S. government as a partner in order to guarantee the neutrality of the route, but the appropriation of land was eliminated. In February 1853, the Mexican government also agreed to sign a contract with one A. G. Sloo, also from New Orleans. The contract did not include any land and it required a $600,000 guarantee, apparently a sticking point. The railroad was never built.

The arguments over Tehuantepec and Mesilla induced the U.S. government to dispatch James Gadsden to Mexico as a special negotiator. Gadsden had a long-time interest in transcontinental railroads and was an advocate of expansion to the south. His instructions were moderate, considering the bombastic demands of the U.S. press. Although Mexico had been weakened by Santa Anna's resumption of the presidency in 1853, it benefited from a strong current of sympathy in the Unites States, particularly in New England. President Franklin Pierce wanted more land and, aware of Santa Anna's lack of funds or scruples during the most decadent phase of his political life, he decided he could buy what he really wanted. Pierce sought a peaceful agreement that would settle all mutual claims, a border that would allow for the construction of a Southern railroad to the Pacific, a release from the obligation to stop Indian incursions, measures to improve trade, and U.S. rights in Tehuantepec.

Most of the U.S. claims were highly debatable. Secretary of State Marcy maintained that the border of the Territory of New Mexico worked out by the joint commission was not final because it was drawn up by a substitute topographer. He insisted that both countries should abstain from occupying the disputed territory by force and he announced that his government was more interested in negotiating an adjustment of the border than in claiming its rights to the disputed territory. The U.S. government disclaimed responsibility for violations of Article 11 of the Treaty of Guadalupe on the grounds that Mexico had not maintained adequate vigilance of its border and had thus been inviting attacks; nevertheless, the U.S. government was willing to pay to be released of this claim.

Gadsden proved less moderate than his instructions. He maintained an aggressive and cynical attitude. To the note written by the minister of foreign affairs, Manuel Díaz de Bonilla concerning compensation for Indian incursions in the north, he replied that the United States had done everything possible to defend the Mexicans and that the article should be interpreted as an impossible demand. When an obligation written into an international agreements was not mutual, it could hardly be sustained for long.

After his first meetings with Santa Anna, it was clear that Gadsden was not willing to yield anything not strictly necessary to the solution of the border problem and to provide for the construction of the railway. A few days later, he received new instructions from Washington through Christopher L. Ward, a lawyer interested in the Garay concession. These instructions listed five possible acquisitions of territory and specified the compensation to be granted. The alternatives ranged from simply obtaining the Mesilla territory for a payment of $15 million to a cession that would include the states of Tamaulipas, Coahuila, Nuevo León, part of Chihuahua and Sonora, and the whole Peninsula of Baja California for $50 million.

By then, Gadsden had suggested to Washington that military forces be concentrated as a warning to the Mexican authorities. Thus, when negotiations began, the Mexicans were again at a disadvantage. However, William Walker's incursions occurred at this time, placing Gadsden in an embarassing position; furthermore, the stubbornness of the Mexican negotiators extended the talks for so long that the U.S. minister halted them. Afraid of military action, the Mexican government finally agreed to sign the Gadsden Treaty (called the Treaty of Mesilla in Mexico and "of clarification of the Treaty of Guadalupe," in the diplomatic notes). The disputed territory was sold for $10 million and Article 11 of the Treaty of Guadalupe was repealed. The possibility of withholding $5 million dollars in payment of U.S. claims, including Garay's concession, was considered, but this punitive clause was finally dropped, and the problem remained unsolved. Mexico's counterclaims were not considered.

Gadsden presented President Pierce with the signed treaty in January 1854 and, although the president and his cabinet had doubts about it, it was sent to the Senate for ratification. The Senate made some amendments, such as one to Article 18 granting the right of transit across the Isthmus of Tehuantepec to U.S. citizens and to U.S. government effects, free of taxes and passports, and ratification proceeded slowly. It was not formalized until 30 June 1854, when Juan Nepomuceno Almonte, the Mexican minister to Washington, received the first payment of $7 million.

The Senate's amendments left the U.S. claims unsettled, and it also refused to take a stand on the filibusters. The U.S. Army did not wait for the joint commission to finish tracing the border—a task that was not concluded until 1857—but immediately occupied the Mesilla territory. The border established by the Gadsden Treaty eventually proved definitive.

The Plan of Ayutla and Liberal Reform

As map 2 shows, Mexico had lost half of its territory to the United States in a period of six years. The signing of the Gadsden Treaty was therefore met by a public outcry in Mexico. His Most Serene Highness Santa Anna was abusing his position as president in many ways and the sale of yet another piece of territory was considered intolerable.

The discontent was quickly expressed in the Plan de Ayutla, proclaimed by Santa Anna's political enemies on 1 March 1854 and supported by the few prominent liberals still in the country (a great number had been exiled by Santa Anna and were in New Orleans). The plan was one of reform, but carrying it out meant internal war and revolution.

One of the leaders, Juan Alvarez, immediately asked Gadsden to have the U.S. government stop the payment of $3 million still due for the Mesilla cession. Nevertheless, the Ayutla revolution needed arms and money to buy them, and Ignacio Comonfort, a Mexican general and a liberal, was sent to the United States to negotiate a loan. The United States was willing to grant the loan, but only if Mexican territory was mortgaged, and Comonfort finally obtained a loan from Gregorio Ajuria, a Spanish resident of New York and guaranteed it with half the income of the customhouse of Acapulco. The struggle against Santa Anna's dictatorship lasted more than a year. On 17 August 1855, Santa Anna left Mexico and disappeared from Mexican politics forever.

The civil war in Mexico, which convulsed the country from 1855 to 1857, entailed not only new bloodshed, but also new opportunities for bandits and filibusters on the northern border. A group of U.S. adventurers, led by Jean Napoleon Zerman and Samuel L. Dennison, sailed from California to take advantage of the chaos and of the Liberal's search for support. They settled in Baja California to capture ships, purportedly authorized to do so by Juan Alvarez, but the authorities imprisoned the 108 members of the group, who had caused much damage and annoyance. Their imprisonment was added to the long list of U.S. claims. The last important filibuster to Mexico occurred in 1856. It was led by Californian Henry A. Crabb, in Sonora, and ended with the death of 93 adventurers. These deaths were also included in the long list of damages claimed by the United States.

Other incidents occurred on the border during this period. Bandits took advantage of the confusion, and several slave owners crossed the border illegally to chase fugitive slaves. The protection that was sometimes given to the U.S. slaves created hostility that endangered the Mexican inhabitants of Texas.

Almonte presented several complaints about these incidents, but the U.S. government did not accept any responsibility, not even in extreme cases like Crabb's filibuster or when bandits such as J. H. Callahan and W. R. Henry, who claimed they were under orders from the governor of Texas to search for Indians, set fire to the town of Piedras Negras in 1855. On the other hand, the U.S. government pressed its own claims hard, and as soon as Gadsden returned to the United States, he started pushing for the payment of claims that had been accumulating since 1848. Besides forced loans, these included trade irregularities, breaches of contracts as in the Garay concession— damages from Indian incursions into the United States from Mexican territory, and damages suffered by filibusters.

Santa Anna was defeated and left Mexico in August 1855 and was succeeded by Juan Alvarez. Gadsden, still the U.S. minister, hastily recognized Alvarez's government, even before it was established in the capital, and attempted to extradite the fugitive slaves living in Mexico. This ill-advised effort soured diplomatic relations and accomplished nothing. Nor did Alvarez's presidency last long: he resigned in December, when a junta of Liberals named a new provisional president, Comonfort. Gadsden's relationship with Comonfort was even poorer. He succeeded in signing a postal convention but created so many problems that the Mexican government finally requested that he be removed. He was replaced by John Forsyth in October 1856. That year the reform was inaugurated with the *Ley Juárez* (Juárez Law), which abolished the fueros (special privileges of the military and the clergy, and the *Ley Lerdo*, which disentailed the estates owned by the church. In the same year, two laws affecting relations with the United States were enacted: the decree of 1856 prohibited foreigners from acquiring real estate in the border areas, and the General Customs Ordinance removed most of the existing obstacles to trade, simplified transactions, and decreased taxes to stimulate trade. (The new customs ordinance remained in force until 1916.)

By 1857, the country had a new Constitution which changed many policies of the past. Some changes aroused U.S. objections. Article 2, for example declared that "All born in the Republic are free." It also confirmed the practice of not returning slaves and declared that they would be protected: *"Slaves who enter national territory regain,* for that sole fact, *their liberty and have the right to be protected by the laws."* Article 30 was also objectionable: it declared that foreigners who brought real estate in Mexico or had Mexican children would be regarded as Mexicans "whenever they did not manifest the resolution to retain their own nationality."

John Forsyth, the U.S. minister to Mexico City, had instructions to negotiate agreements on the Tehuantepec issue, trade, and claims, and he did negotiate several treaties. One provided for a commission to discuss the claims and another granted a loan to Mexico—a necessary measure to help stabilize the country—but President Pierce did not support these agreements. In 1857, James Buchanan became president of the United States and sent new instructions to Forsyth, authorizing him to offer $12 to $15 million for Baja California, a large part of Sonora and Chihuahua, and a perpetual right of transit across the Isthmus of Tehuantepec. In his message to the U.S. Senate on 7 January 1858, Buchanan mentioned William Walker's expedition to Nicaragua and stated:

It is beyond question the destiny of our race to spread themselves over the continent of North America, and this at no distant day should events be permitted to take their natural course. The tide of emigrants will flow to the south, and nothing can eventually arrest its progress.

Manifest destiny had affected not only the president; in February 1858, Senator Sam Houston of Texas moved to appoint a committee to investigate the feasibility of setting up a protectorate in Mexico and in Central America.

Although Comonfort, the Liberal provisional president, became Mexico's constitutional president in 1857, the political situation was anything but stable. Felix Zuloaga, a leading Conservative, rebelled, and Comonfort, only a moderate Liberal, began to doubt that the country could be governed under the new Liberal constitution. After only two years of a Liberal administration, he suspended the Constitution and jailed Juárez, who, as president of the Supreme Court, was his constitutional successor. Zuloaga denounced Comonfort anyway, and the president, realizing his error, reinstated Juárez and resigned. Juárez did succeed Comonfort as president, but Zuloaga's rebellion succeeded to the extent that a military junta occupied Mexico and installed him as president. Juárez retreated, first to Guadalajara, and thence to Veracruz, a Liberal stronghold. From there he directed the hostilities, known as the War of the Reform, which lasted almost three years.

Mexico thus had two presidents—the constitutionally designated Liberal, Juárez, who governed from Veracruz, and the Conservative, Zuloaga, who governed from Mexico City. Zuloaga had the support of a large part of the Mexican Army and the clergy, and his position was strengthened by the de facto recognition accorded him by the United States and other countries. Juárez, on the other hand, had popular support. In mid-1859 he issued his famous Reform Laws which called for a complete separation of church and state; confiscation of all church wealth; creation of a civil registry of births, deaths, and civil marriages; suppression of monasteries and nunneries; and religious tolerance. These laws increased his popular support and gained for him the support of another group, the Mexican bourgeoisie, who were interested in buying the newly nationalized church properties. Conversely, Zuloaga, who at first appeared to be leading the winning side, lost the support of these capitalists by attempting to set the new laws aside. The U.S. government's support had already begun to waver.

Forsyth, having arranged for Zuloaga's recognition by the United States, had proceeded to explore the possibility of buying Mexican territory, as President Buchanan had instructed him to do. He soon found out that the conservatives would not relinquish any land whatsoever, even though the money was badly needed. By April, desperate because he was not able to achieve anything, Forsyth urged his government to intervene militarily in Mexico. He then broke diplomatic relations with Zuloaga, stating that he considered the tax on property owned by Mexican and foreigners as a forced loan.

Instead of sending troops into Mexico, as Forsyth had requested, President Buchanan sent a special agent, William Churchwell, to Mexico City in December 1858 to survey the situation. Churchwell's advice was to recognize Juárez's government. Buchanan then appointed Robert M. McLane his new minister to Mexico; he was instructed to recognize the liberal government, to negotiate a trade treaty, and to offer $10 million for Baja California and the privilege of free right of transit through several parts of the Republic.

The Liberals were as stubborn as the Conservatives about selling territory, particularly since they were hoping that Miguel Lerdo de Tejada, who was Juárez's envoy to the United States at the time, could obtain a loan to finance the war. McLane, like Forsyth, advised Washington to intervene militarily to protect the lives and interests of U.S. citizens. By December, the president recommended that Congress

pass a law authorizing the President . . . to employ a sufficient military force to enter Mexico for the purpose of obtaining indemnity for the past and security for the future . . .

I repeat the recommendation contained in my last message that the authority may be given to the President to establish one or more temporary military posts across the line in Sonora and Chihuahua . . .

When all hope of obtaining a loan had vanished, the Liberals became more receptive to negotiation. In December, Melchor Ocampo, Juárez's foreign relations secretary, signed a treaty with McLane which made him infamous. By this treaty, Mexico granted the United States a perpetual right of transit across the Isthmus of

Tehuantepec, with the proviso that fees charged for U.S. freight would be the same as the Mexican. It also allowed the U.S. to intervene in that area in the event that the neutrality guaranteed by the treaty was upset. The right of transit was also granted through several points that linked the northern border to the Gulf of Mexico and the Gulf of California, as well as virtually free trade between both countries. In exchange for all these privileges, the Liberal government was to receive $4 million. The treaty was rejected by the U.S. Senate, 27 votes to 18, however. Twenty-three negative votes were cast by senators from the north who considered the treaty a southern effort to increase its zone of influence. Mexican sovereignty was saved, but fortuitously.

There was feverish Liberal activity during 1859. The radical wing of the Liberal Party won out, and political reform was consolidated when the Laws of Reform were proclaimed, because the liberal measures attracted the sympathy of some in the United States to Juárez's party and generated support for him which was sometimes decisive. The most remarkable show of support was an incident at Anton Lizardo. The Conservatives bought two Cuban warships and tried to attack Veracruz by sea as well as by land. Juárez denounced the ships as pirate ships and successfully appealed to the United States for assistance. A U.S. naval force stopped the boats, detained them in Anton Lizardo, and took them to New Orleans, foiling the Conservative attempt to take over Veracruz. Although it would be an oversimplification to attribute the Liberal victory to this incident, it no doubt helped. On 25 December 1860, Liberal troops occupied Mexico City.

Like all civil war, the War of the Reform left its country in a pitiful state. The whole Republic had been divided by the opposing armies: the Liberals were strong in the north and the coast, Michoacan, Jalisco, and Zacatecas; the Conservatives, in the capital and center. Reuniting the country was not a simple matter under the best of circumstances. And circumstances were not to prove the best. The frustrated Conservatives conspired in Europe to promote foreign intervention, using as their rationale the precarious financial situation of the country.

European Intervention

President Juárez tried to guide the country back to normality, and the foreign ministry announced that all claims would be heard and offered guarantees to foreigners. Nationalized property continued to be sold but, owing to the scarcity of capital, could not be converted to cash nor could the former tenants be properly compensated. Bankruptcy was imminent. On 17 June 1861, the government suspended payments on its foreign debts, and France reacted by summoning Spain and Great Britain to a convention in London that condemned the Mexican action. At the meeting, which was held in October, the three powers decided to force Mexico to fulfill its international commitments by sending a joint fleet. The fleet arrived at Veracruz before the year's end.

Other external events also affected Mexico. As the civil war in Mexico ended, one began in the United States. The election of Abraham Lincoln as president provoked the secession of South Carolina and, by the beginning of 1861, the southern states united to form a Confederacy. Lincoln's decision to maintain the Union made a civil war inevitable. The bitterly fought struggle lasted until 1865.

The Civil War in the United States affected its relations with Mexico at various levels. The United States was in no position to prevent the European powers from intervening in Mexico. On the other hand, both the Union and the Confederacy were interested in maintaining relations with their southern neighbor. Deciding which side to support was rather difficult for the Mexican government.

Ideologically, Juárez's followers were sympathetic to the North, but Mexico shared a long border with the Confederacy. At the beginning of the war, a southern victory looked probable: the textile industries of Great Britain and France depended on U.S. cotton, and these countries seemed likely to support the Confederacy. The Union, however, won British support largely because the North looked like a winner and because the U.S. minister to London, Charles Francis Adams, skillfully exploited the issue of slavery in the English press at a time when the British government had assumed a moralistic stance on the problem. The French, who cared little about slavery, did not wish to support the Confederacy without England.

In April 1861, Lincoln appointed Thomas Corwin his minister to Mexico. Although Corwin's instructions still reflected the expansionist inclinations of Secretary of State William H. Seward to some extent, his most important mission was to neutralize the offers made by the Confederates and to offer military support if the Confederacy attacked the northern states of Mexico. He was to inform the Mexican government that the United States was not really interested in obtaining Mexican territory, but was willing to buy Baja California if that was the only way to prevent it from falling into the hands of the Confederates.

The Confederacy also sent a representative to Mexico, John T.

Pickett. His mission was to negotiate commercial treaties that would enable the southern states to send cotton to Europe through Mexican ports and to prevent the Union from using Mexican territory to attack the South. Pickett was not a good choice; his indiscreet conduct and condescending attitude toward the Mexicans guaranteed his failure. The Mexican government declared its neutrality, but did not really maintain this position: in August 1861, it authorized Union troops to cross through Mexican territory from Guaymas to Arizona. The affinity with the Union was not entirely ideological. Corwin was even then trying to obtain a loan of $11 million for Mexico, and the hope of raising it did not vanish until the following year.

The Confederacy made gains, however, by sending a special envoy to the northern states of Mexico, José Joaquín Quintero. He was able to establish good relations with the governor of Nuevo León, Santiago Vidaurri, cacique of a vast region of the northeast, who agreed to the annexation of his domain to the Confederacy. Although this proposal had to wait on a Confederate victory, active trade developed on the border strip. Southern cotton was loaded in Matamoros for transit to Europe and arms and munitions were regularly received from Europe for trans-shipment to the Confederates. In Piedras Negras, Laredo, and other towns, trade flourished and their populations increased owing to the work of maintaining the very large wagon trains that carried cotton to Mexico and returned wheat, textiles, shoes, and other Mexican goods to the Confederate states.

Vidaurri set and controlled the customhouse duties and enforced peace and quiet on the border, not an easy task, since Juárez's people were strong in Matamoros, and trouble-making leaders, such as Cortina, who was suspected of cattle rustling, and José Ma. Carvajal, who was suspected of separatism, operated in the border area. Nor did the Texans halt their incursions in pursuit of fugitive slaves. Still, his distance from Mexico City enabled Vidaurri to disregard the orders of the Republican government to maintain neutrality.

Meanwhile, the Mexican government was facing intervention threatened by the Europeans. Juárez, who believed in the power of reasoned discussion, invited the representatives of Spain, England, and France to meet with his foreign secretary. He even authorized the disembarkation of the foreign troops at Veracruz so they would be less exposed to the tropical fevers that plagued the Mexican coasts, but with the understanding that they would reembark if an agreement was not reached. Spain and Great Britain signed the subsequent Soledad Agreements, in which Mexico pledged to resume payment of the foreign debt as soon as possible, but France, which had other plans, did not. The French refused to obligate themselves to reembark if no agreement was reached, and they began their attack on Mexico with the advantage of already being on land.

The reaction of the Mexican people reflected their experience in the war with the United States. The city of Puebla controlled the route from Veracruz to Mexico City, and the new national consciousness prompted a mobilization of troops sufficient to turn the French attempt to capture Puebla on 5 May 1862 into a sharp defeat and to send the French army back to Orizaba.

The setback at Puebla injured Napoleon III's pride. He reinforced his troops, and a year later they defeated the Republican army concentrated in Puebla. The French followed this victory with one in Mexico City, and Juárez was again forced to leave the capital. All attempts to obtain U.S. support failed.

The popular and capable Peruvian ambassador to Mexico, Manuel Nicolás Corpancho, approached Secretary of State Seward and proposed an inter-American alliance to expel the French from Mexico; the Chilean ambassador made a similar attempt later on; and even U.S. envoys in Europe called for some action; but Seward was convinced that the Union's precarious situation precluded any attempt to enforce the Monroe Doctrine. He decided on neutrality. Actually, this policy was only applied to Juárez, who had no funds to pay for arms; the Mexican ambassador in Washington objected without success to the sale of arms and supplies to the French. Although Matías Romero, Juárez's envoy, gained no official support in the United States, he did succeed in obtaining help from many individuals, and Seward was forced to respond to various protests which were made in Congress.

The military superiority of the French was overwhelming, and in 1864, the Republican Army's response became a guerilla war. When he retired to the north, Juárez had to face the northern leaders who had enjoyed almost complete freedom of action and he encountered disloyal governors such as Vidaurri. Juárez's first attempt to make Monterrey the Republican center of operations failed, and he withdrew to Saltillo. There, his troops succeeded in defeating Vidaurri, who fled to Texas.

Maximilian, the Emperor of Mexico

The Conservative Mexicans in Europe, both the older exiles and the new ones who joined them after the Liberal victory in 1860, had long been pressing the idea that Mexico should become a monarchy.

France was ready to help by installing on the throne Maximilian of Hapsburg, brother of the Austrian emperor, who was also the choice of the exiles. Maximilian did not, however, agree immediately: he insisted on receiving a letter with sufficient signatures to prove that the Mexican people were calling him. The signatures were produced and, finally, in June 1864, when the French troops were already in possession of the capital and Juárez had fled, he arrived in Mexico City to take over the reigns of government. He soon disappointed his Conservative supporters by proving to be a monarch of liberal persuasion.

He also disappointed the Confederates to the north. The Confederacy had hoped to be recognized by Mexico when Maximilian established his Mexican empire. Active trade across the border had continued despite the Yankee blockade of the Confederate ports, nor had it been disturbed by Juárez's temporary presence in Monterrey. Local officials in the cities of Matamoros and Monterrey maintained close contact with the southerners. But Maximilian was not inclined to follow suit; even though he was not recognized by the Union, he maintained Mexico's neutrality. When the Confederacy was defeated, his empire welcomed many refugees, especially to its northern states, and he tried to establish an agrarian colony in the State of Veracruz, near Cordoba, but that was all.

The defeat of the South changed the fortunes of Juárez and the Republicans. Important politicians in the United States began to demand that the Monroe Doctrine be enforced and that the French be forced out of Mexico immediately. Seward, although in far greater agreement than he admitted publicly, was a cautious man. He much preferred that the French leave of their own volition, without having their national pride involved in a nasty dispute with the United States, and he restricted his country to the use of diplomatic pressure in Paris.

Meanwhile, the Mexican minister Romero was receiving indications of support and offers to enlist in the Juárist troops. General Ulysses S. Grant, the Union Civil War hero, sponsored the idea of forming a U.S. army to help expel the French, and the Mexican ambassador convinced J. M. Schonfield, a Civil War general, to consent to leading that army. The plan failed because Schonfield consulted with Seward, who convinced him to make a diplomatic effort in France before acting.

The days of Maximilian's empire were numbered, and not only because the Civil War in the United States had ended. In Europe,

Napoleon III was having problems with Prussia, and in Mexico there was constant pressure on the French army from the Juárists. When, at the end of 1865, Seward observed that the French invasion of Mexico was harmful to U.S. friendship with France, Napoleon made plans to withdraw his troops. His timetable, less than two years, was much shortened by pressure from Washington. The French did attempt to secure U.S. recognition of the Mexican empire on the grounds that it would facilitate the withdrawal of the French troops, but this reasoning was unacceptable in Washington.

Seward, besides appointing an agent who would be close to the Mexican Republic's leadership, prevented the Austrians from sending troops to help Maximilian and he hindered Juárez's enemies in the north.

At the same time, Seward continued to press U.S. claims against the Republican government. On 26 March 1867, while Maximilian was on the run, Seward reminded Romero of the many old claims against Mexico. Even though the United States had not pressed for their resolution when Mexico was weak and unstable, the situation would change with the imminent Republican victory, and the unresolved claims would strain relations with the restored Liberal regime. Seward suggested a treaty in which Mexico would bind itself to the payment of these claims and which would exempt U.S. citizens from forced loans and military service. Romero, an expert on the U.S. scene, delayed his response, hoping that if Grant was elected president of the United States, it would make a difference for Mexico. Nevertheless, before he returned to Mexico in 1868, the Mexican ambassador signed an agreement with the secretary of state.

The Mexican empire died in mid-1867, when Maximilian was taken prisoner. Seward joined those who asked for mercy for the emperor, but the Republicans paid no attention.

The politicians of both countries then entered one of those fleeting periods of warm friendship.

5

Toward an Understanding with the Mexican Liberals: 1868–1898

A Cordial Relationship

In most relationships between two countries, even two of such un-equal force as Mexico and the United States, there have been inter-ludes of cordiality. The year 1867 marked the beginning of one of these periods. The Mexican liberals were, despite some fallings-out, satisfied with their political ascendance and the Union had won its Civil War. In both countries, it was time to turn attention to consolidating their hard-won internal peace and to making economic progress. Despite political changes in both countries, and despite some unsolved problems—and the new ones that inevitably arose— the United States and Mexico remained on fairly amicable terms from 1867 until after 1904. The United States did continue to expand its territory, but not at Mexico's direct expense. In 1867, it bought Alaska from Russia; in 1898, Hawaii was annexed; and, that same year, after a war with Spain, the United States acquired the Philip-pines, Guam, and Puerto Rico, and won the right to intervene in Cuba.

Between the end of the Civil War in the United States in 1865 and 1910, the year from which the Mexican Revolution is dated, the United States had eleven presidents. Three were assassinated. The changes in Mexico, less frequent and less violent, nevertheless merit a short review before our story of U.S.–Mexican relations is resumed.

In 1867, following the defeat of Emperor Maximilian and the expulsion of the French troops from Mexico, Benito Juárez, the civilian leader who had been provisional president during the rebel-lion, succeeded to the presidency and continued the liberal reforms begun earlier. Juárez succeeded, for a time, in bringing the military leaders under control, but when, following his death in 1871, he was succeeded by another civilian, Sebastian Lerdo de Tejada, General Porfirio Díaz organized a revolt. Lerdo succeeded in putting it down and served as president until 1876, at which time Díaz again rebelled, this time successfully: the Tuxtepec rebellion which he led, brought him to power. In 1880, since his slogan had been "no reelection," Díaz turned the presidency over to General Manuel Gonzalez, who served until 1884. After resuming office that year, Díaz stayed in power until 1911, being careful to make the necessary amendments to the Constitution to legalize hs reelections. Adding to the stability of his administration were the long terms of service of several key members of the Mexican foreign ministry.

Díaz's dictatorship, although it did not solve Mexico's social problems, brought the country decades of peace and permitted it to place itself on a sounder financial footing, promote economic growth, and occupy an honorable and respected place among nations. Mexico, for almost the first time, became able to honor its international commitments.

In the United States, the conclusion of the Civil War favored an industrial development until then unheard of, thanks to its enormous natural resources, the availability of labor, and European capital. That development also favored corruption in public life that plagued the country until the end of the century.

At the beginning of this period, the problems at their mutual border dominated the relationship between the two countries. Little by little, as trade and investment grew, the economic needs of both countries became more complementary. Mexico needed capital with which to exploit its resources and build railroads, and the United States was willing to invest its recently generated capital. Its industrialization required markets and raw materials; its neighbor to the south needed tools, locomotives, and machinery. Proximity and the railroad system resulted in the replacement of many European products used in Mexico by U.S. products.

Thanks to the political stability and economic liberalism on which it was founded, this complementarity changed a difficult relationship into one of cooperation, as is illustrated by their agreement, during this period, that troops of both countries could cross the border in order to pursue bandits or combat Indian raiders. The new relationship had its ups and downs, but never, until the end of Porfirio Díaz's regime, was it ruptured.

The Claims Arbitration

On 4 July 1868, U.S. Secretary of State William Seward and Mexican Ambassador Matías Romero signed an agreement (referred to in the previous chapter) to settle all the claims for damages presented by citizens of both countries since the signing of the Treaty of Guadalupe in 1848. Each president was to appoint a commissioner who would then appoint an arbiter to pronounce judgment on any disputed cases. President Juárez immediately approved the agreement, but President Grant did not sign it until February 1869 and the joint commission was not convened until August 1869. The time allowed for its deliberations proved too short; four protocols extended its duration. The commission examined 2,075 claims: 1,017 from the United States and 998 from Mexico. Of this total, only 186 claims from the United States and 167 from Mexico were upheld.

Over a third of the Mexican claims, and the most important ones, derived from the commitment to protect Mexico from Indian raids launched from the United States and stated in Article 11 of the Treaty of Guadalupe, which the U.S. commissioner eluded by means of various arguments. First he argued that the commission had no jurisdiction over these claims. Then he declared that the damages had been produced by individuals, not by U.S. authorities. Finally he insisted that Article 2 of the Mesilla Treaty had relieved the United States of all responsibility. The Mexican commissioner, for his part, argued that this release from responsibility was intended for the future and did not apply to the period between 1848 and 1853. The disagreement was so severe that the talks were suspended in mid-1873. Nevertheless, Sebastian Lerdo de Tejada's government was confronted with many problems and wanted to be rid of this one. He appointed a new commissioner to carry on the negotiations, and the work proceeded.

Some of the cases decided by the arbiter were successfully protested by Mexico. One was the claim of a mining company, La Abra, which began operations in Sinaloa in 1865 but was compelled to suspend work because of its high cost. Owing to the difficulty of transportation in the mountrain range, the company abandoned its machinery. In 1870, the investors, in hopes that the commission might help them recoup some of their capital, claimed that the equipment had been left behind because of the hostility of regional authorities who wanted to take over the mines. The arbiter awarded them $600,000 even though they adduced no evidence in support of their allegations.

A similar case, concerning an alleged cotton embargo, netted one Benjamin Weil $334,950. Weil, a U.S. entrepreneur and merchant, also offered no evidence. Years later, these cases were reconsidered and the Mexican government's payments were refunded.

The most famous case was brought by the Pious Fund of the Californias, represented by Tadeus Amat and Joseph Alemany. This claim had to do with property owned by the Jesuits, the rents from which they used to support their missions in the Californias during the colonial period. When the order was expelled from the Spanish empire in 1767, the government of Spain took charge of its central fund; later, the rents were transferred to the Franciscans and Dominicans who took charge of the missions. After 1821, when Mexico had gained its independence from Spain, the Mexican government, pursuing a policy of secularizing these missions, seized and gradually began to sell some of the missions' possessions, and in 1842 President Santa Anna authorized their total sale. The Mexican government was obligated to pay 6 percent interest on the money originally belonging to the missions, but this interest had never been kept current, or paid at all, in view of the poor financial health of the country, war, and the loss of territory. In 1868, the Diocese of Upper California began to press for the payment of two-thirds of the interest that the Pious Fund's properties should have produced since 1842.

Mexico contested this claim by pointing out that Articles 13, 14, and 15 of the Treaty of Guadalupe had cancelled all further claims of U.S citizens against the Mexican Republic and obligated the United States to make payment with money withheld for that purpose. The Mexican commissioner also argued that the purpose of the Pious Fund—the conversion of Indians—had ceased to exist, for they had already been converted or killed off; that the old province of California, the beneficiary of the fund, had disappeared. He rejected the amount of the claim as exorbitant, since it had not been calculated on the basis of the Indian population. Besides, he argued that the estates of this claim were located within the Mexican Republic and that the claim should therefore be presented before internal courts. The arbiter nevertheless awarded the Pious Fund a little more than $904 thousand.

Another decision exonerated the U.S. government of any responsibility for filibusters' attacks. The only case in which Mexico succeeded was in relation to the contract for building a railroad across the Isthmus of Tehuantepec. Various concessionaries were demanding no less than $320 million, but their claim was ruled inadmissable.

The joint commission's work ended on 20 November 1877. Mexico had been obligated to pay a total of $4,125,622.20 and had been awarded only $150,498.42 for its own claims against the United States. The justice of many of the awards was much questioned in Mexico since most of the claims were not acknowledged as derived from incursions at the border, but the country had rid itself a great nuisance.

Border Problems

The Treaty of Guadalupe set the border between the United States and Mexico nearer to the populated area of Mexico, a circumstance that resulted in the creation of new settlements on both sides of the dividing line and in a brisk trade. In 1852, Mexico established a duty-free border zone in the state of Tamaulipas. This permitted the free entry of all kinds of products, but it was also used to smuggle goods into Texas and, in 1868, Edward Lee Plumb, in charge of U.S. affairs in Mexico City, began to press the Mexican government to close down the zone.

President Juárez and other Mexican officials were in favor of doing so; when the U.S. Congress appointed a committee to investigate the problems at the border, Matías Romero, the Mexican minister to Washington, spoke against the continuance of the duty-free zone before the Senate committee. His position was that it also harmed the Mexican economy, for not all the smuggling was into Texas; quite a bit of the duty-free goods ended up in Mexico. Nevertheless, the Mexican Congress, more sensitive to the opinion of the states favored by the duty-free system, actually extended the franchise to Coahuila, Chihuahua, and Nuevo León in 1870.

The most important U.S. complaints about border problems were not about contraband, however, but about raids by Indians settled on the Mexican side and about the rustling of Texan cattle. The increase in cattle stealing was attributed to the appointment of Juan N. Cortina (accused of various felonies on both sides of the border) as military commander of Tamaulipas. He was dismissed, but the complaints about cattle rustling persisted.

The exaggerated issue of Indian raids on U.S. territory had mainly to do with small communities of Lipanes, Mezcaleros, Kikapus, and Mascogo Indians, devoted to agriculture, who had settled in Chihuahua and Coahuila; extremely poor, they stole cattle during the winter. Some U.S. agents who visited them in 1868 and in subse-

quent years were witness to their poverty. Nevertheless, cattle rustling was not to be tolerated and Juárez's government urged the
northern states to collaborate with U.S. authorities to prevent these
Indians from slipping back into Mexico with their plunder. The
Mexican government also permitted some U.S. agents to enter the
country to try to convince some of the tribes, such as the Mascogo, to
return to their reservations, and the crossing of the border by U.S.
troops in pursuit of Mexican Indians began to be unofficially tolerated. On the other hand, when Colonel Joaquin Terrazas and his men
crossed over from Chihuahua in the opposite direction and for the
same reasons, the reaction in Washington was negative and sharp.

In 1872, the U.S. president appointed a commission to investigate
the situation at the Rio Grande, and Mexico appointed a parallel
commission which made a careful and detailed investigation. The first
report of the Northeast Border Investigating Commission appointed
by Mexico was submitted in December 1872. It estimated that two
hundred thousand head of cattle had been stolen and that the number
of lives lost in Indian raids was considerable, although uncountable.
In reference to cattle stealing, the commission wrote that "each side of
the border assumes that the ones to perpetrate or protect this rustling
are neighbors or authorities of the opposite side." It took notice, also,
of the mistreatment of Mexicans in Texas and the transgression of the
border by citizens of both countries.

Their second report, presented in November 1873, delved further
into Indian raids and cattle stealing. It pointed out that cattle raising
on the Mexican side of the border had been insecure since 1848 and
that it was only after 1865 that U.S. raiders had begun to suffer
similar depredations.

According to the Mexican report, the guilty parties were Texan
bandits, U.S. Indians who had taken refuge in Mexico, Mexicans
living in Texas, or all of the above—and it named cattle buyers and
U.S. officers who were covering up these crimes.

The Mexican commission, having consulted archives in Texan
courts, discovered that the rustling perpetrated by U.S. citizens had
never been punished. Contrary to the conclusion of the U.S. commission, the Mexicans, after analyzing data on cattle and Texan leather
exports, also discovered a large discrepancy between the number of
cattle previously in Texas and the number exported from that state,
and made detailed reference to a Texan rancher, Richard King, an
alleged expert in stealing unbranded cattle. Data found in the *Texas
Almanac* from 1869 to 1872 contradicted that offered by the U.S.

Commission about the reduction of cattle in Cameron and Nueces counties; instead they pointed to a slight increase. The report also described the constant state of alarm of Mexican cattle breeders living on the Texan side because of thefts perpetrated by white U.S. citizens whom the authorities protected. Their conclusion was that the Mexican side of the border had suffered more than the U.S. side, despite the raids by Mexican Indians on Texas, and that reports in the U.S. press had been exaggerated in order to justify possible further annexations of territory.

The Mexican commission recommended joint policing of the border by federal troops of both countries, reform of the treaty of extradition, and modification of the laws regarding cattle theft both in Texas and in the northeastern states of Mexico.

The government of Mexico was at least equally concerned about the security of its border farther west. Apache and Comanche Indians were devastating Sonora, and problems there led the Mexican government to appoint an investigating commission for the Northwest in 1874. In its report, presented at the end of that year, the commission described less frequent cattle theft but far more serious assaults, offenses against Mexicans, filibusters, and incursions by displaced Indians. The commission advised the military commanders in the north to cooperate with the U.S. Army to put down Indians that attacked either side.

Pressure from Texas (as well as steady pressure from Washington) did not ease during this period. In 1875, the Texan legislature appointed its own investigating committee to look into border troubles, and in due course received a report covering the disturbances at Corpus Christi, which it blamed on the Mexicans. In its own defense, the Mexican State of Tamaulipas, just across the line, conducted its own investigation and issued its own report, which blamed U.S. gangs for the troubles. Tamaulipas pointed out that, even by U.S. accounts, most of the dead and most of the burned ranches were Mexican. Among the U.S. complaints was a renewed one against General Cortina, now municipal president of Matamoros. The Mexican government tried to explain the political difficulties of removing him, but in the end Cortina was arrested by Servando Canales, the governor of Tamaulipas, and sent to the capital.

Meanwhile the U.S. minister to Mexico City was pressing for agreement to the occasional crossing over of U.S. troops, and the Mexicans turned him down. However, even if national agreements could not be reached, local agreements could be, for the Comanche were a problem to both sides. General E. O. C. Ord, the U.S. military commander in Texas, succeeded in reaching an agreement with the governors of Sonora and Chihuahua to allow troops of both countries to cross the dividing line in emergencies. There was no corresponding agreement in the eastern sector.

The situation at the border became even more complicated in 1876, when General Porfirio Díaz and General Manuel González, in the pattern of many other revolutionaries before and after them, decided to cross the border to organize their rebellion against the Mexican government. The U.S. government turned a deaf ear to notes delivered to the State Department by Minister Ignacio Mariscal requesting that the laws of neutrality against the rebels be enforced. History repeated itself: the arms obtained in the United States aided Díaz and his followers to grasp power and González became president of Mexico in 1884.

Díaz and the Hayes Regime

In April 1876, Porfirio Díaz occupied Matamoros with the help of General Juan Cortina, who had fled the capital after Sebastian Lerdo de Tejada's government had freed him on bail. Díaz's victory was uncertain; despite his popularity as a hero of the wars against the Conservatives and imperialists and his anti-imperialist and anti-reelectionist rhetoric, he had been unsuccessful in two previous attempts.

On 26 September 1876, Díaz issued a decree from Oaxaca in which he declared void all contracts which resulted "in mortgage of the nation." Lerdo had authorized a series of concessions to foreigners, particularly the railroad concession, that were as imprudent as most granted during that period by other nonindustrialized countries and that were very unpopular in the Mexican Congress; Díaz was a popular cause. On the other hand, among the grantees was the former U.S. minister, Edward Lee Plumb, whose enmity did not help Diaz's popularity in that country.

After the mid-year elections, Lerdo declared himself reelected but it was Díaz who dominated the greater part of the country. The situation was further complicated by José María Iglesias, the president of the Supreme Court of Justice, who declared himself temporary president on the grounds that Lerdo de Tejada's reelection was illegal. This situation evoked old times. In November, Díaz won out over Lerdo's troops and tried to induce Iglesias to recognize the Tuxtepec

Plan, which banned a president's reelection. He did not succeed, and both Lerdo and Iglesias were exiled to the United States.

Díaz moved cautiously after his victory and declared himself provisional president pending new elections. The international situation was still uncertain; the whole country was isolated because of damage to the telegraph lines through Matamoros; moreover, Lerdo and Iglesias, both in the United States, were trying to prevent U.S. recognition of Díaz.

Don Porfirio Díaz, aware of all of Mexico's difficulties vis-à-vis Washington, decided to make a great effort to pay the first installment due on the Mexican–U.S. claims debt. On 27 November, he called together the richer traders and businessmen and requested their collaboration through a "voluntary" loan at an interest rate of 1 percent a month. In this way, 189,000 pesos were collected, but the amount due was 300,000. José María Mata was appointed special presidential agent to carry out the burdensome task of delivering the money.

President Ulysses S. Grant decided, in line with the tradition of recognizing de facto governments in Mexico, to give discretionary instructions to his minister, John W. Foster. Foster was wary: the situation was complex and Díaz's tenure seemed uncertain. He waited and decided to take advantage of the occasion to press for the solution of the border problems. The Mexican foreign minister, Ignacio L. Vallarta, was firmly convinced that U.S. recognition should be granted unconditionally; he insisted, throughout his term, that only full recognition would alter the situation sufficiently to facilitate negotiation of the differences in which the U.S. minister appeared to be so interested.

But U.S. politics further complicated relations between the two countries. The 1876 presidential election had resulted in the disputed victory of Rutherford B. Hayes, and some diversion of national attention seemed in order. On the day of Hayes' inauguration, 4 March 1877, perhaps not by coincidence, newspapers in New York, Washington, and Philadelphia published comments on the border situation in which they concluded that Mexico could not achieve political stability and in which they called for the establishment of a protectorate.

Foster, who had nothing to do with any of this and was his government's closest observer of the Mexican scene, recommended, in March 1877, that Díaz's government be recognized. The new secretary of state, William M. Evarts, told him to wait.

Díaz, anxious to prove that his was an efficient and orderly government, turned his attention to the border problems. He appointed General Jerónimo Treviño to head the forces guarding the northeastern border and strengthened his troops; he also transferred Juan N. Cortina, the ex-mayor who had assisted him, to a post outside Tamaulipas. Nevertheless, the incidents continued. When Mexico complained about Lt. Col. W.R. Shafter's armed incursion from Texas into Piedras Negras—not to pursue criminals but to rescue two Mexicans being held by Mexican authorities—it received no reply.

In May 1877, the Mexican Congress declared Porfirio Díaz the country's constitutional president, and Foster hastened to send telegrams and dispatches to Washington recommending recognition. Several European countries had already so acted, and the moment seemed appropriate. Hayes was playing to popular opinion in Texas, however, and instead of an authorization Foster received a copy of the orders that the secretary of war sent to the border troops in June 1877:

> The *President* desires that utmost vigilance on the part of the military forces in Texas be exercised . . . General Ord will at once notify the Mexican authorities along the Texan border, of the great desire of the President to unite with them in efforts to suppress the long continental lawlessness. At the same time he will inform those authorities that if the Government of Mexico shall continue to neglect the duty of suppressing these outrages, that duty will devolve upon this government, and will be performed; even if the performance should render necessary the occasional crossing of the border by our troops. You will, therefore, direct General Ord that in case the lawless incursions continue he will be at liberty, in his discretion, when in pursuit of a band of marauders . . . to follow them across the Rio Grande, and to overtake and punish them, as well as retake stolen property . . .

Lerdo and Iglesias were the first to protest—exiled in the United States, they were the first Mexicans to learn about this—but the wave of indignation that swept the country helped to strengthen Díaz, for he appeared to be a leader capable of standing up to his northern neighbor's aggressiveness. His minister of war immediately ordered General Treviño to inform General Ord "that the Mexican government, unable to allow a foreign army to penetrate national territory . . . would repel force by force."

Lerdo's minister to Washington, Ignacio Mariscal, who was still serving (Díaz's own confidential agent, José María Mata, had not yet arrived) presented Mexico's official protest to the assistant secretary of state, who tried to calm him by stating that the order was not meant to provoke Mexico but "only" to appease U.S. public opinion, particularly in Texas, and to force Mexico to act. This seemed correct, for General Philip Sheridan, then in command of U.S. western and southwestern troops, advised Ord not to cross the border unless he found it necessary; Treviño and Ord had maintained a cordial interchange; and U.S. troops had even collaborated in arresting a Lerdist, General Mariano Escobedo, who opposed Díaz. Some time later, when Mexican troops crossed the border to chase other Lerdists, Mexico apologized, the guilty were punished, and the matter was dropped.

Foster, for his part, tried to convince Vallarta that the Mexicans had interpreted General Ord's directive erroneously; but he also decided to talk to Díaz directly. This initiative led to a series of long discussions of all the disagreements between Foster and Vallarta. Besides requesting agreement on reciprocal crossing of the troops, Foster asked for the suppression of Indian raids, of cattle stealing, of compulsory loans from U.S. citizens, of the duty-free zones, and of the laws prohibiting foreigners from buying real estate in border areas.

Vallarta, an experienced jurist, reminded Foster that the policy of requiring compulsory loans derived from Article 9 of the Treaty of 1831 and that its suspension could condemn the Mexicans to an inferior status within their own country. As to the border problems, Vallarta advanced José Mata's proposals: to watch in a coordinated way both banks of the river, to tighten up the treaty of extradition in both countries, to have both countries declare it compulsory to hand over any nationals accused of rustling cattle, and to force federal and local authorities to collaborate in identifying criminals and in recouping stolen property. Mata acknowledged the damage being done in the duty-free zone, but declared it impossible to convince the Mexican Congress to abolish it. It was made clear that the Mexican government considered recognition and the revocation of the order to Ord as prerequisite to any agreement.

When he arrived in Washington, Mata was unable to discuss the Mexican proposal for solving the border problems. On 17 July 1877, the *New York Herald* published a map including the territories that its publisher thought the United States should annex: Baja California, Sonora, Chihuahua, Coahuila, part of Nuevo León, Sinaloa, and

Durango. In Mexico City, the public was upset and relations between Vallarta and Foster worsened abruptly.

Vallarta consulted Díaz and Matías Romero and outlined a treaty draft which he transmitted to Foster on 10 September. It authorized the presidents of both countries to agree to reciprocal border crossing by troops in pursuit of bellicose Indians or rustlers, specifying the period of time that any particular force would be in the other country and just where it would be. Each government was to punish any abuses by its own troops and to respect the territorial rights of the other. These discussions had to be suspended, and Vallarta was politically embarrassed by having to allow U.S. troops to cross into Mexico. Five years later, and on the terms Vallarta had specified, such permits were granted.

Díaz's government perceived great interest in the country among U.S. investors and decided to use it in the push for recognition. The man chosen as a confidential agent to Washington was Manuel de Zamacona, who had been a member of the Joint Claims Commission and who was well acquainted, as Romero was, with the neighboring country. Zamacona's instructions were to insist on the protests and to enlighten U.S. opinion. He had his own ideas of how to move President Hayes' supporters in Washington off dead center and he organized the opinion and influence of those who had a stake in Mexico's economic development.

Zamacona was not mistaken. The railroads and industrial interests were growing daily more impatient with Hayes' delay in recognizing Díaz, and they succeeded in persuading Congress to appoint a committee to study the "Mexican matter." Congress invited Evarts, the secretary of state; General Sheridan, now secretary of war; General Ord; Foster, the minister to Mexico; and even Zamacona to advise the committee. Evarts' hostility to Díaz's regime was exposed and he finally directed Foster to communicate U.S. recognition of the Mexican government. Recognition was announced on 18 April 1878, eighteen months after Díaz had become president.

It must be admitted that Porfirio Díaz found this initial U.S. hostility useful in securing his position and gathering support for his policy of uniting the country. In addition, Mexico, whose diplomatic relations since 1858 had been confined to the United States, was forced to seek separate and independent relations with European countries and to break away from its complete diplomatic dependence on its northern neighbor. Recognition did not immediately improve relations between the two countries, however. Vallarta insisted on having the orders previously issued to Ord formally revoked. And although Díaz and his cabinet were initially willing to grant limited crossing permits to the U.S. Army, the proposition caused such an uproar in Mexico that it became useful propoganda for the Lerdists and Zamacona had to resign.

Nevertheless, Zamacona had been able to move closer to important U.S. commercial circles. Groups interested in obtaining concessions began to appear, and Matías Romero supported his arguments for opening Mexico's doors to international trade with a book full of statistical, geographic, economic, and legal data. Its publication indeed marked the official opening of Mexico's doors to foreign investment.

In accordance with diplomatic practice at the time, as the policy of the U.S. government toward Mexico changed, so did its minister. Foster had worked hard and done his best, but he had to press difficult and unpopular policies and to suffer the consequences of his country's transgression of the border. At the end of 1879, Foster toured the northern states in Mexico and was able to report that the situation had improved. He was then transferred to Moscow, just as the controversial directive to General Ord was revoked.

Foster was succeeded by Philip H. Morgan, who presented his credentials on 15 April. Morgan's instructions were simple: he was to maintain good relations and to work for U.S. interests. In order to achieve this second objective it seemed imperative to obtain authorization for reciprocal border crossing of the troops; Díaz managed to end his first term in office without agreeing to it.

Old Problems and New Attitudes

The four years of Manuel González's term (1880–84) led to further improvements in Mexican–U.S. relations which would reach a peak between 1898—when Mexico and the United States raised their legations to embassies—and 1901–02, when the Second Pan–American Conference was held in Mexico.

This period was dominated by Díaz's long presidency and by the permanence of his surrounding staff. Ignacio Mariscal acted as foreign minister for nearly thirty years, from 1880 to 1910 (with brief absence from 1883 to 1885), and Matías Romero was minister to Washington from 1882 till his death in 1898. The two were a good combination. Mariscal, according to Cosío Villegas in his *Historia*

Moderna de México, was irrationally anti-United States, but he had valuable diplomatic experience and he capitalized on every opportunity to secure whatever independence was possible for Mexico. Romero, knowledgeable about the United States was an efficient watchdog, vigilant of Mexican interests. This combination produced victories such as the review of the rulings on the Weil and LaAbra claims (1889), the acceptance of Mexican ownership of the Guano Islands off the Yucatán Peninsula (1886) and of Passion Island in the Pacific (1897), both of which the United States claimed to have discovered and, above all, U.S. official agreement that all U.S. citizens must submit their claims to Mexican courts before appealing through diplomatic channels.

The dominating factor in the relations between the two countries continued to be the flow of U.S. investments into Mexico. Businessmen had been visiting the National Palace since Juárez's times, when some concessions had been granted to foreigners. Lerdo followed the same pattern. Even anti-imperialist Díaz, influenced by his conviction that economic development could be attained only through the construction of a railway system, began to grant concessions. General Díaz's hospitality had also created pressure by private enterprises on the U.S. Congress for recognition of his government. Three months before the end of his first term in office in 1880, the two most important railroad concessions were signed: the lines connecting Mexico City with Ciudad Juárez and Laredo, which were to seal the fate of the Mexican economy as complementary to that of the United States.

Other problems also required attention in 1880. Border problems still troubled both governments, and the policy of the new secretary of state, James A. Blaine, was a reaffirmation of U.S. interests in Central America, which generated new opposition within the Mexican government. In order to maintain a respectable national and international image, Mexico had to resist U.S. pressure as well as maintain a record of regular and timely payments on the foreign debt. The Mexican government did a good job of defending the Mexican position. It also harshly punished violations of law and order at the border. And it met its financial commitments. All this improved the relations between the two countries.

Although Minister Foster, before leaving Mexico, witnessed an improvement in conditions on the northeastern border, the border problem to which the United States paid most attention, Indian raids in the northwest—in Sonora, West Texas, and Arizona—had increased. In 1882, General D. S. Stanley, in Nueces County, Texas, expressed his intention of crossing the border as often as necessary in pursuit of Indian raiders. It was evident that Mexico would have to adopt a more realistic policy toward border crossing. United States troops were going to cross the dividing line with or without permission; moreover, ever since the 1850s Mexican governors in this zone had been saying that the prohibition of pursuit simply favored delinquents on both sides. In addition, General Manuel González, to whom Díaz had turned over the presidency in 1880, did not need to adopt an anti-U.S. stance. It was actually in his interest to improve relations in the north, even at the cost of giving Washington some of what it wanted, because the administration was facing problems with Guatemala on its southern border. It had become possible to compromise with Washington, especially in the context of improved Mexican–U.S. relations.

On 3 May 1882, the U.S. State Department telegraphed a request for a permit to cross the border after an Indian raid into Texas. Instead of sending back the customary rejection, Foreign Minister Mariscal agreed to the request on the condition that the permission be reciprocal. On 31 May, the U.S. War Department agreed to the conditions that had been set forth by Vallarta in 1877 talks.

On the Mexican side of the border, Sonora continued to be the chief victim of Indian raids originating in the United States. It was only through an increase in population on the U.S. side, military vigilance on both sides, and confinement of the descendants of the oldest inhabitants of the country on reservations that the situation finally improved about 1890.

The borderline created other problems as well: changes in the course of the Rio Grande, the disappearance or moving of boundary stones, and the distribution of water in common rivers. A convention held on 12 November 1884 recognized an invariable border, and only the problem of Chamizal—left on the U.S. side when the river changed its course in 1867—remained, and had to wait a century to be solved. That, and the other problems on the northern borders, simmered but did not boil over.

The distribution of water was complicated by the construction, in the United States, of dams along the upper parts of the rivers that ran through U.S. territory and which reduced the amount of water received in Mexico. Although Washington agreed, in 1899, to the naming of a commission to study the international use of the waters, the construction continued. Mexico lodged a formal protest in 1895 and brought its case before the International Border Commission. The decision was in Mexico's favor, but the United States ignored it and, in 1906, Mexico felt forced to sign an agreement which accepted the situation.

Some problems, like the duty-free zones, which the Mexican legislators had so stubbornly defended, simply disappeared. As early as the 1880's, it became clear that they were only harmful to Mexico; they were abolished in 1905. Goods from the United States continued to enter Mexico illegally, however—a problem which has not yet been solved.

The more urgent problem was on Mexico's southern border. This situation had a long history. In accordance with the Plan de Iguala by which the independence of Mexico from Spain was proclaimed in 1821, Guatemala remained part of the Mexican empire. In 1823, when Emperor Iturbide abdicated, the empire broke up and several states declared themselves sovereign. Central America was in favor of permanent separation from Mexico. When the Mexican federal constitution of 1824 was adopted, however, Chiapas—which had been the northernmost section of the Spanish captaincy general of Guatemala—chose to be reincorporated into Mexico; the rest of Central America went its own way and organized itself into several republics. Guatemala never accepted Chiapas's decision to join Mexico and, when negotiations between Mexico and Guatemala first opened and a binational commission was named, they gave rise to a long dispute which almost resulted in a war over Chiapas.

Guatemala's dictator, Justo Rufino Barrios, in power from 1873 to 1885, opened his country to U.S. investors and felt he could count on their support to balance the superior strength of Mexico. Barrios was willing to bargain away territory he did not possess: he attempted to sell the Honduran islands of the Fonseca Bay to the Hayes administration, and he was willing to cede the Soconusco region of Chiapas (if he could obtain it from Mexico) to the United States in exchange for protection in case of war.

The United States did not take Barrios' generous offers seriously, but Secretary of State Blaine was willing to use the situation to promote his project of building a trans-isthmus canal in Nicaragua. He therefore tried to fill the role that the Guatemalans had bestowed upon him: "natural protector of the integrity of Central American territory." Blaine instructed his minister to Mexico, Philip H. Morgan, to inform the Mexican government of his friendly interest in the dispute between Mexico and Guatemala, and to reassure the González government that he had no intention of becoming the arbiter of the destiny of either of the two nations. By then, Mexico had mobilized troops on its southern border; Blaine, in a warning note, declared that any military action against Guatemala would be considered contrary to U.S. interests.

The Mexican government rejected Blaine's offer of mediation. Mariscal, Mexico's foreign minister, replied that there was nothing to arbitrate, since Mexico did not accept any revision of its rights to Chiapas. The Mexican foreign office also sent to the U.S. minister, Philip Morgan, several volumes of documents that established Mexican rights over Chiapas. Morgan insisted it would be convenient to have commissioners from the three countries review the question and then establish the exact border. Mariscal was willing to accept this proposal, but only on the condition that Guatemala would accept, in advance, Mexico's rights to Chiapas.

Since Barrios was occupied, at that time, with a project to unify Central America, Guatemala's minister to Mexico announced that very likely his government would officially accept the "loss" of Chiapas. The Mexican government kept its army mobilized. Blaine proposed an inter-American peace conference, but Mexico decided to transfer the negotiations to Washington (It was then that Díaz named Matías Romero his minister to the United States.) At first, Romero accepted the U.S. offer of arbitration, but he backed off when he learned that the Guatemalans expected a payoff of $4 million.

The assasination of President James A. Garfield in 1881 changed the political scene. Blaine was replaced by Frederick Frelinghuysen at the State Department, and Guatemala offered the new secretary a treaty granting the United States the right to station troops in El Salvador, Honduras, and Guatemala, as well as to occupy ports, in exchange for protection and for the recognition of the union of the three countries. The United States declined. Barrios, worried, decided to travel to Washington in July 1882; there he learned that Frelinghuysen was willing to intercede if both Mexico and Guatemala requested it. That response left Barrios no alternative but to reopen talks with the Mexican minister to the United States. Romero succeeded in getting Barrios to recognize Mexican rights over Chiapas and, in order to prevent any change of heart on such an important point, signed a preliminary treaty. But U.S. mediation was accepted in this document, and, in consequence, the Mexican government did not ratify it. Deliberations were transferred to Mexico and, in September 1882, the Guatemalan minister signed a treaty in which the Mexican position was accepted: direct negotiations between the two countries.

The Growth of Commerce and Immigration

Economic development in the United States was bolstered by a new philosophy. Social Darwinism, a new argument for the dominance of the strongest, swept the United States and Europe during the last decades of the nineteenth century and triggered a new expansionist movement. The old rhetoric of Manifest Destiny was revived; in 1885, John Fiske spoke of the inevitable fate of the English race to impose on all the world its language, religion, habits, and traditions. At that time, Europe was more imperialistic than the United States. The United States had become a continental power with shores on both oceans and had acquired Alaska, but had no colonies. The United States was not yet ready to embark on an aggressive program of territorial expansion, although it had bought Alaska from Russia in 1867.

Now, times were different. By and large, the U.S. government preferred economic penetration and followed its corporations' guidelines. In 1880, Washington's ministers to Mexico were emphasizing trade. That year, when Mexico denounced the old treaty of 1831 as out of date, it opened the way for a new treaty more in accord with the new reality.

The U.S. railroads had reached the border towns, creating new opportunities for trade in finished products and raw materials. Mexico became the center of attention of U.S. capital, and the first of the "reciprocal" treaties initiated by Secretary Frelinghuysen was negotiated with Mexico. Even before the idea was accepted in principle, Frelinghuysen named two commissioners for that task: one was the former U.S. president, Ulysses Grant, who had become a railroad concessionaire in Mexico. Matías Romero, faithful to his liberal beliefs in economic expansion, managed to overcome Mexican reluctance and wrote a draft that served as a basis for discussions held in Washington in 1883.

The heart of the proposed treaty consisted of two lists of duty-free products. The reciprocity "consisted in the fact that the United States admitted 28 Mexican products tax free, in exchange for 73 products tax-exempted by Mexico for their importation." The most important exempted Mexican exports were henequen, leather, vanilla, and coffee; the U.S. imports included railroad wagons and track, tools, steam engines, coal, and oil. Despite protests from protectionists in both countries, the treaty was ratified.

Even more important than the treaty was the Liberals' conviction that Mexico's economic progress depended on immigration, construction of railroads, and foreign investment. The plan was not new: Juárez, Lerdo, and even Díaz had all granted large concessions to foreigners, and Matías Romero had taken advantage of his controversy with Foster to advertise the country as a favorable field for foreign investment. Thus, developments in the 1880's were quite in accord with Liberal policies. In 1880, concessions, subsidies, franchises, and lands had been granted to foreign individuals and enterprises; more, Díaz's government had renegotiated the public debt, maintained payments to foreign creditors, suppressed excise taxes, and reformed the country's laws in order to further economic development.

Mexico's first colonization law, promulgated in 1875, was designed to attract immigrants and thus propel this program ahead. In truth, the law brought in only a few hundred Mormons and similar groups, always in small numbers. Some other Protestants came, but their proselytising precipitated some violent incidents. Mexico did not seem destined to become a country of immigrants.

Nevertheless, in 1883, the government expanded its immigration policy with a new law designed to populate and utilize empty land, especially in the northern states. The unfortunate result was that large landowners, rather than new settlers, occupied empty land and even seized property to which there was no written title but which had traditionally been used by a particular village or smaller community; the villagers, poor and illiterate, were usually helpless in the face of such action. This was the origin of the development of large cattle haciendas in the north. Even some U.S. citizens found ways to circumvent the prohibition against owning real estate near the border; they also acquired estates.

The most important legislative changes during the last decade of the nineteenth century concerned mining. The Mining Code of 1884 declared that all subsoil resources were the property of the nation, thus eliminating interference by Mexican states, and in 1887 another law authorized the president to extend concessions, and also exempted bullion and coins from all taxes. Finally, the law of 1892 modified the old Spanish tradition that all resources in the subsoil belonged to the state, by stating that ownership of land would perpetually include the hydrocarbons and coal in the subsoil. Another law, promulgated in 1898, allowed the president to authorize the extraction of oil.

In 1889, the Commercial Code eliminated the old taxes that had obstructed trade. It stimulated the use of the railroad system and permitted trade between Mexico and the United States—only $9 million in 1870—to rise to $36 million in 1890 and to $117 million in 1910. The trade balance was initially unfavorable to Mexico, which imported more than it exported, but the situation changed by the end of the century and exports began to surpass imports in value.

Part of the liberal dream of stimulating economical development by eliminating interventionism had, for a half-century, included the development of an extensive railroad system that would link isolated areas of the country with the center, one that would serve as a cheap means of transportation for national goods. Díaz set this task as one of the main goals of his regime. One of his dictatorship's achievements was to have taken over a country with only 640 kilometers of railways and to have left it with almost twenty-thousand. Even though the first two concessions were granted to U.S. companies, British capital predominated in the railroads up to 1900. About that time, in response to the attempt of a U.S. company to link Mexican lines to one of the large U.S. railroad systems, José I. Limantour—secretary of the treasury—created the Ferrocarriles Nacionales de México. The stocks of the Central, Inter-oceánico, and Nacional railroad companies were transferred to the new government corporation, which became their principal shareholder.

There was no plan that reflected the country's needs, however, with the result that the routes of the railroad lines served the interests of the U.S. mining companies rather than Mexico's. Railways followed parallel routes through uninhabited areas while places in urgent need of transportation were ignored. Moreover, the construction, subsidized by the Mexican government, was expensive: it cost an average of more than $8,000 per kilometer, in addition to the franchises, land, and exemptions. Moreover, it fanned the flames of anti-U.S. sentiment because the important posts went to foreigners.

Nevertheless, knowledgeable observers consider the profits reaped by foreign investors modest. Some of them paid hardly any dividends to their shareholders. The reasons advanced are overcapitalization, poor administration, lack of knowledge of the market and of the Mexican labor force, and anti-U.S. prejudice. Historian David Pletcher has emphasized the negative effect of the fall in the price of silver until 1905.*

*"The Trade of Silver in Mexico, 1870–1910 and Its Effects on American Investments," *Journal of Economic History,* vol. 18 (1958), pp. 33–55.

Railroads proved to be the least profitable investment; mining, although better, yielded an uncertain return; industrial investments did somewhat better. There were, of course, some exceptions—successful enterprises such as Doheny's Mexican Petroleum Company; the American Smelting and Refining Company (Asarco), which belonged to the Guggenheim family; and the Mexican Telegraph Company. Perhaps it was the luck of these remarkable companies that encouraged other U.S. investments: they continued to grow at a constant level and reached $646,200,000 by 1911.

It is difficult to judge the effect that the expansion of these investments had on the country. Fernando Rosenzweig has insisted that they turned the Mexican economy into a complement of the U.S. economy. Luis Nicolau D'Olwer points out that, in all of Latin America, only in Mexico did the U.S. investment, which constituted 45.5 percent of the total of all U.S. investments in the continent, surpass the British.* These investments, highly visible and bringing them with them considerable U.S. foreign staff—never assimilated—rekindled anti-U.S. sentiment and lessened the popularity of the Díaz government which, people thought, was turning over the resources of the country to foreigners. In response, the government enacted corrective measures, such as the creation of the Ferrocarriles Nacionales de México and the mining law of 1909 which prohibited mining near the border.

Cosío Villegas, the expert on the Díaz dictatorship, insists that Díaz was not a lackey of foreign or, particularly, U.S. interests. He contends that Díaz had his own ideas of the national interest and acted effectively to carry them out.* If so, perhaps Díaz relied too completely on his belief that U.S. investments, railroads, industry, and commerce would work a miracle in Mexico. This was especially difficult within the framework of Darwinian imperialism. Given the socioeconomic abyss between the two countries, the idea was at best problematic.

---

*Fernando Rosenzweig, "El Comercio Exterior," and Luis Nicolau d'Olwer, "Las inversiones extranjeras," in *Historia Moderna de México*. Vol. 7, *El Profiriato: Vida Económica*, ed. Daniel Cosío Villegas.

†*Historia Moderna de México*. Vol. 9, *El Porfiriato: La Vida Politica Exterior*.

Lorenzo Meyer

Part Two

6

The Fall of Díaz and the End of a Good Relationship: 1904–1910

The Last Years of Tranquility

On 16 September 1904—before the beginning of his sixth presidential term—General Porfirio Díaz opened the sessions of the Twenty-second Congress. In his message before the representatives of the nation, Díaz listed the various material and legislative steps his government had taken to improve conditions in the country and pointed out that, thanks to peace and legal order, Mexico had entered "the route towards unquestionable progress," an image that was "already generalized throughout the whole world." Thus, Mexico had prospered in peace and improved its image in the international community. Relations with the United States, so difficult in the past, now seemed to be so normal and routine that the president considered it unnecessary to make any specific reference to them.

In conclusion, Díaz emphasized his belief that national prosperity, of which he was so proud and on which the modernization of the country was based, would continue only as long as there was peace and legal order. Implicit in his statement—and that is how his audience understood it—was that Díaz's permanence in office was the best guarantee of order. Few national or foreign observers could have known then that the *Pax Porfiriana* was about to end. To the majority of Mexicans, Díaz and his regime appeared so solid as to be eternal. However, some members of the political elite were concerned about the consequences of a regime which was more personal than institutionalized, and their fears were shared by some U.S. politicians. Díaz was seventy-four years old and he still had not provided for his own succession or apparently given the matter any serious thought. The reins of government, which he had handled with such strength and intelligence, were slipping into the hands of others. Coming into particular prominence was a small informal group of intellectuals known as the *científicos*, established by Manuel Romero Rubio, secretary of the interior.

This group, which included some governors and prominent members of the federal administration, openly recognized the secretary of finance, the efficient, elegant, and powerful José Ives Limantour, as its leader. However, the *científicos* were not popular and, with the covert encouragement of the president, were opposed by another faction of the governing family led by General Bernardo Reyes. Reyes, who had spent many years in the field and as head of the War Department, had served Díaz as a loyal and forceful instrument in his efforts to pacify the country and to concentrate power. His group had both a solid geographical base of power—the north—and a functional one, the army itself.

In the struggle between Limantour of the Department of Finance and Reyes of the Deparment of War, Limantour had the advantage. In this stage of Porfirism, the economy was the center of politics. The conflict between the two factions did not solve the problem of succession but, instead, created an irreparable split within the governing elite.

This power struggle coincided with the first steps taken to organize an opposition to the regime elsewhere in the country. At the beginning of the century, the iron circle of the Porfirist oligarchy had obstructed the social and political mobility that the country's modernization required. A large number of the middle class, which had emerged as a result of the country's material progress, was increasingly resentful of the way the landowners and the leaders of large foreign enterprises had taken over practically all decisions—establishing new positions, both in and out of government, and blocking the advancement of members of the middle class into the ranks of the elite. Many engineers, doctors, teachers, ranchers, and merchants reacted enthusiastically to the appeal of anti-Porfirist and anti-reelectionist organizations, whether they were radicals (such as the anarchist group that published *Regeneración*, moderates (such as those who formed the liberal clubs organized by Camilo Arriaga), or frank conservatives (such as the supporters of General Reyes for the presidency). The visibility of large foreign enterprises and their close ties with the regime inevitably tinged the opposition to Díaz with a nationalist sentiment which was clearly anti-United States. All these political movements were occuring in a society within which a rising working class was also searching, by different means, for its place in the sun, while many peasant communities were struggling to defend their ancestral communal lands from the great encroaching haciendas and latifundia.

Vested Interests

By 1900, there was already a marked contrast between the economics of Mexico and the United States. The Industrial Revolution dominated the economy of the United States: 40 percent of its 76 million inhabitants lived in urban areas and the industrial labor force exceeded 20 million workers. Mexico, with fewer than 14 million inhabitants, was still an agricultural country. Although some of its farming and cattle-raising activities were relatively advanced, its rudimentary industry employed little more than a half-million people and only 20 percent of its inhabitants lived in urban areas. A simple way of confirming the disparity between both societies is to note that in 1910 the *per capita* income in the United States was estimated as almost nine times that of Mexico.*

Capital invested in Mexico at the beginning of the century by U.S. interests constituted a substantial part of the total foreign investment in the country. Estimates by the U.S. consulate were $511.5 million in 1902 and $646.2 million in 1911. In 1911, then, U.S. investors controlled 38 percent of the total foreign investment in Mexico: 41.3 percent of that investment was in railroads, 36.6 percent in mines and metallurgy, and the remaining 22 percent in real estate, public debt, oil, banks, and insurance. Investment in manufacturing, public utilities, and commerce was insignificant.

It is important to note that the fields in which U.S. investments were centered were also the ones the United States dominated. Of the total foreign money invested in railroads in 1911, 47.3 percent came from the United States, followed by 35.5 percent from England. In mining, the United States controlled 61.7 percent of total foreign investment; France, second in importance, trailed with only 21.8 percent. Mexican investment in mining was insignificant.

The aggressiveness of U.S. investors, which turned some of the modern sectors of Mexican economy into true enclaves—particularly mining and the rising oil industry—was remarkable, especially when we consider that the United States was itself still a net importer of

* John H. Coatsworth, "Obstacles to Economic Growth in Nineteenth-Century Mexico", *American Historical Review*, vol. 83, no. 1 (February 1978), p. 82.

capital. Before the First World War, foreign investment in the United States, mainly British, was estimated at approximately $7 billion. This figure, greater than the capital invested abroad by the United States, was exceeded only, and only slightly, by the sum the British devoted to Canada.

Political relations between Mexico and the United States, just before the fall of the Díaz regime, were good. Some authors have insisted as did the dictator's own son after Díaz's overthrow, that U.S. influence was a decisive factor in the fall of the Porfirist regime in 1911. The available facts do not support such a conclusion. The problems between Mexico City and Washington awaiting solution before the Mexican Revolution broke out in 1910 were varied but relatively minor, and could not have justified an attempt to destabilize the Díaz regime. The remaining problems were the use of Magdalena Bay by the U.S. Navy, the dispute between the Compañía Agrícola e Industrial del Tlahualilo and the Mexican government over water for irrigation, the border strip in dispute at El Chamizal, and certain differences of policy toward Central America.

The issue of Magdalena Bay stemmed from a permit requested in 1897 for some U.S. warships to maneuver for a few days off that almost uninhabited part of the Mexican Pacific coast. These petitions were renewed annually until they became routine. The situation changed when the Mexican press raised the question of Mexican sovereignty. Díaz's government, sensitive to such criticism, suggested to the United States in 1910 that it was not convenient to continue the arrangement. Washington apparently accepted the Mexican decision quietly.

The problem regarding the Compañía Agrícola e Industrial del Tlahualilo emerged after the Mexican government reduced the flow of water that this Anglo–United States company could divert from the Nazas River for the irrigation of its 18,000 hectares planted in cotton and wheat. In 1909, the company demanded a compensation of 11,300 pesos from the Díaz government. Mexico, which had been trying to achieve a more equitable distribution of the scarcest resource of the region—water—refused to pay, although it was probably legally bound to come to some arrangement with the Compañía Agrícola.

The dispute concerning the 250 hectares (about six hundred acres) known as the Chamizal, very near the city of El Paso, originated earlier. The Rio Grande changed its course in 1864, stranding the Chamizal on the northern or U.S. side of the river, then as now the accepted international boundary. Since the property was valuable, Mexico continued to claim it, and in 1910 Washington agreed (although not very enthusiastically) to submit the dispute to international arbitration. The award—favorable to Mexico—was finally made when Díaz was no longer in power.

The last problem concerned Central America. The United States suggested to the Mexican government, in 1907, that it would be convenient to jointly guarantee the peace and integrity of the countries occupying that region. President Díaz considered it unwise to risk becoming a tail to a kite flown by the United States and declined the invitation, arguing that Mexico had no national interests to protect south of Guatemala. Nevertheless, in 1909, Díaz sent a naval ship to Nicaragua to assist President José Santos Zelaya when he was overthrown by a rebellion supported by the U.S. government.

These matters did not amount to serious conflicts between the two countries. Nor were relations much affected by Díaz's efforts to slow U.S. economic expansion in Mexico, such as his creation in 1906 of Ferrocarriles Nacionales de México, mentioned in the previous chapter. This quasi-governmental company controlled about two-thirds of the railroad's existing mileage, and the Mexican government held a half-share of its total capitalization of 460 million pesos. In a similar situation, the Mexican government granted a concession to the British company of Weetman Pearson, rather than a U.S. company, to look for oil in a vast area of public lands: the concession included a long-term tax exemption. In one instance, the Mexican government prevented a U.S. railway from controlling Mexican railways; in the other, it prevented a U.S. group from controlling the production and sale of oil. In the latter instance, however, the Mexican government tried to forestall Standard Oil's efforts to create a monopoly in the country by bringing in the British as a counterweight.

At the end of the first decade of the twentieth century, the United States was not worried about its relations with Mexico, about the political differences between the two countries, or about vehement Mexican expressions of economic nationalism. It was more concerned about the stability of the Díaz regime. In 1906, there had already been a small demonstration of what could happen were this stability lost. In that year, a labor conflict took place in the great copper-mining center of Cananea, owned by a U.S. company. It ended in a violent clash between the Mexican workers and the U.S. administrators. Property was destroyed and lives were lost on both sides. The U.S. government became alarmed to the point that Cananea was briefly invaded by a troop of rangers from Arizona and Washington offered Díaz military help, which the Mexican president firmly refused; at the same time, he ordered Mexican troops to move into Cananea to restore order.

In October 1909, when a regime headed by a man of seventy-nine years seemed precarious, the first meeting ever between the presidents of Mexico and the United States took place. Although no direct evidence was left of the discussion, President William Taft considered it his contribution to the security of Díaz's position. If there was anything that the U.S. president feared in Mexico, it was precisely the destabilization that Díaz's death could cause. Taft could do very little about this problem; he simply hoped he would not have to face, during his administration, the Mexican crisis that would probably occur when the dictator died. To President Taft, the simple fact that his country had an investment of "a billion dollars" in Mexico (as he told his wife in a letter) meant that the United States would be inevitably involved if disorder overtook that country.

Taft was not lucky. In November 1910, an armed movement was organized to prevent Díaz from reelecting himself to the presidency for the seventh time, that is to say, for the period 1910–16.

The Maderist Revolution

The rebellion that, in a little more than five months, put an end to a government that had lasted more than thirty years cannot be fully understood if we do not take into account the complex and powerful role played by the United States. For many years, following a tradition, the leaders of the anti-Porfirist movement found shelter north of the border, just as Díaz had in his own time. There, protected by U.S. laws or communities of Mexicans who resided in the United States, they found refuge. The vast, uninhabited, and not very well-policed border zone made it an ideal region for conspiracies and for organizing armed groups. Such a group was the anarchist organization *Regeneración*. Other groups were formed by the diverse sympathizers of the antireelectionist party which, in 1910, had nominated Francisco I. Madero, a young member of one of the most powerful families in the country, as their presidential candidate. Their party did not accept the triumphal reelection of Díaz in 1910, and it called for an insurrection on 20 November 1910. The United States became, once more, the operational base of a conspiracy against the Mexican government.

President Díaz closely followed the activities of the opposition groups that operated in the United States, both through his consulates and with the help of U.S. private detectives. On many occasions, the Foreign Relations Department sent notes to the U.S. government asking it to detain conspirators and to prevent men and supplies destined for the rebels from entering Mexico. Díaz could not accept the fact that U.S. officials had not arrested the conspirators immediately because they were legally unable to do so without proof that anti-Porfiristas active on their side of the border were really violating U.S. laws regarding neutrality. He suspected that Washington was not acting in good faith and was encouraging, for undisclosed reasons, the enemies of his government. Díaz's suspicions were unfounded because, with the possible exception of certain petroleum interests that resented his favoring of British competition, neither the government nor the powerful business executives of the United States desired his downfall. To the contrary, the United States wanted to maintain Mexico's peace so that its own mines, railroads, plantations, and other interests would prosper in an atmosphere of law and order. Indeed, they zealously persecuted violators of U.S. neutrality.

When the first combat between revolutionary groups and Mexican federal troops took place in the north of the country, U.S. authorities were already aware of the strong anti-Porfirist feeling in Mexican communities on both sides of the border—a possible seedbed for a generalized rebellion in the north. However, the dispatches reporting this sentiment were lost in the heavy flow of everyday reports received by the Department of State and other U.S. agencies in charge of border security. When the revolt began, the U.S. ambassador to Mexico expressed cautious confidence that the authorities would achieve a rapid triumph, a confidence which diminished as the revolutionaries were not immediately liquidated. By February, the ambassador began to consider the possibility that the army might not be able to put down the rebellion, and the lengthening struggle aroused fear in the U.S. community. It was perhaps for this reason that the U.S. government decided something had to be done, even if it was merely initiating military maneuvers in Texas involving twenty thousand men and some ships stationed in Mexican ports. This mobilization would have been insufficient for an occupation of Mexico, but it aroused the collective memory and the fear of a new invasion, both in government circles and among the insurgents, and the Mexican press echoed their apprehensions. None of this strengthened the Díaz regime, however, and the revolution grew.

The U.S. authorities were concerned not only about the civil war but also about their citizens' substantial investments in Mexico. They were worried that foreign powers might take advantage of the situation to undermine the Monroe Doctrine, and also about more immediate concerns: the protection of U.S. laborers and of the construction work in the Colorado River to protect the Imperial Valley of California from floods; and the damage that the struggle could cause in border towns, as indeed occurred in the areas of Ciudad Juárez, across from El Paso, and in Agua Prieta, near Douglas.

The rebels of 1910 faced an old and arthritic regime, internally divided and incapable of responding to the challenge with the requisite force and urgency. Owing to the perceived threat of an invasion from the United States and to the weakening of social control, news of the lynching of a Mexican citizen in Texas produced an unforeseen and violent reaction. Mass demonstrations against the United States took place in Mexico City, Guadalajara, San Luis Potosí, Morelia, Oaxaca, Puebla, Pachuca, Chihuahua, and smaller cities. More than once, these demonstrations turned into uprisings. According to some observers, the unusual reaction of the Mexican public was not due merely to the incident in Texas, but to something more profound and therefore dangerous: the existence of a strong anti-U.S. sentiment throughout Mexico. It was the product, among other things, of the resentment created by the remarkable economic penetration of U.S. capital. This feeling did not disappear when the police dispersed the rioters. To the contrary, as the years went by, it became stronger.

On 10 May 1911, the federal garrison of Ciudad Juárez surrendered to the rebels. Two weeks later, President Díaz left office. In his letter of resignation to the Congress, the old president stated that he had made his decision in order to put an end to the civil war, to prevent the nation's credit from deteriorating, and to avoid exposing Mexico to the danger of "international conflicts" (which must be considered an oblique reference to the United States). This was how—despite the fact that his army was almost intact—Díaz forsook power and a whole stage in the history of Mexico ended.

7

The Civil War and the American Intervention: 1910–1920

Madero's Term

As Berta Ulloa has correctly stated, the Mexican Revolution was an "intervened-in revolution."* At every decisive moment of the lengthy and complex Mexican civil struggle, U.S. influence was exerted. This did not mean that the final result of the struggle was determined by the United States, but there is no doubt that its development can be explained only by taking into account the effects of geographic proximity, and the various and often contradictory policies of the U.S. public and government toward the Mexican conflict.

According to the peace treaty of Ciudad Juárez, signed by the representatives of General Díaz and the insurgents in May 1911, Francisco León de la Barra, secretary of foreign relations of the old regime, assumed provisional charge of the federal executive function. This government, presided over by a man who not so long ago had been Díaz's ambassador to the United States, was a compromise between the old the new styles. De la Barra's main task was to hold new presidential elections in October and, at the same time, try to reestablish social peace by coming to an arrangement with the rebel guerrilla groups who had still not laid down their arms.

This provisional presidential term was brief, lasting only five months. De la Barra understood the United States and had no difficulty in obtaining support from Washington. His chief problem was that the new government still had armed opponents who persisted in organizing incursions into Mexican territory from the United States. General Bernardo Reyes, for example, worked openly

*La revolución intervenida (Mexico: El Colegio de México), 1976.

in Texas to overthrow the new authorities. Washington responded favorably to the Mexican government's demands and Reyes's project failed.

From Washington's point of view, the first task of the provisional government was to guarantee the security of U.S. citizens and their property, especially in areas where armed rebel groups were operating, as in Tamaulipas. As much as possible, De la Barra responded positively to the sometimes exaggerated demands for protection from U.S. Ambassador Henry Lane Wilson. All things considered, there were no serious incidents between the two countries during those months. United States groups with interests in Mexico waited with cautious optimism for the coming of Madero's administration, which was openly committed to a policy of democratic political reform but nothing more.

When Madero formally assumed power in November 1911, he had no friends in the U.S. embassy. Even before he moved into Chapultepec castle to take over the presidency, the U.S. ambassador to Mexico, the unbending and arrogant Henry Lane Wilson, was writing the Department of State that Madero's project of bringing democracy to Mexico was not practicable: democratic reforms could not be carried out in the social context of the poverty and illiteracy of the Mexican people. Wilson foresaw, instead, the beginning of a lengthy period of corruption and violence that could adversely affect U.S. interests in Mexico. The ambassador's opinions were particularly important because of their influence on President Taft, just as he was formulating his policies toward Mexico.

In dealing with Washington Madero encountered the same problems that León de la Barra had faced—but in a more acute form—and new ones emerged. To begin with, the rebel groups became more active, and U.S. fears increased accordingly. These rebels were, on the one hand, Maderist revolutionaries of an older school who were not happy with his compromise with the old order; on the other hand, they were Porfirists trying to regain lost privileges.

The rebellion in southern Mexico was centered in the peasant forces in Puebla and Morelos led by Emiliano Zapata. He demanded substantial and quick changes in the landholding system—the principal determinant of the social structure of the country. Pascual Orozco, another popular leader, but less of a reformist, was operating in the north. He had defeated the Porfirists in Ciudad Juárez the previous year and was now inflaming other ex-Maderists who believed themselves unjustly relegated to a subordinate role in the new distribution of power.

In addition to the groups led by these popular rebels, two new movements inspired by Porfirist military officers, emerged. The insurrections led by generals Bernardo Reyes and Félix Díaz (Porfirio's nephew) in 1911 and 1912, respectively, were reactionary.

The insurrections led by the generals were quickly quelled—the army did not provide the support they had counted on, and both rebels were captured and sent to prison—but the problems posed by the popular movements were not solved that easily. Zapata lost control of the main southern cities but continued to mount intense guerrilla warfare in the countryside. On a smaller scale, the Orozquists followed a similar pattern in the north after their defeat at Bachimba in 1912. There was much more social interest in Madero's Mexico than in the Mexico of a few years earlier, when the rigorous discipline imposed by Porfirio had maintained political order.

The reaction of the U.S. ambassador was increasing irritation over the inability of Madero's government to restore civil tranquility, so essential to the prosperity of U.S. economic activities in Mexico. He also felt that local peace and quiet were necessary to discourage other powers from acting on their own initiative in a sphere of U.S. influence. Nor did the ambassador approve of the nationalist sentiment that was beginning to prevail in Mexico. Thus far, it had been limited to modest measures, such as requiring foreign personnel who worked on the railroads to be able to speak and write Spanish, but he viewed this as the camel's nose under the tent and tried to get the rule changed.

Like his predecessors, Madero had to keep an eye on the colony of Mexicans exiled in the United States. It was from there that Reyes finally launched his unsuccessful revolt; it was there that Pascual Orozco took refuge for some time, after his defeat; and it was there that Emilio Vázquez Gómez, an important leader in the first stage of Maderism, later conspired against Madero. As they had during De la Barra's administration, U.S. authorities attempted to prevent the organization and arming of anti-Maderist expeditions in the border zone.

All things considered, Madero's opponents posed no serious threats from the other side of the Rio Grande. On the other hand, the United States was not satisfied with the Mexican government's good faith and diligence in protecting U.S. citizens and their property. The problem existed in various parts of Mexico, but it was particularly acute in the north, along the U.S. border, where Orozco's operations were strongest. United States officials therefore began to consider ways and means of interfering in the situation, including wondering aloud if they should not move in some troops and, in March 1912, Ambassador Wilson obtained authorization from Washington to advise some nine thousand U.S. citizens to withdraw temporarily from particular Mexican states designated as danger zones. Four northern states and parts of five others fell into this category, and by April a large number of U.S. citizens had left these areas. Actually, U.S. business suffered more damage from the resulting stagnation and general neglect than from the direct effect of the civil war.

The U.S. ambassador continued to press Washington to advance its preparations for military action, but President William Howard Taft was at no time sympathetic to this proposal. Instead, the U.S. government sent a formal protest to the government of Mexico, deploring the damage the war was inflicting on its citizens. Surprisingly, the U.S. government also sent a similar demarche directly to Orozco, who must have been thunderstruck to receive such a communication from Washington. Direct communication of this sort with Orozco did nothing to improve relations between Washington and Mexico City.

Orozco's military defeat should have lessened the tension between the two governments, but did not. By that time, Ambassador Wilson was convinced that Madero's government was unable to maintain sufficient order to provide the necessary protection to U.S. interests. On 28 August 1912, in a report to Washington, Wilson described the Mexican government as "apathetic, inefficient, cynically indifferent or stupidly optimistic." His influence helps to explain why the Department of State sent, in September—just as the internal situation in Mexico was improving—one of the harshest notes in the history of relations between the two countries. In it, Madero's government was directly accused of not providing adequate protection for U.S. citizens, of neglecting to investigate the deaths of seventeen of them, of sanctioning "frivolous" or unfounded legal action against others, and of discriminating against certain U.S. companies. Regarding this last point, the note referred to a tax of twenty cents per ton on crude oil, to the old problem of the Tlahualilo Company, to a decision that affected the Associated Press, to the subsidy of the *Mexican Herald*, and to an indemnity requested by the Mexican Packing Company. The U.S. government declared that it reserved the right to take necessary action in each case and concluded with a demand that Mexico state the measures it was planning to take to solve the problems listed in the message. Such a sharp reprimand is rarely sent by one government to another.

The note was a blow to the precarious revolutionary government: the United States doubted Mexico's ability to fulfill its basic duties and suggested it might do the job itself. Despite its weakness, Madero's government rose to the occasion when it replied in November. The Mexican reply stated that four of the seventeen "murders" had occurred even before Madero had assumed power, that three others had actually been legally executed for participating in filibusters in Baja California, and that still others were in custody and under investigation. While it deplored the loss of U.S. lives in Mexico, it was impossible to provide absolute security—difficult even when there were no rebellions, as U.S. authorities, who had not been able to prevent the lynching and murder of Mexicans in the United States, well knew. The government acknowledged it had not been able to put an end to the revolts. But that was a difficult task; again, this should be well-known to the government of the United States, since it had not been able to put a stop to the subversive and illegal activities carried out by Mexican rebels in U.S. territory. The government denied that it discriminated against any U.S. person or enterpirse. Finally, some of the complaints were simply the result of the termination of some government subsidies (e.g., the *Mexican Herald*) or monopolies (e.g., the wireless monopoly of the Associated Press).

Mexico's response did not decrease the tension. The U.S. ambassador was still convinced that the perpetuation of Madero's government was contrary to U.S. interests, and by then, U.S. ships were once more stationed outside Mexican ports.

A few months later, however, Madero's government seemed to be en route to stability: the basis for Ambassador Wilson's criticism—the uncontrolled rebel activities—was disappearing. Nevertheless, in February 1913, part of the army decided that the time was ripe for a coup d'etat. Certain officers who were in command of troops in Mexico City freed the two insurgent generals—Bernardo Reyes and Félix Díaz—whom Madero had pardoned, sending them to prison instead of executing them by firing squad in accordance with the directives of the two courts-martials. Reyes and Díaz were thus enabled to lead a new revolt.

The revolt, although unsuccessful at the outset, was never entirely crushed, particularly in the capital itself, and the confused military situation permitted the commander of the government troops, General Victoriano Huerta, to become the arbiter of the political life of the country by shifting his influence and military strength from one side to the other. Huerta reached a secret agreement with the insurgents and accomplished, for his own benefit, the coup originally planned by Reyes and Félix Díaz. Madero was placed in confinement at the National Palace on 17 February 1913 and Huerta was named interim president by Congress. On 22 February, Madero and the vice president were assassinated on Huerta's orders. Mexico then began to suffer not the reinstatement of the old Porfirist system, but the bitter reality of a military dictatorship.

For the United States and the European powers, the coup d'etat could not have occurred at a better moment. According to those governments, Mexico needed stern social discipline rather than democracy: the alternative to Huerta was anarchy. Their diplomats, especially the U.S. ambassador, played an active role in the military coup and congratulated themselves on the outcome.

Shortly after the revolt began, Ambassador Wilson asked his government to once again send warships to the Mexican coasts to protect the U.S. colony living in the capital, and he even threatened Madero with the disembarkation of troops if the lives of U.S. citizens in Mexico City could not be guaranteed. In his desire to finish off the constituted government, Wilson exceeded himself: he had not been instructed to make such a threat, but the State Department backed him up. Immediately after presenting this ultimatum, the ambassador, as dean of the diplomatic corp, succeeded in uniting the other important diplomats in a demand for the president's resignation as the only solution to the crisis. This interference in domestic affairs was immediately rejected by the Mexican president, who reminded the foreign representatives that they had no right to proceed as they had—an observation that did not stop Wilson. Four days later, on 18 February, he met secretly with the rebel leaders, General Félix Díaz and General Huerta, in his embassy, where the terms and details of the coup were concluded. When it actually took place, the satisfied ambassador informed his government: "Our position here is stronger than ever."

Madero's relatives, who knew of Wilson's influence with those engineering the coup, appealed directly to him to save the overthrown president's life. Wilson acknowledged no responsibility and, when he learned of Madero's assassination, accepted the implausible official explanation that he had been killed while trying to escape. For Wilson, the outcome—the destruction of Madero's government— was important; the violence with which it was carried out was irrelevant. His view was that Madero had presided over an anti-U.S. and incompetent government, more despotic than that of Porfirio

Díaz, and now it had finally been replaced by a new and better one. True, Huerta had initially resorted to the use of force, but he had subsequently assumed command in a constitutional manner, which was the most important consideration.

To Ambassador Wilson, it was only natural for the Mexican government to be a dictatorship. This explains his initial optimism after the coup: everything, in his opinion, was back to normal. Wilson never realized that his efforts had not served to restore the status quo ante but that, to the contrary, they had hastened the arrival of the real revolution.

The Great Turn: The United States and the Military Dictatorship

The regime of General Victoriano Huerta lasted only from February 1913 to July 1914. According to Huerta, his coup d'etat had been mounted with U.S. approval and support. But although the major European countries recognized the new government promptly, the United States did not act to do so. Ambassador Wilson asked his consuls to try to induce regional Mexican authorities in their respective districts to recognize Huerta's administration. The ambassador hoped to legitimize his conduct in Mexico ex post facto, through U.S. recognition of Huerta's government, and he knew that a quick solution of the problems pending between the two countries—the Chamizal, Tlahualilo, and so forth—would help. Huerta did not reject this idea, but he needed time. Moreover, Taft's term in office was ending; the U.S. president decided to leave the question of Mexican recognition for his Democratic successor, Woodrow Wilson.

The election of Woodrow Wilson in 1912 restored the Democratic Party to a position of power for the first time since 1896. During his campaign, Wilson had lashed out against the Republican Party's conduct of foreign affairs and had declared a moral view of how the U.S. government should conduct business abroad. Wilson maintained that the Christian principles of "obligation," "service," and "rectitude" were generally valid, and that they should apply to the conduct of international affairs as much as in the personal conduct of individuals. In a nutshell, relations between the United States and the rest of the world should be ruled by moral principles. It was in this atmosphere that the Mexican problem was taken under consideration by the new administration in Washington.

The U.S. press followed the problem south of the border closely and reported the death of Madero and his vice president in detail. Few people placed any credence in the official version of this dramatic event, including President Wilson, who declined to legitimize Huerta's seizure of power by sponsoring U.S. recognition of his regime.

By May 1913, the political situation of Henry Lane Wilson in Mexico had become untenable. From Huerta's point of view, the ambassador had failed to deliver the expected formal recognition from Washington, and in Washington he was considered a moral accomplice to the violent overthrow of a constitutional regime and to the assassination of its leaders. The U.S. condemnation of the coup d'etat took Victoriano Huerta, Ambassador Wilson, the European powers, and a goodly number of foreign investors in Mexico by surprise. For a while, Mexican revolutionaries were to be the beneficiaries of foreign intervention and not its target. At the beginning of July, the ambassador was recalled to Washington for consultation; there he ended his mission to Mexico. United States policies toward Mexico had taken a 180-degree turn.

Contrary to Ambassador Wilson's original predictions, Huerta's government never exercised effective control over the whole country. Once the confusion entailed by Madero's downfall had subsided, an important group of his followers in the north organized in the name of constitutional legality under the formal leadership of Coahuila's governor, Venustiano Carranza. Very soon, the Constitutionalists, as they called themselves, formed an army of considerable size and bought supplies in the United States with funds collected from taxes, compulsory loans, and the sale north of the border of requisitioned minerals, agricultural products, and cattle. In the south, Zapatism recovered its vitality and joined the anti-Huertist movement. President Wilson soon established contact with the rebel leaders through a network of special envoys who acted as a channel of communication parallel to the embassy (a representative there was still in charge of business matters) and the consulates in Mexico. In this way, the U.S. government was able to follow the complex Mexican situation closely, to converse with the revolutionary leaders, and to stay in touch with Huerta's government. Wilson also sent a personal agent, John Lind, a former governor of Minnesota, to assess the general situation in Mexico and to convey his views to Washington as necessary.

Lind's unfavorable view of Huertism, coincided with President Wilson's own view. In Lind's opinion, the social stability required by Mexico and Latin America was best guaranteed, in the long run, by democratic governments, not by military dictatorships. And for

democracy to flourish, it was essential to have some minimum of
equity and social justice. In agrarian societies like Mexico, land was
the most important source of wealth; it was therefore urgent to
confront the problem of latifundism. It was essential to deconcentrate
the estates if there was to be a society in which the extremes of wealth
and poverty were less pronounced and where workers would have the
minimum rights accepted in the modern world: only under these
conditions could democracy, stability, and commerce flourish. To
Wilson, as to some members of his cabinet, the defense of the status
quo at all costs was not the best way to secure the economic and
political interests of the United States in Mexico and Latin America.
It was for these reasons that the U.S. president could not accept
Huertism.

Naturally, Huerta considered Wilson's views utopian, since they
did not take into account the reality of a country whose social base was
antagonistic to the establishment of democracy. However, for some
time, the dictator tried to maintain the appearance of legality through
the Mexican Congress and even by holding elections. This did not
satisfy Wilson's government, which asked something else—that the
usurper leave office immediately. Huerta soon abandoned all pretense
of legality and began to govern without regard for constitutional
forms: he dissolved Congress, annulled his dubious election of October 1913, and retained office as provisional president—in effect, as
dictator of Mexico.

President Wilson's decision to depose Huerta was strengthened
when Huerta decided to seek British support. In view of the hostility
of the U.S. government, Huerta turned to Europe for legitimacy,
arms and credit. At first, the Europeans responded positively—
especially the British, who were convinced of the suitability of
Huerta's government. But pressed by U.S. protests that the British
were violating the Monroe Doctrine, they withdrew their support
despite their conviction that President Wilson's policy toward Mexico was not realistic. In exchange for not intervening in Mexico, Great
Britain received equal treatment from the United States in the use of
the Panama Canal.

As a result of the Anglo–U.S. agreement, the doors to European
credit were closed to Huerta and he could no longer meet the
scheduled payments on the debt owed to foreign creditors. The
maintenance of Mexico's credit in the major banking centers of
Europe had been one of the supporting pillars of Porfirio's economic

policies. This pillar had collapsed within two years of his departure, as did many others, and the economy of Mexico did not fully recover until the Second World War.*

In 1914, it became evident that diplomatic moves, the embargo on the sale of arms to the Mexican government, and the lack of foreign credit were not unseating Huerta with the swiftness desired by Wilson, who decided to increase the pressure. General Leonard Wood had prepared a contingency plan to invade Mexico in October 1913; the opportunity to use it finally arrived in April 1914, when some members of th crew of the U.S. Navy's *Dolphin*, anchored in Tampico, disembarked without permission in a zone under Mexican military control (the Constitutionalists were besieging the town) and were arrested and briefly held. Rear Admiral Henry Mayo considered this trivial episode an insult to national honor, and with his government's support, turned it into a *casus belli*: either Huerta's government made public amends (a gun salute) to the U.S. flag or armed force would be used against him.

On 22 April, Veracruz, the most important port in the country, was occupied, not as a follow-up to the Tampico affair, but to prevent the unloading of a cargo of U.S. arms consigned to Huerta from a German ship in the harbor. The incident in Tampico was not mentioned again; instead, all military and diplomatic activity was concentrated on obtaining Huerta's resignation and in determining the type of government that was to succeed him. Negotiations to this effect took place between the months of April and July, and the governments of Argentina, Brazil, and Chile participated. Huerta's government recognized no right of the United States to dictate the terms by which Mexico should govern itself, but it could not ignore the occupation of part of the national territory, nor could it hope to recover that territory by force.

Huerta resigned himself to negotiating with the United States the conditions of his departure from the presidency. The Constitutionalists were invited to participate in the negotiations and they kept themselves well-informed of what was going on, but they never formally acknowledged the right of the United States or the other mediators to discuss the domestic problems of the country, and never sat down with them. Meanwhile, the Constitutionalist forces advanced in the north.

---

*From 1914 to 1942, Mexican governments were consistently unable to meet the debt service on money owed abroad or to secure access to foreign credit.

On 23 June 1914, following a victory in battle, the Constitutionalists won control of the city of Zacatecas. The federal army began to fall back on all fronts and, on 10 July, still without having reached any agreement with the United States, Huerta resigned and left for Europe.

It is important to note the role that the Constitutionalists and their leader, Venustiano Carranza, played in this international imbroglio. The rebels were certainly assisted by the United States, notably by its occupation of Veracruz. Nevertheless, Carranza never accepted the occupation; instead, he denied that the United States had any right to intervene in Mexico's domestic affairs and demanded the unconditional and immediate evaucation of the city. The Carrancists, unlike the Huertists, never participated in direct talks with the United States and the South American mediators, precisely because it was in those meetings that the nature of the Mexican government that was to succeed Huerta was being discussed. Their position was that the only legitimate topic for discussion was the evacuation of Veracruz, and as the U.S. government insisted in discussing other topics, the Carrancists boycotted the negotiations. Huerta was therefore unable to use against them the wave of nationalism and anti-U.S. sentiment that swept the country after the bombardment and occupation of Veracruz.

Following Huerta's downfall, the revolutionaries seized power unconditionally—without subscribing to any agreement with the United States, which would have cost them their legitimacy in the eyes of Mexican people. President Wilson, surprised and bothered by what he considered Carranza's intransigent and uncooperative attitude, had no alternative but to accept it. By the end of 1914, the U.S. forces evacuated Veracruz without linking their departure to the pretext for their arrival: the Mexican refusal to make amends to their flag for a fancied insult. By this time, also, President Wilson was preoccupied with the European crisis and the beginning of the First World War. Policy toward Mexico became more and more the responsibility of the State Department and the Wilsonian moral tone diminished.

Divisions among the Constitutionalists

The triumph of Constitutionalism and its most immediate result, the dissolution of the regular standing army and its replacement by the forces organized by the revolutionaries, did not bring peace. To

the contrary, the different factions of the Constitutionalist movement—variously led by Carranza, Villa, and Zapata—were soon
engaged in a struggle as fierce and ruthless as the one that had just
ended. Efforts to create some sort of central authority, a working
compromise among the three principal leaders, proved fruitless. The
worst imaginings of President Taft before the downfall of General
Díaz came true. The very appearance of centralized power vanished
and Mexico entered upon the most difficult years of its contemporary
history, characterized by economic crisis, nationwide social disorder
and civil struggle, hunger, and epidemics. The United States' immediate problem in Mexico was to protect the lives and property of its
citizens; the most important longer-term problem was to decide with
which faction to negotiate and cooperate so as to restore order, create a
new national government, and secure U.S. interests in Mexico.

In the great conference that the revolutionary leaders held at the
end of 1914 in the town of Aguascalientes, the followers of Zapata
succeeded in inducing the followers of Villa to accept the Plan of
Ayala—that is, agrarian reform. The two factions formally allied
themselves against Carranza, who responded with the law of 6 January, 1915, which also permitted some change in the structure of land
ownership in the country. The alliance between Villa and Zapata was
never a solid one, however, and each fought Carranza separately. The
whole struggle was a mixture of class conflicts and a fierce battle
between figures and groups for the profits of power.

As before, the U.S. government organized another network of
confidential agents close to the main leaders of the different factions.
At a certain moment Villa, or rather Villism, seemed the best
alternative. After all, Villa had never revealed himself as anti-United
States, and his manifesto of November 1914, which promised a series
of social reforms, also contained assurances that he would not occupy
the presidency once constitutional government had been restored.

Still, President Wilson decided not to commit himself just yet. On
2 June 1915, he issued a statement about the situation in Mexico.
According to this document, Mexico lacked an effective government,
a situation which entailed extensive economic damage both to natives
and foreigners. In view of this, the U.S. government appealed to the
factions in the struggle to come to an understanding so as to establish
a government with which the rest of the world could deal. In the
event they did not, the United States would then decide what means
were to be considered appropriate "to help Mexico save itself." Thus,

the possibility of military intervention in Mexico was again posed, as was perfectly clear to all interested parties.

Wilson's warning was issued after the battles of Irapuato and Celaya between Villa's and Carranza's forces, which the Villists lost. This victory helps to explain why Carranza ignored Wilson's appeal and refused to seek or accept a truce with his rivals. Moreover, only days later, a new battle was fought in León, and Villism received the *coup de grace*. From that moment on, and through a difficult and long process, the Carrancists began to rise militarily above their various enemies, who included not only Villa and Zapata but also many other independent groups that operated more like bandits than political factions, and some openly reactionary minor movements such as the one led by Félix Díaz, nephew of the deposed dictator, and the troops led by General Manuel Peláez in the oil zone.

Carranza's victory over his rivals turned him into the man to restore order—the "new order" that Wilson was supposedly seeking. Nevertheless, because of Carranza's nationalistic arrogance and his contempt for U.S. recommendations, President Wilson and the State Department preferred to look for an alternative. Argentina, Brazil, Chile, Uruguay, Bolivia, and Guatemala were all summoned to confer; these countries, together with the United States, were to try to find the right person and group to receive international recognition and support for constituting a provisional but effective government. To this effect, new mediation among the main Mexican factions was proposed. If it failed—as it was almost sure to—then the seven countries would proceed to support a government of their own choosing.

Carranza rejected this new inter-American intervention that was designed to nullify or dilute his military victory and which he considered interference with national sovereignty. The mediating conference was convoked for August 1915, and although the Villists and Zapatists were willing to meet with the conferees, Carranza was not and his generals supported him. In September, the remnants of Villism were defeated in the north by the Carrancists. In October, the U.S. State Department informed the Latin American Conferees that there was no other alternative but to the recognition of Carranza's government. A new protagonist—Germany—had impelled the U.S. government toward a new policy. To the U.S. diplomats it was clear that Germany was intent on keeping alive the struggle between the different Mexican factions in order to prevent order from being restored in the Mexican–U.S. border. For this reason, Carranza, despite Washington's eagerness to reject him, succeeded in obtaining recognition of his de facto government on his own terms.

A New Invasion and a New Constitution

The immediate effect of the recognition of the Carrancist government by the United States, was on the one hand, to encourage the European and Latin American countries to follow suit and, on the other hand, to ban the export of arms and ammunition to any Mexican group other than the goverment. Both measures helped to stabilize Carranza's regime; still, it took some time for the new government to establish normal international relations.

At the end of 1915, Villism was defeated but not destroyed. Although Villa no longer had the powerful Northern Division under his command, he still had a few hundred faithful followers ready to fight formal battles with their enemies; instead, they fought a guerrilla war that threatened the central government's capacity to restore and maintain order in the northern states.

On 10 January, 1916, a Villist gang stopped a train at Santa Isabel, Sonora, on which sixteen U.S. mine employees were traveling, their mission to reopen the mine so that Carranza would not cancel the concession. The assailants made them step off the train, and then and there, without further formalities, shot them. The news created a wave of indignation throughout the United States. Wilson's enemies took advantage of this sentiment to denounce his Mexican policy, and public pressure grew to invade Mexico and to end, once and for all, the disorder in that country. At dawn on 9 March 1916, a group of three to five hundred Villists attacked the town of Columbus, New Mexico, where a detachment of the Thirteenth Regiment of the U.S. Cavalry was stationed. Villist losses were heavy indeed, but the attack could have meant the end of Carranza, for it created a crisis in the U.S.–Mexican relations. The reasons for this attack are obscure; the possibilities range from retaliation against some arms dealers living in Columbus who had cheated Villa to Villa's desire to forestall an alliance between Carranza and the U.S. government which would turn Mexico into a U.S. protectorate. It could also have been the work of a German political agent who, pretending serve Villa, was in reality following orders from the German embassy in the United States to provoke a war between the two countries in order to prevent, delay, or diminish possible U.S. participation in the First World War.

The Villist attack provoked a much stronger wave of protest in the United States than the one produced by the murders in Santa Isabel. President Wilson replied to this aggression with a second military incursion into Mexican territory: his policy of "watchful waiting" had been shown to be ineffective. Carranza ordered Villa's arrest and, anticipating the worst, put his generals on the alert along the border. Officially, Mexico deplored the incident and proposed an agreement with the U.S. government similar to the one of the nineteenth century, which allowed the troops of both countries to cross the border to pursue gangs of bandits such as the Villists. The government in Washington could not agree to give Carranza such an easy way out; it prepared an expedition under the command of General John Pershing to pursue and eliminate Villa "without impairing Mexican sovereignty." Carranza maintained his position: U.S. troops could not enter Mexico if the principle—even a theoretical one—of reciprocity was not accepted beforehand. General Pershing's troops entered Mexico on March 15, causing great commotion and apprehension among the Mexican public and placing Carranza in a very uncomfortable position.

Pershing's "punitive expedition" began with 4,800 men, but as time went by it involved more than ten thousand. Its action was not as swift as some people expected, for the expedition stayed within Mexican territory for ten months; it was not as efficient either, for it never captured Villa. And it led to many incidents that made relations between the two countries even more tense. In April, in Parral, Chihuahua, the population rioted and attacked a U.S. detachment; the natives suffered 40 casualties; the U.S. soldiers, 2. From the beginning, Carranza tried to restrict the territory in which Pershing's troops could operate; however, on 21 June, a cavalry detachment moved farther south than the established limit. The Carrancists drove them back in a place called El Carrizal, also in Chihuahua. The Mexicans lost 74 men; the U.S. Army, 12, and 23 prisoners. Interventionist groups demanded that punishment not be confined to Villa but include Carranza, too; Mexico, however, returned the prisoners immediately and Wilson was able to resist this pressure. In the end, after many negotiations in the United States, Pershing withdrew, leaving behind substantially increased resentment of the United States and distrust of its motives.

While Pershing's forces were unsuccessfully searching for Villa, Carranza's government convoked elections to regularize its situation and the political life of the country. These elections were unusual; parts of the country were still in the hands of enemies of the government; moreover, the Congress that resulted as its main task the redrafting of the Constitution of 1857 to reflect new political and social realities.

The Constitutional Congress that assembled in November 1916 in Querétaro revealed the heterogeneity of the Carrancist group; radicals with socialist doctrines and those who still insisted on ideas and structures inherited from the nineteenth century were both present. In general, the group called Renovators, formed by Carranza's close followers, supported a draft constitution presented by him which was not too distant from the earlier constitution. Another group, the Jacobins, asked for substantial changes. The longest part of the debate in Querétaro was about the rules that should govern the future conduct of the church, indentified as an ally of the enemies of the Revolution; once this matter was settled—with a victory for the Jacobins—the discussion turned to such other vital matters as the nature and function of private property in general, of land and water in particular, of the ownership of oil in the subsoil, of the rights of the working class, of presidential powers, and so forth.

The U.S. government suspected that many things that directly affected its interests would be discussed in Querétaro. Since September, when representatives from Mexico and the United States had met successively in New London, Atlantic City, and Philadelphia, it had tried to reach an agreement not only on how Pershing and his men were to leave Mexico, but also on how Mexico was to guarantee respect for the life and property of U.S. citizens in the future. The United States set several conditions before ordering its troops to leave Mexico: the protection of the life and property of foreigners in the event of sudden attacks in the civil war; an explicit recognition of the rights of foreigners to own property; the creation of joint commissions to examine the pending claims between the two countries; the guarantee of religious freedom for foreign citizens; and more minor matters. As expected, the Carrancists refused to discuss any matter other than the departure of U.S. troops from Mexican territory. The U.S. government threatened to withdraw its recognition of Carranza's government and the discussions reached a stalemate.

By November 1916, when Congress was discussing at Querétaro

the new rules of the political scheme, the U.S. commissioners' demands had become more specific. Before Pershing was ordered to leave Mexico, an agreement had to be reached on issues as concrete as those expounded in the mining decree of 14 September 1915, a decree that threatened to cancel the mining contracts of those enterprises that would not resume operations immediately; the decree of 15 August 1915, by which all foreigners had to renounce diplomatic protection before being allowed to acquire real estate; and the oil decree of 7 January 1915, which forbade new drilling until legislation authorizing it was approved. Under pressure from the U.S. commissioners, the Mexican delegates accepted the demand that their government rescind these measures. But Carranza did not give his approval and, by 18 September 1916, the negotiations had returned to their starting point.

At the beginning of 1917, the new Constitution was in effect and the United States had become concerned about the First World War. The international crisis helped Carranza. On January 3, Wilson's delegates to the conference advised him to order the unconditional withdrawal of the troops, since the alternative was to strengthen them, possibly by posting as many as a half-million men in Mexico. By February 5, when the new Mexican Constitution was formally promulgated, the last U.S. troops had left Mexico.

The U.S. government's apprehensions about the new Constitution were justified. The articles regarding religious issues greatly increased the restrictions on the religious liberty of foreigners and on the education of their children. Article 27 placed conditions on the right of foreigners to acquire real estate and made it possible to expropriate rural property belonging to natives and foreigners; it also made it possible to deprive foreign oil companies of the ownership of subsoil petroleum reserves. Article 33 provided for extraditing foreigners without trial or appeal (as it does to this day). Article 123 granted the workers political, social, and economic prerogatives that until then had appeared in no other legislation in the world; this article led eventually to an increase in the cost of labor in the modern sector of the economy, diminishing—for some—Mexico's attractiveness as a place for investment.

The Constitution of 1917 was considered by many capitalists to be the work of radical socialists and some chancelleries saw it as the work of German agents. A few months later, the Bolshevik Revolution in Russia deposed Mexico as Enemy No. 1 of international capitalism;

however, in years to come, the revolutionary Mexican government followed the U.S.S.R. very closely on the blacklist of foreign investors and their governments.

In 1913–14 the U.S. government's actions against Huerta had been justified by the argument that Mexico needed social reform to prevent future ruptures of the political order, but by 1917 this diagnosis had been forgotten. After that time, U.S. activities in Mexico were directed mainly at ameliorating the effect of the revolutionary reforms on foreign interest.

A European Intrigue

When the First World War began, Mexico lost some of its importance to Washington, but gained in other places, particularly Germany and England. There were two basic reasons for this European interest. First, Mexico had become an important producer of oil at a time when the great world fleets had replaced coal with oil. The demand for oil increased the producer's strategic importance, as did the increased mechanization of the armies at war and the rise of aviation. It is true that the output of the Mexican oilfields could not be compared to that of the United States, but it is also true that the United States consumed a great part of what it produced while Mexico exported nearly all of its output. In 1914, the production of crude oil in Mexico was 26.2 million barrels; by 1918, in response to the demand generated by the First World War, it had increased to 63.8 million barrels. By then, Mexico had become the leading world exporter of hydrocarbons. Most of this oil was destined for the United States, enabling it in turn to export great quantities of fuel to the Allies, particularly England.

The great powers were in sharp competition in Mexico. The Anglo–U.S. objective was to maintain control of their enterprises in the country, while Germany's objective was to deny Mexican oil to the Allies by any means available, be it an embargo or sabotage of the oil fields. The clandestine services of both sides were very active in Mexico. The wells were never destroyed or even damaged, nor did the new Mexican legislation interfere with the production and export of the fuel. However, both the U.S. and British general staffs drew up contingency plans in the event of an invasion of the oil zone, but the potential invaders were discouraged by to the distance from the coast to the oilfields and by the poor condition of the roads. The presence in the oil zone of the forces commanded by the anti-Carrancist, General Manuel Peláez, a supporter of the Allies, was also considered helpful.

Second, the great powers were interested in Mexico not only for its oil but also because of its proximity to the United States. From the beginning of the First World War, several countries either desired or feared that the Mexican Revolution might lead to a new war between Mexico and the United States, in which event the United States would have to divert an army of occupation to Mexico. This is why Germany sought to bring about such a conflict, while Great Britain and pro-Allied circles in the United States did not. Villa's attack on Columbus could have been linked to this German plan, but in any case it was not the only one. German efforts to bring Victoriano Huerta back from European exile to lead a revolt against Carranza were based on the hope that Wilson would not tolerate Huerta's presence in Mexico and would have to resort to an invasion in order to get rid of him. Unfortunately for the Germans, the British became aware of the scheme at its very beginning in 1915, followed the dictator on his return trip to the American continent, and managed to have U.S. authorities arrest him when he headed toward the border with Mexico. Huerta died in Texas in January 1916 still in the custody of U.S. authorities.

Huerta's death and the reduction of Villism to a handful of skirmishers led the Germans to modify their Mexican strategy substantially: instead of supporting Carranza's enemies, they decided to effect an alliance with him in the hope that his defensive nationalism could be turned into an anti-U.S. offensive. There is evidence that, beginning in 1916, Carranza and the German envoys discussed the possibility of having Germany grant material support to Carranza's government in exchange for an alliance between the two countries. The negotiations did not prosper.

However, as the war in Europe continued and since Germany had decided to use submarines to eliminate trade between its enemies and the United States—which would surely lead to U.S. intervention on the Allied side—the possibility of persuading Carranza to set aside his neutrality and ally himself with the Central Powers became very attractive to German Secretary of Foreign Affairs Arthur Zimmermann. These circumstances led German representatives in Mexico to formulate a tentative offer of help to Carranza in exchange for renunciation of Mexican neutrality. Carranza could expect to receive financial aid directly from Germany, but not military support; this might well have had to come through Japan, for it was difficult for German ships to get past the Allied patrols and reach Mexico.

At the end of 1916, most neutral observers were not sure of an Anglo-French victory in Europe; there were possibilities of a German victory. However, Carranza did not hasten: Japan's ability to furnish Mexico with arms was limited. The Germans nevertheless pressed on and, in January 1917, Zimmermann sent his minister in Mexico a telegram informing him that Germany had decided to start unlimited submarine warfare. If the United States reacted against this decision and made an alliance with the empire's enemies, then the minister was to formalize the offer made to Carranza. He was to propose an offensive-defensive alliance with the promise that, by the end of the war, Mexico would recover the territories lost in the conflict with the United States in the previous century. His message was sent in code through his Washington embassy, but it was intercepted and deciphered by the British secret services and delivered to the United States just when Wilson needed additional arguments to bolster public support for entering the war on the Allied side. The "Zimmerman telegram," long considered a classic diplomatic fiasco, served this purpose. Mexico never responded to the German offer but the United States and England had delivered the Central Powers a punishing blow.

The New Constitution and Foreign Interests

By 1917, the main problems between the United States and Mexico were not Mexican neutrality in the war, nor the violence that still affected some regions of Mexico, nor compensation for the damages caused during the revolutionary struggle, nor the resumption of payments on the foreign debt, but those regarding the interpretation of the nationalistic aspects of the new constitution. Using the horrible example of the Russian Revolution as a text, Wilson pointed out to a skeptical Carranza that any revolutionary attack against international capitalism was no less than an attack on democracy and on civilization itself. In his view, the new Mexican Constitution was dangerously leftist and anticapitalistic and the United States could not cooperate with Mexico in effectuating its provisions.

Carranza, for his part, was not over-eager to put into practice the agrarian reform or the labor legislation. He did insist, however, on the Calvo Doctrine embodied in the new constitution. According to this doctrine, foreigners were subjected to the same juridical processes as Mexicans, and could not ask for diplomatic protection and preferential treatment, because this would amount to discrimination against the natives. If foreigners decided to try their luck in Mexico, then they should think of themselves as Mexicans and they should share with the rest of the country's population the fluctuations of fortune. The United States and European countries did not accept this interpretation of international equity, affirming that even if their citizens—as individuals—renounced their right to diplomatic protection, as the Constitution required, their governments were not compelled to imitate them. In the event of a clear denial of justice, these foreign governments had the right to extend their protection even if the affected party failed to ask for it, since this protection was, according the the U.S. government, an unrenounceable right of their citizens and a permanent obligation of their government.

These disagreements, which foreshadowed later disputes over the ownership of oil rights during the regime of Lázaro Cárdenas, were phrased and expressed as matters of high principle, but the nub of the problem was control of Mexican oil resources. The foreign powers—not just the United States, since Great Britain was equally concerned—were particularly apprehensive about legislation pending before the Mexican Congress that would apply retroactively to foreign-owned deposits of oil and reclaim them for the government of Mexico. The U.S. government accepted Mexico's right to declare as government property the deposits of hydrocarbons that were not owned by individuals, but by no means those that had been legitimately acquired under the oil laws of the old regime—around 2.1 million hectares, virtually all of the Mexican oil zones then known.

Carranza used the special powers to deal with financial matters that Congress conferred on him and worked out a series of decrees, in particular the one of 19 February 1918, which explicitly stated that all oil deposits belonged to the nation, regardless of whatever rights to them individuals had held until that moment. Both the powerful Anglo–U.S. enterprises that controlled over 90 percent of regular production and the State Department declined to accept this retroactive interpretation of the Constitution and they refused to comply with the crucial part of the decrees, which required them to submit to the government their old titles of ownership and have them exchanged for mere state concessions. According to the companies and to the U.S. government, this was confiscation: to accept Mexico's position would be to establish a precedent that would affect the legitimacy of foreign investments in every part of the world.

In view of the realities of power—the United States had emerged from the First World War as the world's strongest state—Carranza decided to suspend his decrees, waiting indefinitely for Congress to "issue a law to implement Article 27 concerning oil." Congress, always responsive to Carranza, never passed this legislation, and by 1919, pressure from those groups in the United States that demanded military intervention in Mexico had increased. A final determination of Mexico's control of the country's oil was left pending, awaiting a better moment.

Many powerful groups in the United States wanted to settle accounts with Carranza, who had, after all, once considered forming an alliance with Germany who had taken advantage of the international crisis of the First World War to install an antiforeign constitution. Confronted with the interventionist attitude of the U.S. government once the war in Europe was over, and with no hope of obtaining help from the European powers, Carranza turned momentarily to Latin America. This policy, which became known as the Carranza Doctrine, enunciated the following fundamental principles: (1) not to permit foreigners to attain a predominant position in relation to natives; (2) to maintain judicial equality among the states; (3) to disown the Monroe Doctrine as constituting interference in the domestic affairs of Latin American countries; (4) to establish a relationship of true solidarity among Latin American countries based on the principle of nonintervention; (5) to set up treaties and alliances between Latin America and any country or group of countries when it so suited their interests; (6) to gain control over national resources and to promote industrialization as the best way to secure independence.

There is no doubt that the Carranza Doctrine was aimed against U.S. hegemony in the Western Hemisphere, but it never produced any practical results. Most of the Latin American governments, unlike Mexico, did not see the advantages of seeking a showdown with the greatest world power, so they continued to seek an accommodation with it, leaving Mexico as isolated as before.

In the last stages of his regime, which ended in 1920, Carranza was less aggressive in his search for a readjustment of the rights held by foreigners in general and by U.S. citizens in particular. Confrontation was replaced by a search for an adjustment. Even if in practice the importance of U.S. interests in the Mexican economy did not diminish—by 1919 American investments in Mexico were estimated to surpass $900 million—it is also true that the antiforeign articles of the new constitution were maintained. They were not enforced, but neither were they abrogated.

It was at about this time, October 1919, that William O. Jenkins, a wealthy businessman and consular agent for the United States in Puebla, was kidnapped by a rebel party loyal to Félix Díaz. The incident provided a new excuse for the interventionists to demand that the United States issue a stern warning to the Mexican government for not providing adequate protection to foreigners. After a week, Jenkins—a notorious enemy of the Revolution—was set free, but the Mexican authorities then arrested him on charges of kidnapping himself in order to create a political incident between Mexico and the United States. Tensions between the two countries reached a dangerous level at the beginning of 1920, then both governments decided to drop the case.

Undoubtedly, the Mexican Revolution, as a reaction against the great economic and cultural penetration of foreign interests and values during the Porfirist period, unleased a tremendous wave of nationalism. This nationalism frequently degenerated into xenophobia, but in its positive aspect and perhaps for the first time, it gave real content to the idea of a Mexican nation.

The Revolution affected both U.S. and European interests; but by 1920, once the most violent stage of the civil war was over, it was evident that the Europeans had accepted the fact that in Mexico the main foreign interests were the United States, and that it would be very difficult for any European state to try to establish a policy of its own in that country. Thus, for all practical purposes, after the First World War, Mexico and the United States stood facing each other with no intermediaries. For a long time thereafter, Mexico's political and economic relations with the rest of the world could be equated with its relations with the United States, precisely the situation that Mexican rulers had traditionally tried to avoid.

8

Revolutionary Nationalism and Imperialism: A Difficult Coexistence: 1920-1940

In Search of Recognition

In 1920, in the United States, the presidential candidate of the Republican Party, Warren G. Harding, overwhelmingly defeated his Democratic rival, James M. Cox, in a national election. In Mexico, the successor to the first government elected under the new revolutionary Constitution was decided in the traditional way: by force.

General Alvaro Obregón, undoubtedly the strongest and most charismatic military leader of the day, revolted against Carranza; his followers included an important part of the federal army as well as most of the anti-Carrancist rebels still active in Mexico. With a base in his home state of Sonora, a rich mining and farming territory in the extreme northwest, and well-equipped with slogans and manifestos labelling Carranza an enemy of democracy all too fond of imposing his own solutions, Obregón and his followers took over the country rapidly and without difficulty.

Carranza tried to repeat one of his earlier strategies: withdrawal and the organization of the counterattack. He accordingly struck out for Veracruz with what followers he had and a good part of the federal bureaucracy. His luck had run out, and on 21 May 1920, he was killed in the small mountain village of Tlaxcalantongo by a group of armed counterrevolutionary adherents of Manuel Peláez.

Obregón's triumph marked the ascendance of the so-called Sonora group, which had contributed the main force against Carranza, and the political predominance of the northwest was maintained until 1935. The victory of the Sonorans did not usher in any fundamental change in governmental policies, although Obregón and his successor, General Plutarco Elías Calles, were more inclined to incorporate into their governments the leaders, groups, and factions who supposedly represented the interests of peasants, workers, and lower–middle-class people—the so-called popular sectors.

The first internal measures taken by the victors were to reestablish civil order and legal processes, and Adolfo de la Huerta, governor of the state of Sonora and titular chief of the rebellion, was declared provisional president. His immediate tasks were to call for elections from which General Obregón would emerge victorious, and to arrange for the surrender of various groups which were still in revolt against the federal government, the best-known of which was the irregular force led by Francisco Villa. De la Huerta successfully pacified the country, and on 1 December 1920 he handed the presidency over to the true caudillo of the victors: Alvaro Obregón.

On the international scene, the Sonorans' most important task was to obtain recognition of the new regime from Washington. Recognition by the United States would lead the way for European countries; itself an important matter: it would also facilitate the economic and fiscal arrangements with the outside world—in particular, with the United States—without which the Mexican economy could hardly breathe.

Carranza's fall was not deplored in the United States. To the contrary, the U.S. government's abstention from the brief civil struggle which overthrew him was a meaningful one. From the beginning, the Sonoran rebels appeared to the United States as more amenable to negotiations. This time, however, the U.S. groups that were pushing for a long-range solution to the Mexican problem were demanding more than promises or gestures of goodwill. They wanted a formal agreement—a treaty—which would protect the rights and privileges that they had acquired in Mexico. The value of U.S. investments in Mexico—around twelve-hundred million dollars, was even greater than when the Revolution had begun, partly because of the growing importance of the oil industry. The oil companies' representatives headed those who demanded a strong U.S. hand in dealing with Mexico and its new Constitution.

In the last years of President Wilson's government, there remained very little of his early sympathy with Mexican reforms. By 1920. the most influential voice speaking about Mexico was not that of the president; it was that of Congress, particularly that of Republican Senator Albert Fall, an authentic counterrevolutionary. He had presided over a series of hearings dealing with Mexican problems in which points of view opposing the Mexican Revolution predominated. The senator, who was very concerned about U.S. oil interests, recommended that a new treaty with Mexico be concluded, one which undid the harm inflicted on foreign interests by the 1917 Constitution, particularly in articles 3, 27, 33, and 130, and that, if Mexico refused to accept such a treaty, the US government should proceed to occupy the country militarily and install more compliant regime.

President Wilson adopted a position similar to Fall's. He informed De la Huerta's envoys that his government would extend its recognition only when the existing problems between the two countries were solved. These problems ranged from respecting the property rights of foreigners in Mexico to the removal of the Mexican ambassador in Buenos Aires owing to his openly anti-U.S. attitude. The new Mexican leaders assured the White House they were willing to consider the demands, but they insisted that formal recognition be granted first. Wilson's cabinet turned them down. If the failure to recognize the new regime diminished Obregón's standing both in and out of his country, that was the Mexican government's problem and not the United States'.

For internal reasons, the need to obtain diplomatic recognition from Washington was substantial. The suspension of political relations had not hindered normal economic exchanges between the two countries, nor the resolution of routine issues, since their embassies continued to operate with lower-ranking personnel and consular services, where maintained. But lack of recognition of the new Mexican government did mean that the United States had no obligation to prevent anti-Obregón groups from operating in its territory and no obligation to stop the flow of arms to dissident groups in Mexico. Moreover, the threat of recognizing the belligerent status of the enemies of the Sonorans, who were not few, remained alive. In addition, without U.S endorsement, the Obregón government could not reestablish Mexico's credit in the world's money markets and thus could not borrow money.

On the other hand, to waive important provisions of the Constitution would be tantamount to acknowledging that Mexican sovereignty existed only on paper and that the country was ineffect a protectorate of the United States. Until then, the Revolution had served to strengthen the nationalist spirit. The main elements of the Carranza Doctrine—nonintervention in the internal affairs of any nation and the juridical equality of all nations Mexico—had transcended its author. Obregón had to respect these principles.

Obregón decided to try to consolidate his government without either accepting or rejecting the U.S. demands. He chose a third way:

to assure the United States, by sovereign acts, that its acquired rights would be respected and so convince it that the proposed treaty was unnecessary.

This is why, on 20 August 1921, the Mexican Supreme Court of Justice ruled favorably on an appeal which had been made years earlier by the Texas Oil Company against Carranza's decrees of 1918. The verdict was that Article 27 of the Constitution, as it applied to oil, was not retroactive, since retroactive application was expressly prohibited by Article 14. Nevertheless, the court also ruled that the previous Porfirist oil legislation remained valid when the companies that were exploiting hydrocarbons had failed to take some "positive act" prior to the enactment of the Constitution of 1917. Those lands, that is, that were simply maintained as reserves would have to be governed according to the Constitution. In this and in four parallel rulings, Mexico's highest court committed its government to a conservative interpretation of the Constitution with respect to oil (even though Obregón refused to convert the interpretation into new regulatory legislation). The specter of nationalization vanished, but the oil companies remained unconvinced of the desirability of granting unconditional diplomatic recognition to Mexico.

Obregón not only curtailed the scope of Carranza's oil reform but, in view of the stubbornness of the oil companies, he decided to woo U.S. traders and bankers and turn them into his advocates in Washington. To that end, the president invited to Mexico City, on several occasions, a large number of U.S. exporters. He assured them that, once full diplomatic relations were resumed, there would be improved opportunities for them in the Mexican market. The bankers were most important in the effort to dissuade President Harding from trying to give Mexico only conditional recognition. But in order to obtain the support of the bankers, Obregón first had to reach an agreement on the payment of the already substantial foreign debt and the interest that had accumulated since 1914, a difficult undertaking in view of the depleted Mexican treasury.

At the end of 1921, Obregón invited Thomas Lamont, president of the International Committee of Bankers on Mexico (ICBM) to initiate talks about the debt. Lamont left Mexico without reaching any final understanding, but the following year, Obregón sent De la Huerta, at that time his secretary of the treasury, to Washington to continue negotiations. Both Lamont and De la Huerta seem to have handled the negotiations well, and a cordial atmosphere was maintained.

The talks were not simple, but in June 1922, the De la Huerta–

Lamont agreement, whereby Mexico recognized a debt to the ICBM of $508,830,321, of which $243,734,321 represented railroad bonds, was signed. (An additional $207 million, claimed as interest, was eliminated). By the terms of the agreement, Mexico would pay $30 million annually for four years and an increased amount after that. The terms were difficult: $30 million was almost a fourth of the annual income of the federal government. Despite the difficulty and internal critcism, the agreement was ratified by Obregón on 7 August and by Congress on 29 September. The Mexican president was confident that it would lead to formal recognition and to a renewal of foreign loans in order to refinance the debt.

Agrarian reform was not one of Obregón's chief concerns. The president himself owned rural property and was convinced that Mexican agriculture could prosper only within a private-property system, although one purged of the excesses of the latifundia.* Nevertheless, his government needed the support of the peasants, and there was more expropriation and distribution of land—in accordance with Article 27 of the Constitution—than in the previous administration. Some of the expropriations affected U.S. interests, although not many, and not very important ones. Even so, Washington complained that they were not adequately compensated for.

By 1923, the governments of Mexico and of the United States were aware that their irregular relations could not continue indefinitely and that a reconsideration of their respective positions was inevitable. For Obregón, the situation was urgent; the presidential succession had to be decided that year and no great vision was needed to predict that the losers would be tempted to resort to rebellion. In that event, the Mexican government would require strict enforcement of U.S. neutrality laws to deny sanctuary to rebels and to prevent them from acquiring arms in the United States and dispatching them to Mexico.

For the United States, the situation was not so urgent, but it would be awkward if the Mexican government could prove to the world that it could hold power without Washington's approval. The longer it took to recognize Obregón, the less effective a weapon diplomatic recognition would be in the future. In addition, the secretary of state was being pressured by some European governments, mainly France,

---

*He was born into a family of modest Sonora farmers and his main activity before the revolution was growing and selling chick-peas. He invented a simple and effective machine for planting them and organized their export to the principal markets: Spain and the United States.

and by U.S. business executives who were hoping to obtain some benefits from Obregón's goodwill once diplomatic relations were reestablished.

The opportunity to resume negotiations arose when James A. Ryan, a retired U.S. general with interests in Mexico who knew the presidents of both countries, offered to act as an intermediary. On 9 April 1923, Obregón handed Ryan a document in which he agreed to the suggestion that the differences between his governments and that of the United States be discussed through personal representatives of the two presidents. Obregón stated, however, that existing Mexican legislation could not be the object of negotiations, a condition intended only to keep up appearances. President Harding must have understood it so, since he offered no objection and accepted Obregón's entire proposal. Obregón appointed a friend to represent him, Ramón Ross, and a skillful lawyer, Fernando González Roa. Harding's representatives were Charles B. Warren and John B. Payne, both lawyers.

The negotiations, known as the Bucareli conferences because of the place in Mexico City, where they were held lasted three months, beginning 14 May. They were private conferences, and only the points of agreement reached in the fifteen formal sessions were ever published. The minutes made no reference to the numerous informal meetings that were the heart of the negotiations.

According to the minutes, there were three categories of agreements. The first designated a Special Mixed Claims Commission, which was to determine the validity and amount of the U.S. claims stemming from the civil war in Mexico between 1910 and 1920. The second covered the creation of a General Mixed Claims Commission, which would examine the civil claims accumulated by the citizens of each country against the other after 1868, when the last claims convention between Mexico and the United States had been signed. The third agreement—the most controversial—was known as the "unofficial pact." It was an agreement reached by the commissioners about the way Mexico would apply its oil and agrarian legislation to U.S. interests in the future.

With respect to the agrarian problem, it was agreed that the Mexican government would pay with government bonds those U.S. citizens whose property was affected, but only if the area did not exceed 1,755 hectares. Whenever this limit was surpassed, compensation would have to be made immediately, in cash and at market prices. This clause seems rather strange, almost as if it should be the other way round, but the commissioners knew very well what they were about. Since the federal treasury was nearly empty and there were no funds to compensate the foreign holders of really large estates, confiscation of such rural property belonging to U.S. citizens would have to be a rare event.

The Mexican commissioners reaffirmed that Article 27, regarding nationalization of hydrocarbons, would not apply retroactively to oil deposits—provided that the owners or tenants of oil fields had undertaken, before 1917, some "positive act" proving that they intended to look for and extract fuel. If there was no such proof, the new legislation would apply. Even so, the owners of such land would have preference in obtaining government concessions for their exploitation. The U.S. delegates were not directly opposed to this interpretation, but they did not accept it formally.

On 15 August, the final texts were ready, and the U.S. delegates left for Washington. By then, stormy winds were blowing through the Mexican political scene. President Obregón had given his support to General Plutarco Elías Calles, secretary of the interior, as his successor. This decision was challenged by De la Huerta, secretary of the treasury, who launched his own candidacy, opening the door to rebellion by his followers and other dissatisfied groups. And in the United States, the oil companies were not very pleased about the Bucareli agreements, which did not protect 100 percent of their acquired rights. The secretary of state, on the other hand, believed the delegates had reached the limit that could be obtained without military force, and on 31 August 1923 Washington announced the reestablishment of diplomatic relations.

By September, Charles Warren had returned to Mexico as ambassador and Obregón's political position was strengthened.

The result of the Bucareli agreements was beneficial but ambiguous. On the one hand, the United States had managed to limit the scope of nationalist revolutionary legislation, on the other, Obregón had obtained U.S. recognition without actually changing the Constitution and without subscribing to the kind of treaty that the United States had originally demanded. The unofficial Bucareli agreements were never held to constitute an international instrument. They were not presented to the Congress of either country, and their execution depended solely on the goodwill of the parties involved. The only clauses submitted to the legislatures were the texts of the claims conventions. They were duly approved after relations were reestablished, in December 1923 and February 1924.

As expected, De la Huerta and his followers did not wait on the elections to act against Obregón. With the support of a substantial part of the army, they launched a rebellion in December 1923 and immediately attempted to gain recognition from Washington. Even though the rebels sent an envoy to offer a more advantageous arrangement in case of victory, the U.S. government preferred to support Obregón. Thus, Obregón was able to acquire arms in the United States and to push for strict enforcement of the U.S. neutrality laws. When De la Huerta realized that he would get no help from the United States and that the rebel movement was losing force, he used the Bucareli agreements as a basis for accusing Obregón of selling the national sovereignty in exchange for U.S. support. The charge diminished the legitimacy of the government, but not enough to save the rebels.

In 1924, after De la Huerta was defeated and the stability of the Obregón leadership was reestablished, the oil companies decided to reach a direct agreement with the Mexican government. In September, talks were held in Mexico City to seek a "definite solution" to the disagreement that still existed. The companies wanted legislation that would end all ambiguities and increase their guarantees. In exchange, they were willing to increase production, which had begun to fall drastically, affecting the federal treasury most adversely.

Despite this blackmail, the oil companies were able to obtain only a tax reduction and no legislative concessions. Obregón's government was coming to an end and the new president, General Calles, would have to assume responsibility for any new decisions. Moreoever, everything seemed to indicate that Mexican–U.S. relations were beginning to settle down. The reformist and nationalist storm seemed to be over and Washington had weathered it. European countries, with the exception of Great Britain, which insisted on more explicit guarantees and prompt compensation for the damages suffered by British subjects, proceeded to recognize the Obregón government as soon as Washington had pointed the way.

The Oil Legislation

General Plutarco Elías Calles, who then had the reputation of being a radical and perhaps even a socialist, assumed power on 1 December 1924. Obregón, the great caudillo, retired to private life to attend to his agrarian and business interests. Calles then sought more support among farm and, particularly, labor groups and put the

Ministry of Industry, Commerce and Labor, which included the
Department of Oil, in the hands of Luis N. Morones, the leader of the
largest labor organization in the country, the CROM.

In 1925, the production of hydrocarbons in Mexico continued to
decline, greatly increasing the government's irritation with the oil
companies. From the Mexican leaders' point of view, the decline in
production could have only one cause: a decision by the foreign
companies to exploit oil in other countries where the bothersome
specter of nationalism had not yet emerged—particularly Venezuela—and to punish Mexico by leaving its oil in reserve. What the
companies wanted, the Mexicans decided, was to force Mexico to
make further concessions: the Bucareli pacts had left Mexico its own
master, not a situation agreeable to the companies. Calles's government became exasperated and proceeded to shape the first legislation
to effectuate paragraph 4, Article 27 of the Constitution—that is, oil
legislation—without consulting the companies or the U.S. government.

A new problem began to emerge: the federal government had used
up practically all its money putting down the De la Huertist rebellion
of 1923–24. Obregón could not meet the second annual payment on
the foreign debt and, on 30 June 1924, just before he was due to turn
over power to Calles, he declared that the agreement with the bankers
had to be temporarily suspended. Calles tried to solve this problem in
1925, but found it was financially impossible. He asked his secertary
of finance, Alberto J. Pani, to attempt a more realistic agreement
which did not require more than Mexico could pay.

Pani was successful. The Pani-Lamont agreement of 23 October
separated the railroad debt from the public debt; the railroad debt
became once more the direct responsibility of Ferrocarriles
Nacionales, an enterprise in which the government was the principal
shareholder. In return, the government promised to deliver to Ferrocarriles Nacionales, at the end of that year, the railroad lines that the
government controlled. The new public debt amounted to 998.2
million pesos, $499 million. Calles made the first payment of $10.7
million in 1926, thus avoiding a confrontation with the bankers.

In mid-1925, U.S. authorities were notified that Mexico was
preparing new oil legislation which did not conform to the Bucareli
agreements. By then, the U.S. president was yet another Republican,
Calvin Coolidge, whose position on U.S interests abroad was as firm
as his predecessor's. Relations between the two nations soon became
less cordial; it was still possible to appoint an arbiter to each of the two

claims commissions—a Panamanian to the general commission and a Brazilian to the special commission—but that was all.

The U.S. government notified Calles on several occasions that it opposed the new oil legislation being considered by the Mexican Congress. On 12 June 1925, the Department of State declared publicly that "the Mexican government is being judged by the world"; nevertheless, on 31 December, the first legislation concerning hydrocarbons based on the Constitution of 1917 took effect. In April 1926, regulatory legislation was promulgated. The so-called alien law became effective at the same time as the oil legislation. Neither of these laws was well received in Washington or in business circles with interests in Mexico.

The alien law was opposed because it prohibited foreigners, and companies owned mainly by foreigners, to continue to own real estate within 50 kilometers of the coastline and 100 kilometers of either border, and stipulated the ways in which such property was to be marketed so that it could be acquired only by nationals.

However, what displeased the U.S. government and the oil enterprises most was the oil legislation. This law required the owners of oilfields to exchange property titles dated earlier than 1917 for government concessions with a life limited to fifty years following the last "positive act." The same law gave the companies one year to complete all action required by the law; a company that missed the deadline would lose all its rights.

Washington could not effectively argue that the unofficial pact of 1923 should be respected, since the Mexicans could reply that it was not a treaty, and once more the two sides disagreed about the constitutional meaning of "retroactivity." This time, however, there was a new ambassador, James Rockwell Sheffield, who was unwilling to negotiate with Mexico because such action was contrary to his "principles."

Sheffield believed, as he wrote a friend, that the obligation of the Anglo-Saxon people toward societies such as the Mexican, a "non white" society, was to serve as guides so the natives would eventually understand their true interests and obligations, which could never be contrary to U.S. interests; if persuasion failed, force would become morally justified. Coolidge agreed. From the U.S. government's point of view, Calles was attempting to confiscate—steal—legitimate rights from foreigners in an industry that only their effort and inventiveness had created. This could not be permitted.

The oil producers decided, with the support of U.S. authorities and the concurrence of the British and the Dutch governments, not to comply with the oil legislation, which they considered unconstitutional. The British oil companies had considered a compromise whereby concessions in Mexico's oilfields would be balanced against fiscal advantages in other areas, but in the end, they maintained a united front with their U.S. colleagues. In November 1926, the U.S. press began to speculate about the possibility of breaking diplomatic relations with Mexico. Calles then suggested that the differences between the two countries be submitted to international arbitration, but the U.S. government rejected the proposal. The oil companies and Ambassador Sheffield agreed that the moment to act firmly had come.

President Calles was also interfering with Washington's policies elsewhere in Central America: he was politically and materially supporting the Liberal Party of Nicaragua against Adolfo Díaz's Conservatives, who had the backing of the U.S. marines. The official U.S. point of view was that the Mexican government was serving Bolshevik interests in Latin America, conduct Washington could not accept.

Calles had his hands full. He was already facing the Cristeros in central Mexico. That rebellion, mounted and carried forward by peasants and ranchers in defense of their own property rights and those of the Catholic Church, was widespread, intense, and—like all religious conflicts—highly emotional. The Cristeros affected Mexico's image in the United States adversely: Mexico was widely portrayed as a chaotic country led by bloodthirsty and dishonest leaders who were enemies of private property and the church, men with no fear of God or respect for religion. Some Mexican observers, noting how Mexico's image was being manipulated in the U.S., concluded that the ground was being prepared for military action against Mexico similar to the action being taken in Nicaragua.

But U.S. opinion was not monolithic. A contrary view—that negotiation was more effective and less costly—was held by U.S. senators William Borah and Robert M. La Follette, Jr., who led a group that opposed military intervention and was interested in Calles's proposal of arbitration. In February 1927, U.S. Army manuevers on the border created widespread apprehension in Mexico, but by March the anti-interventionists had won out. Congress did not support a new armed action in Latin America for the benefit of the oil or banana companies: its members were convinced that trying to turn Mexico into a larger Nicaragua would not solve the problem but

would only complicate it. By then, too, the leading representative of
the oil companies in the U.S. cabinet, Harding's former Secretary of
the Interior Albert B. Fall, was serving a term in jail for an illegal
transfer of oil reserves from the U.S. Navy to private enterprise. The
poor public image of the oil companies in the United States during
those years made it easier to convince Coolidge to initiate negotiations, a position that had been supported for some time by the new
British minister to Mexico City, who was convinced that Sheffield's
intransigeance had unnecessarily prolonged the crisis with Mexico.

An important factor in Coolidge's decision to change his ambassador and his policy in Mexico in mid-1927 was the attitutde of U.S.
financiers. The ICBM, particularly J.P. Morgan's firm, believed that
intervention would merely postpone Mexico's capacity to face its
international obligations. Indeed, the Mexican government had not
suspended the Pani-Lamont agreement, which the bankers thought
reflected a genuine desire to normalize Mexico's foreign relations:
patience, not conflict, was needed. Moreover, since the bankers had
nothing to lose from Mexico's modifications of foreigners' rights to
oil, they did not consider that problem a *casus belli*. Coolidge finally
accepted this point of view and authorized one of Morgan's partners
to find some solutions. Dwight Morrow replaced Sheffield as U.S.
ambassador to Mexico, to the relief of many.

Morrow came to Mexico at the end of 1927 with instructions to
avoid a conflict, and immediately proceeded to change the focus of
Mexican–U.S. relations. The change was perhaps more in form than
in content, but the result was remarkable. To begin with, Morrow
was careful not to display the arrogance and racism of his predecessors; to the contrary, he initiated a public-relations campaign to
demonstrate that the United States had every intention of treating
Mexico with all the respect due a sovereign nation in possession of a
valuable culture. The new ambassador believed that the Mexican
Revolution was over, that radicalism was a thing of the past; and that
Mexico's leaders, particularly Calles, could be educated in the com-
plexities of international economics and convinced that the best way
to modernize Mexico was to join their interests to those of the United
States, the strongest economy in the world.

In November, Morrow accompanied Calles on a tour to the north
of the country to inspect the government's new irrigation works, a
public demonstration of U.S. support for Calles that impressed the
Roman Catholics of both countries, many of whom had regarded
Calles as anti-Catholic. Immediately afterward, the ambassador sug-

gested that it would be expedient to modify the oil legislation by
persuading the Mexican courts to rule that it was not retroactive. On
17 November, the Supreme Court handed down the verdict that
Morrow had been hoping for. Immediately, both the U.S. embassy
and the Mexican Department of Commerce, Industry and Labor
began to draw up a new law that would translate the court's decision
into action and that would meet with approval in Washington. On
26 December, President Calles sent to Congress modifications of
Articles 14 and 15 of the oil legislation of 1925 and the legislators
approved them. The changes provided for concessions in perpetuity to
foreigners who had acquired rights before 1917 and who could
demonstrate that they had taken some "positive act," now more
loosely defined. The previous rights of the oil companies would not be
affected by their refusal to obey the law of 1925, but would be if they
did not observe the new law.

The oil companies were still not satisfied: they wanted total
elimination of confirmatory concessions, but the U.S. government
informed them that it would not support their intention to return to
the status quo ante. A new phase in international relations required
some concessions to the sovereignty and nationalism of countries such
as Mexico. The Department of State regarded the oil crisis as over and
done with; in the future, any problems the companies had with the
Mexican government were to be dealt with in the local courts and no
longer via diplomatic channels.

Internal Rebellions

Carrying out the Morrow-Calles agreement required political stability, and Ambassador Morrow was eager to negotiate an end to the
Cristero rebellion. With the help of the U.S. priest John J. Burke, a
representative of the U.S. bishops and of the Vatican, he became the
mediator between the Mexican government, on the one hand, and the
Mexican bishops and the Vatican, on the other. While it was obvious
that the rebels could not easily be defeated, it was also clear that they
could not seize power from a government supported by the United
States. The negotiations were difficult.

Presidential elections were being held in Mexico, and Alvaro
Obregón was elected for the second time owing to a change in the
Constitution to permit reelection. In mid-1928, before he assumed
office, he was murdered by a Catholic militant, and the talks were
suspended. However, they were soon resumed, primarily because the

Vatican feared that prolonging the civil struggle would only favor the government and cause further suffering to the Mexican church. It took another year to reach an agreement. In mid-1929, when Calles had left the presidency but remained the power behind the throne, the provisional president, Emilio Portes Gil, and the bishop, Leopoldo Ruíz y Flores, finally ended the conflict between the church and the state. By this agreement, drafted partially by Morrow himself, the Mexican government promised to respect the integrity of the church, and the church agreed to observe the constitutional requirement that priests register at the Ministry of the Interior. The Cristeros had to accept the settlement. Their rebellion lost its force and soon ceased to be a problem for the government.

During that crucial year of 1929, however, the federal government faced yet another armed conflict: the insurrection of almost half the army. The leaders of the rebel movement under General Gonzalo Escobar were those supporters of Obregón whose political ambitions had been frustrated. They accused Calles of trying to become a dictator *de facto* by imposing a provisional president and his successor. This time, the United States responded promptly to the Mexican government's requests for military equipment. Some of the weapons came directly from the U.S. Army's arsenals. The U.S. government was also asked to enforce its Neutrality Act, to tighten up its vigilance against the rebels' agents, and to prevent them from importing military equipment into Mexico—and it responded.

In a series of relatively quick actions, Mexican troops also put an end to the uprising of Escobar's followers, centered in the north of the country.

The Foreign Debt

It was only after the oil problem had been solved that Morrow was able to tackle another issue which interested him even more directly: the payment of the foreign debt. The financial hardships of the Mexican government had led to a suspension of the Pani-Lamont in 1928, and in the following year the problem of money worsened. Putting down the rebellion led by Gonzalo Escobar was extremely expensive and the production of oil continued to decline as the oil companies continued to sulk. The Great Depression, a world economic crisis, was beginning to make itself felt in Mexico as elsewhere. The Cristero rebellion, although subsiding, was a continuing drain on both the army and the treasury.

By then, the Mexican government was in possession of a report from two experts appointed by the ICBM to examine Mexico's economic situation and determine its real capacity to pay. According to their report of May 1928, known as the Sterrett-Davis report, the only way Mexico could handle the annual payment of 30 million pesos and the gradual increase to 70 million in 1932 was to reduce its military expenses, virtually suspend all federal construction of roads and dams, and cut back plans for expenditures for education. These recommendations may have made economic sense, but they lacked political realism. As long as the Cristero struggle continued and the government feared new rebellions, it could not cut its military budget. The federal programs were politically essential. The recommendations were not accepted.

In 1930, the secretary of the treasury, Luis Montes de Oca, renegotiated the agreements directly with the ICBM—despite the fact that both the Department of State and Ambassador Morrow had insisted that the new agreement have an enlarged scope that would cover all the holders of Mexico's foreign debt, who were mostly U.S. citizens, and not only those represented by the ICBM, who were mostly Europeans.

In the Montes de Oca–Lamont agreement of 25 July 1930, Mexico acknowledged a consolidated debt of $267,493,240 to be redeemed in forty-five years at an interest rate of between 3 and 5 percent. Interest already overdue, an almost equal sum, was mainly forgiven; only $11,755,000 was pledged. The sums to be paid annually began with $12.5 million and were to rise later on, and Mexico paid $5 million in interest immediately.

The terms of this agreement were more favorable to Mexico than the two previous ones, but the plummeting tax revenues resulting from the Great Depression once again made Mexico incapable of meeting its financial obligations. In January 1931, the Mexican government and ICBM agreed to postpone payments for two more years. In 1932, as world trade continued to deteriorate Mexico suspended all payments to foreign creditors indefinitely. Mexico was not alone; the economic crisis forced many countries to adopt similar measures and there was very little that the creditor countries, the United States in particular, could do except wait.

In 1930, Morrow left Mexico to occupy a seat in the U.S. Senate. During his term as ambassador, relations between Mexico and the United States had improved markedly. Morrow had contributed significantly to the solution of the oil problem, the slowing down of agrarian expropriations, the solution of the Cristero rebellion, and the consolidation of Calles's government. Ironically, the only large problem that the ambassador had not solved was the foreign debt, precisely the one which interested the banker most. J. Reuben Clark, Jr., a lawyer and career diplomat, succeeded Morrow for a short period; he had been Morrow's deputy and colleague in Mexico, and his mission was to safeguard the agreements.

Mexican Emigration to the United States

Mexicans began to migrate to the United States in search of opportunity in the last years of the nineteenth century, when U.S. settlers occupied the land north of the border and the Mexican border states themselves became more populated. As the Mexican population grew and the superior economic development of the United States became more evident, immigration increased. The Mexican Revolution accelerated the process: it led hundreds of thousands of Mexican citizens of all social classes to take refuge and look for a new livelihood in the United States. This current subsided when violence in Mexico decreased, but it never stopped.

As the U.S. economy expanded, Mexican workers found relatively acceptable conditions: they traveled as far as the industrial cities in the north, and established communities in places as distant as the steel towns near Chicago.

Opposition to the growth of Mexican communities in the United States began to appear in the twenties, however. In 1924, the Border Patrol was created to end the free crossing between Mexico and the United States; five years later, spreading unemployment made the Mexicans, indeed all foreigners, undesirable visitors. There were about a million Mexicans living in the neighboring country in the late 1920s, most of them engaged in farming and cattle raising.

In 1930, the United States began repatriating the Mexicans. It was not an official policy, but a "voluntary" procedure: the Mexicans were invited to leave because of the economic crisis and were aided by a variety of private and official organizations that returned them to the border. There the repatriated Mexicans were entrusted to inefficient Mexican bureaucrats and left mainly on their own. In 1930, seventy thousand people returned to Mexico from the United States; in 1931, one hundred twenty-five thousand. In 1932, this number decreased to eighty thousand; in 1933, it fell further, to thirty-six thousand; and by 1934, when the worst of the depression was over, the voluntary repatriation program ceased to be a factor in Mexican–U.S. relations.

The results of the repatriation were various. Some of the newly returned aggravated the unemployment problem in Mexico. Many were absorbed by the traditional economy and some even benefitted from the distribution of land carried out by the Mexican government. Others simply slipped back across the border. The odysseys published in the Mexican press—of ill-treatment and discrimination—hurt the sense of national dignity, deepening even further the anti-U.S. feelings already awakened by the history of conflict between the two countries.

The Power behind the Throne

Between 1929 and mid-1934, political power in Mexico was divided. It was a period of transition. When Obregón was assassinated in 1928, the last great revolutionary caudillo disappeared. The resulting political vacuum made it possible to create an official political party—the National Revolutionary Party (PNR)—in 1929. Its main function was not to win elections but to hold in line the various interest groups that made up the new regime and to institutionalize a peaceful and orderly transition of power at all levels.

It was not easy to institutionalize and bureaucratize the political process. The PNR was initially overshadowed by the power and prestige of the former president of Mexico, Plutarco Elías Calles. It was he who decided to reinstate the antireelection provision in the Constitution but also who was himself to occupy the post of president of the Republic on four occasions. The presidents had little power of their own; Calles, with no formal responsibility, was arbiter of the last instance in all important political matters. He was obeyed by the generals, by the politicians, and by the bureaucracy. The decisions made by Emilio Portes Gil (provisional president from November 1928 to February 1930), by Pascual Ortiz Rubio (president from February 1930 to September 1932), and by Abelardo Rodríguez (provisional president from September 1932 to November 1934) were subject to General Calles's tacit or explicit approval.

To the United States, Calles's maintenance of power was considered helpful. Although he maintained the posture of a nationalistic (and not too pro-U.S.) Mexican general, he was always reasonable. Moreover, his political endurance over a ten-year period was a guarantee that agreements with the United States would remain in force regardless of who occupied the presidency.

Another likeable thing about Calles was his tendency to move to the right as he grew older. In 1929, he and the government broke with the most important workers' organization in the country, the CROM; and the rupture plunged the workers' movement into a crisis from which it did not emerge for several years. And, as Calles and his followers became increasingly skeptical about land reform, expropriations virtually ceased and an important radical segment of the armed agrarian groups was dissolved. Finally, Mexico broke diplomatic relations with the U.S.S.R. Foreign observers, and even some local experts, believed that the social repercussions of the Mexican Revolution had ended and that Mexico's international relations, particularly with the United States, would improve.

After 1928, the Mexican government also stopped infringing on the rights acquired by the oil companies and began to grant confirmatory concessions, though not with the swiftness desired by the enterprises. The government did not, however, entirely drop the idea of gaining greater participation in the oil industry, and in 1933 it created a federal oil enterprise to exploit the so-called federal zones (defined as lands bordering on certain waters, even if within privately held estates) and to break the monopoly held by foreign enterprises in the internal market. The results were less spectacular had been hoped: Petróleos de México (Petromex) never had enough capital to enable it to become a true competitor of the international consortia. After a brief period of uncertainty, the foreign oil enterprises ceased to be concerned about it.

Some action on foreign claims was taken when the agreements reached in the Bucareli conferences of 1923 began to be carried out, but the number of cases to be examined was so great that the commission's work went on for years. The Special Mixed Claims Commission, in charge of investigating the damages caused by the Revolution, received 3,176 U.S. claims totalling $42,300,123; most of these claims were for theft, fires, murders, and compulsory loans. By the beginning of the thirties, Mexico and the United States had already spent several million pesos and dollars maintaining the commissions and the arguments on both sides continued. The special commission decided to settle the matter by agreeing on a total amount, as several European countries had already done. In April 1934, an agreement was reached by which Mexico was to pay 2.64 percent of the claims for damages caused by the Revolution; this amounted to almost five-and-a-half million dollars and Mexico agreed to pay $500,000 dollars annually, beginning in 1935.

The work of the General Mixed Claims Commission was more

complex. This commission began to meet at the end of 1924 and received a total of 3,617 claims. Of these, 2,822 were U.S. claims against Mexico amounting to $389,170,870 and 795 were Mexican claims against the United States amounting to $245,158,395. The commission worked for years without reaching as practical a solution as the one reached by the special commission, and it was estimated that it would take almost twenty years more for it to finish its work.

The Fruits of Reduced Conflict

The construction of roads to and from the United States, the end of the Mexican civil war, and the normalization of relations between Mexico and the United States led to a new type of contact between the two countries, one that in time was to acquire considerable economic and social importance: tourism. In colonial times, Mexico had been virtually closed to foreigners, and in the nineteenth century conditions discouraged all but the most intrepid. The *Pax Porfiriana* improved the situation somewhat, but foreign visitors were still rare until the 1930's. In that decade, large-scale tourism developed. Accounts written by visiting U.S. and European intellectuals and artists aroused curiosity about Mexico's folklore, its pre-Hispanic past, and its muralists. Finally, the end of violence and the acceptance of Mexico as a "civilized" nation led to an increase in the number of U.S. visitors who traveled into the interior. The Ministry of National Economy decided to create the Tourism Office.

By 1935, the effect of nationalism on Mexico's relations with the rest of the world seemed to be relatively modest: a greater sense of identity, a weakening of its economic and cultural ties with Europe, and a reaffirmation of its links with the United States. About 65 percent of Mexico's foreign trade took place with that country. The largest railroads were controlled by the Mexican government, but they held little attraction for foreign investors. Some railroads were, however, still under the control of foreigners, as was the generation of electric energy and other minor activities. The Great Depression encouraged the domestic manufacture of certain imports, such as textiles, but without promoting much industrialization. Traditional agriculture continued to consume the energies of the majority of Mexicans.

In 1935, when the Sonora group lost control of the country, the most obvious results of revolutionary nationalism were symbolic. The Mexican public-school system had successfully propagated the concepts of motherland and nation, and the expression of a more elevated culture—painting, etching, music, dance, novels, and an incipient film industry—reaffirmed the value of what was Mexican. A militant movement to extol the national heritage was recreating a valuable and complex cultural past.

Indeed the cultural growth was far more dramatic than internal economic growth or the growth of economic independence from the United States. In the first half of the thirties, there were efforts to encourage the public to "buy Mexican," and there were some very general programs, such as the Plan Sexenal, a six-year plan that in 1934 served as a political platform in Cárdenas's presidential campaign. But that consisted mainly of a catalog of the frustrated aspirations of Mexican nationalism, and the important foreign interests inside Mexico did not take it very seriously. Nothing could go very far off the rails as long as Calles was around.

Cárdenas and the Renewed Revolution

In 1934, when Lázaro Cárdenas became president of Mexico, he began to form a great coalition of forces that allowed his government to count on the active support of mass organizations. To achieve this, he reactivated the agrarian reform program and did not oppose militant workers' organizations. His view was that, once the worst of the economic crisis was over, the workers should be allowed to regain the ground lost to management; in the process they would strengthen their support of the government.

However, as the workers reestablished their influence over certain vital areas of the economy, they ran head-on into management, particularly in Mexico City, where several foreign companies did not hesitate to push the workers into strikes—not that they needed much pushing. Nor were the strikes always peaceful. The question was whether the workers could get away with such independent actions. Sure enough, Calles interfered, just as he had done for years. He publicly condemned the strikes and issued a warning to the new president.

Calles's show of strength created a political crisis in June 1935, but Cárdenas acted swiftly and decisively. He neutralized Calles's support within the army and the administration, ending the division of authority at the top. By the end of the year, it was clear to all that the Revolution's vitality had not yet been exhausted and that the Mexican Thermidor had been only a pause. Calles was comfortably exiled and ceased to play any part in Mexican politics.

With Calles's disappearance from the political landscape in 1935 the reaffirmation of the army's and the PNR's loyalty, the creation of a new workers confederation linked to Cárdenas (the Mexican Confederation of Workers), and the creation of a peasants' organization for the beneficiaries of agrarian reform, Cárdenas became the president with the greatest personal power in the history of Mexico.

The Good Neighbor Offers a New Deal

Washington's reaction to the revival of the Mexican Revolution was far less hostile than it would have been in the days of presidents Coolidge and Hoover. In 1933, the Democratic Party, led by Franklin D. Roosevelt, defeated the Republicans by promising to lift the country out of the economic mud of the Great Depression. Roosevelt's New Deal was an attempt to reaffirm capitalism by giving the state greater power to intervene in the conduct of economic affairs and to turn it into an instrument with which to mitigate social injustice. Its counterpart in foreign affairs was the Good Neighbor policy, initiated by Herbert Hoover but put into practice by the Democrats.

This policy, intended at first to be global, soon became limited to Latin America. Its objective was to end unilateral U.S. intervention in the hemisphere and establish an alliance whose main objective was to isolate the American continent from the instability that prevailed in Europe and Asia at the time. In practical terms, the United States wished to create an inter-American alliance to confront German and Italian expansionism in Europe and Japanese expansionism in Asia.

Washington had to pay a price for such an alliance: it had to accept the principle of nonintervention and put down the big stick willed it by Theodore Roosevelt. At the Seventh Conference of American States in Montevideo at the end of 1933, and three years later at the Conference of Buenos Aires, the United States committed itself not to intervene unilaterally in the region and to support collective action to defend the integrity of the hemisphere. In January 1933, the U.S. Marines left Nicaragua; in 1934, they left Haiti.

As his ambassador to Mexico, Franklin Roosevelt named a personal friend and former member of Woodrow Wilson's cabinet, Josephus Daniels. Daniels, a Democrat-politician from North Carolina, was a fervent advocate of the inter-American alliance and of the Good Neighbor policy. Like Morrow, he maintained good and close personal relations with Mexican leaders; unlike Morrow, he did not oppose reforms. When Cárdenas began large-scale expropriations of rural property and actively support of workers' organization, Daniels stated publicly that these policies were compatible with his own country's New Deal, and he did not share the apprehensions of representatives of U.S. enterprise in Mexico.

Not everything seemed perfect to him, however, and on occasion the ambassador tried to restrain Cárdenas's enthusiasm for agrarian reform. Following instructions, Daniels made it clear that the United States was strongly opposed to the expropriation of its citizens' rural property without compensation with agrarian reform bonds (Mexico had suspended the issuance of these bonds in 1933). In April 1935, the U.S. government sent a delegation to Mexico to try to solve this problem. According to the government in Washington, Cárdenas should refrain from expropriating any more land owned by U.S. citizens until he had reached an agreement about the land already taken over. The political climate in Mexico did not favor such an understanding and the delegation left without having reached any agreement.

The still unresolved problem became more serious in 1937 when the Mexican government carried out one of its greatest expropriations in the Yaqui River Valley in Sonora to form *ejidos* (common farmlands and pastures). Since about fifty U.S. settlers were affected by this measure, the embassy intervened with legal arguments, but to no avail. The expropriation affected Mexican landowners as well. They were allowed to retain only the 100 hectares to which each of them was entitled, and they received no immediate compensation for the remainder of their property.

The Nationalization of Oil

The differences between Mexico and the United States about the agrarian expropriation did not create a crisis. In 1936, for example, Ambassador Daniels declared that relations between the two countries were better than ever. However, that same year a problem arose that was to test those relations severely: the Mexican Congress passed a law that enabled the government to expropriate any type of property for any reason of public interest and to postpone its compensation for as long as ten years. President Cárdenas assured Daniel that he did not intend to use the law against foreign interests in Mexico.

Still, in response to the government's pro-labor policies, the trade unions in the oil industry decided to merge into a single union and to negotiate their first collective labor contract. Immediately after the Union of Oil Workers of the Mexican Republic (STPRM) was formed, it submitted a list of demands to the oil enterprises: the key demand was for higher wages and benefits amounted to 65 million pesos per year. The companies offered 14 million pesos, and negotiations failed to close the gap. Confronted with the threat of a strike that would seriously affect the economy, the government attempted to mediate, but it was unsuccessful.

By then, the oil companies' directors were disturbed, for they correctly suspected that Cárdenas was planning to ignore the spirit of the Calles-Morrow Agreement. There were many signs that this would happen—among others, the sluggishness with which the confirmatory concessions were being granted and the existence of the draft of a bill in the legislature that would require the enterprises to pay royalties on oil extracted from property acquired before 1917.

In May 1937, the oil workers struck. The government intervened once again; this time not to mediate but to complete a financial analysis to determine the amount—without becoming bankrupt— that the companies could afford to pay their employees. From that moment, the conflict became less one between the union and the companies, and more one between the government and the companies. The government's analysis resulted in two findings: one, the enterprises were capable of granting raises totalling 26 million pesos per year; two, their actions and policies in Mexico had been and were unfavorable to the national interest.

These conclusions were cheerfully accepted by the STPRM but not by the companies, which questioned the legality of the decision in the Mexican courts. The United States, British, and Dutch governments were openly concerned, for the companies insisted that their financial condition did not permit them to grant a raise of 26 million pesos. Not could they accept the STPRM's insistence on unionizing workers who had been considered supervisory or management personnel.

It soon became clear to all the parties involved in the conflict that the Mexican government was determined to gain control of the oil industry and that it had used the power of the union to limit the companies' freedom of action and thus obtain in wages what it could no longer obtain through taxes. Very few believed, however, that this new confrontation would end in anything other than a temporary intervention in the management of the enterprises, for it was believed that Mexico lacked the technical and financial capacity to run the industry itself.

On 1 March 1938, the Supreme Court ruled against the companies and they were given seven days to comply with the decisions reached by the federal authorities. The enterprises, their governments, and Cárdenas became entangled in last-minute negotiations, and on 16 March the companies agreed to pay the 26 million pesos, but demanded some restrictions on future labor policy.

By then, however, Cárdenas had made up his mind. On 18 March, he announced to an astonished world his determination to seize virtually all the foreign oil holdings in Mexico—there were really no Mexican enterprises in that field—in view of their contempt for the decision of the judiciary of a sovereign country. As the U.S. ambassador declared: the news struck like "thunder in a blue sky." Neither the companies nor their governments, not even the Mexican public, had expected so drastic a measure. Following the general astonishment, some expressed fear; some, jubilation; and others, condemnation, anger, and threats.

The 1938 expropriation was the culmination of Mexican revolutionary nationalism. With a single slash it cut the Gordian knot into which Article 27 and its reference to oil had been converted. Suddenly, one of the two great foreign economic enclaves—mining was the other—existed no more. The implementation of this measure required all the power accumulated by the presidency through the support of the army, the official party, and the workers' and peasants' organizations. The church and universities, although distant from the government, offered some support for the measure. Cárdenas offered to compensate those affected—but within the ten years specified in the 1936 law. The first step would be to agree upon the value of what had been expropriated; and then, upon the form of payment, preferably in oil.

The companies rejected everything: the legality of the expropriation, the deferred compensation, and payment in "their oil." As a pamphlet published by Standard Oil of New Jersey stated, the action of the Mexican government was a simple "robbery under the law." The British government's attitude was similar to the companies'—in 1938, the Anglo-Dutch oil enterprise El Aguila had the largest investment in oil in Mexico. Mexico broke diplomatic relations with Great Britain and set aside that part of the problem.

In reality, the Mexican government's was concerned only about the reaction in Washington. Ambassador Daniels recommended acting with moderation, but Secretary of State Cordell Hull proposed to

teach Mexico a lesson and, if possible, force it to return the expropriated property. In the end, Roosevelt acknowledged Mexico's rights in
the matter, but he made it clear that it was essential that compensation be paid immediately and adequately.*

The Mexican government never accepted the U.S. interpretation
of international practice and insisted that there were acceptable
precedents for deferred payments. In any event, an appraisal of the
cash value of the properties would be essential, but impossible to
make because the oil companies declined to cooperate.

Finally, at the beginning of 1939, the Mexican government and a
representative of the oil companies entered into negotiations. Cárdenas intended to proceed directly with the appraisal in order to set
the form of payment. The oil companies, however, sought to establish
the conditions for their return; they were even willing to support the
creation of a great new company in which they would participate
along with the government. Since no agreement about who would
have the final authority over that enterprise's activities could be
reached, the proposal died and the State Department's pressure on
Mexico increased.

Just then, the Sinclair Oil Company, a relatively small company
with only small interests in Mexico, decided to break away from the
others and negotiate a separate indemnification with Cárdenas. In
May 1940, an agreement was signed with the head of this company,
Harry Sinclair, by which Mexico would pay $8.5 million for Sinclair's
property within three years, part of the payment to be in cash and the
rest in oil, though at lower-than-market prices. This victory enabled
Mexico to inform the State Department that the obstacle to agreement was the stubborness of only some of the oil enterprises. Cárdenas
term ended in November 1940, his conflict with both Washington
and the oil companies a complete victory, although the companies
complained for years. The expropriation measure had become the
touchstone of economic independence for Mexico: from then on, it
became increasingly difficult for foreign enterprises to return to
Mexico except in a subordinate role.

The U.S. and European oil companies, but even more so the
chancelleries of their respective countries, wanted the oil enterprises

---

*Since then, the U.S. Department of State has insisted that the seizure of property
without immediate, adequate, and effective payment is not expropriation—a situation accepted by international practice—but confiscation, which constitutes a violation, of international law.

back. It was not so much because of their intrinsic value—Mexico was then an unimportant producer of only 47 million barrels the year before the expropriation—but for future development and to prevent a dangerous precedent from being established: that less-powerful countries might unilaterally impose restrictions on great foreign capital. What had happened in Mexico could happen in Venezuela or in any Latin American country.

However, their effort to force Cárdenas to reverse the action was limited. They could not resort to the force, for that would destroy a policy more vital than oil to the U.S. government: the creation of an inter-American alliance within the setting of the Good Neighbor policy. Nor were they willing to encourage Cárdenas's internal enemies for fear that the resulting instability might lead to the replacement of his administration by a more conservative one. In the Mexican context, that could open the door to fascist and Falangist groups. We must not forget that Cárdenism combined nationalistic policies with a militant antifascism which fitted perfectly with Roosevelt's hemispheric and world strategies.

The only way, then, that the U.S. government and the oil companies could fight was by exerting diplomatic and economic pressure. The economic pressure consisted of interfering with Mexican access to its traditional silver and oil markets, and in denying equipment and aid to the new governmental oil enterprise, Petróleos Mexicanos (PEMEX). Nevertheless, Mexico found an independent contractor, Davis and Company, willing to face the wrath of Jersey Standard and Dutch Shell.

In 1938 and 1939, Mexican oil found its way to Europe—ironically, to Hitler's Germany and Mussolini's Italy—and to certain Latin American countries, but most of PEMEX's production was absorbed by an ever-growing domestic market. In the forties, Mexico almost ceased to be an exporter of oil, partly because of the disruption of international trade during the Second World War, but mostly because its growing industries absorbed practically all of the oil that Mexico produced.*

With the outbreak of the Second World War, at the end of 1939, the attention of the United States became still more focused on matters of national security. Political and military coordination with

---

*After the 1940s, hydrocarbons furnished 90 percent of the energy that Mexico consumed, and PEMEX became a pillar of its modernization by supplying—albeit not without some difficulty—all the required fuel at low prices.

Latin American countries acquired an importance far greater than the economic interest of individual companies. The U.S. decision not to increase pressure on Mexico was also due to the election, in 1940, of General Manuel Avila Camacho, a moderate, to succeed Cárdenas. Once again, there was a feeling that the Mexican Revolution was over, and Henry Wallace, the U.S. vice president, attended Avila Camacho's inauguration. Undoubtedly, the destruction of the international balance of power by Italy, Germany, and Japan had helped Mexican nationalism to emerge victorious this time.

In the mid-twenties, despite the climate of insecurity created by the Mexican Revolution, U.S. investments in Mexico were more than one billion dollars. By 1940, they had been reduced to three hundred million. The foreign presence had lost strength in Mexico, quantitatively and qualitatively. More important, Mexico's self-image had become much more positive and confident.

The Vicissitudes of Normality: 1941–1970

In Search of Economic Modernity

Once Mexico became independent of Spain and through the remainder of the nineteenth century, one of the central ideas of its ruling classes, regardless of their many other differences, was to promote the economic modernization of the new nation. Internal division, foreign invasions, and the lack of infrastructure, as well as capital, made this project almost impossible, and it was only late in the century, under the dictatorship of Porfirio Díaz, that significant progress was achieved. The 1910 Revolution delayed the process of economic modernization, but by 1922 industrial production—the central core of Mexico's development—had recovered to its earlier levels.

By then the worst of the civil war was over, but almost immediately the traditional economic activities—oil, mining, and agriculture—began to face serious problems, some of them because of price fluctuations in the international markets. In short, from 1911 to 1940, Mexico's economy grew very slowly. The situation changed dramatically after 1941 mainly because of the return to economic orthodoxy under the presidency of General Manuel Avila Camacho (1940–46) and the economic stimulus provided by the Second World War. This period saw the beginning of a policy of industrialization which resulted in a relatively high rate of economic growth. The goal was to replace imports with internal production—i.e., manufactured goods, traditionally imported, were to be made in Mexico. In 1940, 68 percent of the labor force was engaged in agriculture; thirty years later only 41 percent was so engaged. Mexican economy and society had indeed experienced a structural change.

The overall economic goal, shared by the governmental and business sector of Mexico, was to use the great power of the presidency to move the country from its agrarian base and concomitantly, to export industrial products and raw materials. This ambitious project required, among many things, protective tariffs to lessen the impact of competition from cheaper and better foreign goods, mainly from the United States. However, the long border shared by Mexico and the United States made it almost impossible to seal off the Mexican market from foreign goods and to impose effective controls on foreign exchange. Industrialization had to proceed almost without the market of the border states—which were linked, for all practical purposes, to the United States—and in the face of a free exchange of currencies.

Tarriffs were necessary but not sufficient to encourage industralization. Mexico also needed capital. While the Second World War enabled Mexican exports to increase greatly—their value more than doubled between 1941 and 1945—the need for imports to support the industrialization program was so great that, by 1946, Mexico's balance of payments was in deficit.

As in the past, the drive toward modernization required foreign participation in those fields that were about to be developed. Direct foreign investment in 1941 was not impressive: that year only $17 million entered Mexico. The memory of expropriation and ill treatment was still fresh in the minds of foreign capitalists and Mexico had a poor reputation in the international money markets. Ten years later the situation had changed almost beyond recognition. The amount of new direct foreign investment (DFI) in 1950 reached $124 million, a flow which continued to increase.

Foreign capital entered Mexico after 1940 not only as direct investment but also as loans from private and public institutions. In 1940, Mexico was still searching for a way to reach satisfactory agreements with its old creditors; the war provided the necessary stimulus for such agreements and the old foreign debt ceased to be a problem.

After 1941, the problem of economic development replaced the quest for political stability as the core of the national political debate in Mexico. The main effort of Mexico's political leadership was devoted to economic growth. South of the border, U.S.–Mexican relations became increasingly colored by the needs of the economy and its industrialization. By the end of the war, however, those in charge of relations with Mexico in the United States did not share Mexico's enthusiasm for industrialization: among other things, it encouraged commercial protectionism and thus interfered with free trade, something very dear to U.S. policy makers. From the vantage point of Washington, it would have been better for Mexico to guide its foreign trade by the laws of "comparative advantage"—which, in practical terms, meant continuing to export mineral and agricultural products and to import manufactured goods, mainly from the United States.

The Second World War

As early as the turn of the century, the United States had begun to realize that it was in its own national interest to preserve a friendly and stable Mexico. Internal stability south of the Rio Grande was essential to the security of a two-thousand-mile border and, by 1940, this interest overshadowed even those of the oil companies.

From the Mexican point of view, the situation was somewhat different. The fervency of the Mexican Revolution had begun to recede, and the legitimacy of the authoritarian system it had produced needed reaffirmation. The construction of a modern capitalist economy in Mexico required that some of the central elements of the regime's ideology—such as democracy or social justice—lose much of their content. For this reason, nationalism remained a source of legitimacy for the regime, as important then as in the more distant past or even more so. Nationalism was vital to the preservation of internal stability, and the United States could not undermine this nationalism—even though it was still basically directed against U.S. influence in Mexico—without weakening Mexico's political stability. Still, Mexican nationalism, in the mid-twentieth century, did not express itself in such dangerous acts as expropriations or open disregard of what the United States considered its special geopolitical interests. Between 1942 and 1945, Mexico and the United States were formal allies against the Axis powers.

President Manuel Avila Camacho, Cárdenas's successor, achieved a delicate but effective political balance between the leftist remnants of Cardenism and the conservative forces, increasingly powerful, that were competing for the country's future leadership. The disruption of the world's balance of power enabled Avila Camacho to appeal to national unity in the face of possible foreign peril. When the conflict spread and Mexico became involved in it, this presidential appeal to postpone struggles based on class interests for the sake of the national interest, became the leitmotiv of his administration.

In the international sphere, Avila Camacho maintained Cárdenas's commitment to the antifascist forces. This pro-Allied policy provided the necessary basis for a resolution of the problems still pending between Mexico and the United States, especially after Washington declared war on the Axis. So far as the United States was concerned, the key countries in Latin American were, as always, Brazil and Mexico, as much for their strategic geographical position as for their production of raw materials. As to Mexico specifically, the United States wished to coordinate the defense of the Pacific coast in the event of a Japanese attack, to use Mexican fields as stopover points for aircraft en route to and from Panama, and to count on an adequate supply of industrial minerals, rubber, oil, and natural fibers. Finally, the collaboration of countries such as Mexico was necessary to U.S. efforts to neutralize the pro-German attitudes of the Argentine government and to encourage the region in the fight against fascism.

During the last years of the Cárdenas administration, and later, the Mexican government had demonstrated its willingness to coordinate its military actions with the United States; in October 1939, a security zone was created in the Western Hemisphere during the Inter-American Assembly held in Panama, as a preventive measure in case of a world conflict. This policy was reaffirmed by a regional collective security treaty at the Conference of Havana in July 1940. However, Mexico delayed extending its full cooperation until the pending bilateral problems, particularly the terms of compensation to the oil companies expropriated in 1938 and the payment of the foreign and railroad debts, were solved.

Talks between Avila Camacho's administration and the United States concerning the oil companies' compensation began immediately after his inauguration, in February 1941. By November of that year, despite the opposition of the companies, the two governments were able to announce the creation of a joint commission to fix the value of the expropriated property and to recommend the terms of payment. The following April, when the United States was already at war, the commission published the results of its investigations: the value of the goods expropriated by Mexico from those U.S. oil companies with which it had not been able to reach direct agreement amounted to $24 million plus $5 million in interest—far less than the hundreds of millions that the companies had claimed—and Mexico was to pay this sum within five years. The oil companies rejected the agreement at first, but the State Department announced that it would no longer support them in their dispute with the Mexican government, for the agreement was an equitable one and the global interests of the United States required close collaboration with Mexico. Much against their will, therefore, Standard Oil and its cohorts finally began to negotiate directly with Mexico on the basis of the joint commission's resolution and, in 1943, final agreement was reached: Mexico increased the compensation owed to the companies to $30 million. Thus ended one of the most dramatic episodes of revolutionary expropriation of foreign capital.

The oil companies' acceptance of the joint commissions' resolution as the basis for negotiation was more of a concession than might appear at first glance. The Mexicans had always been willing to compensate the oil companies for their installations and equipment and, on this basis, $30 million was a fair compromise. But the oil companies had never been primarily concerned about their out-of-pocket expenses: they believed they had a valid claim to all the oil in the subsoil.

At the beginning of President Avila Camacho's administration, Mexico was involved in a debate with the International Bankers Committee (IBC) over the possession of $7 million that Mexico had deposited in the United States some years previously in the name of the IBC. The money was part of the first payments due before the Montes de Oca-Lamont Agreement of 1930 collapsed. The legal complexities suggested that this minor dispute would last for a long time; nevertheless, the Mexican president decided to put it aside and to resume international bidding in the open market for the depreciated bonds of its own debt. By the end of 1945, 25 percent of the debt had already been redeemed in this unorthodox manner. Understandably, it was the IBC which was anxious to stop a process that was draining them of funds, and agreed to discussions. By November 1941, both parties reached a final agreement: Mexico committed itself to settle its old foreign debt within twenty to twenty-five years, beginning in 1948. The amount of the settlement was $49.6 million, about 10 percent of the original debt. Agreement about the railroad debt, more difficult, was postponed until the end of the war, but it was then settled on similar terms: in 1946, Mexico committed itself to pay the holders of this type of bond $50.5 million, about 10 percent of the nominal value of the Mexican paper.

At the end of 1941 and after the Japanese attack on Pearl Harbor, Mexico broke diplomatic relations with the Axis and with those countries occupied by the Germans. In January 1942, the Mexican-American Joint Defense Commission was formed; Avila Camacho also created the Pacific Military Region, comprising all the states on the littoral, from Baja California to Chiapas. The defense of this enormous region was entrusted to the former president, Cárdenas. Avila Comacho thus achieved a double goal: he satisfied the U.S. desire for a coordinated defense of the West Coast and also demonstrated to his constituents and to the United States the limits of this cooperation, for although Cárdenas was recognized as an antifascist, he was even better known as a zealous defender of Mexican sovereignty vis-à-vis the United States.

At this time, the Mexicans were not enthusiastic about collaborating with the United States against the Axis. Mexican nationalism in the twentieth century was founded on the struggle against its northern neighbor and, to a certain extent, against Great Britain. The initial sympathy for the Axis, especially for Germany, was therefore unsurprising, and it was only through an effort on the part of the Mexican government and the departments of propaganda of the Allied countries, particularly of the United States, as well as a growing awareness of the excesses of the Germans in the countries they occupied, that public opinion shifted slowly in favor of the antifascist forces. At the beginning of 1942, Mexico was still neutral but, unlike the administration during the First World War, Avila Camacho's administration had already manifested a clear inclination toward the Allies.

In May 1942, the Mexican oil tanker *Potrero del Llano* was sunk by a German submarine while transporting fuel to the United States. Nationalist and leftist organizations in Mexico immediately called for a declaration of war against the Axis, but the majority did not support such a drastic measure, largely because of a widely held belief that the real attacker was a U.S. U-boat that had acted to force Mexico to enter the war on the Allied side. Avila Camacho protested to the German government and demanded indemnity. When, at the end of the month, a second Mexican tanker, the *Faja de Oro,* was sunk in similar circumstances, he was able to refer to Germany's disregard of Mexico's earlier protest, and declare the existence of a "state of war" between Mexico and the Axis countries. This time there was no important adverse reaction in Mexico and, for the first time, Mexico and the United States became formal allies.

This dramatic change in relations between Mexico and the United States led to close military and political cooperation between the two nations, and to economic collaboration. The person in Mexico who best symbolized this new era of "good neighborliness" was Secretary of Foreign Affairs Ezequiel Padilla, a champion of a close relationship with the Allies. The alliance was not free of contradictions and friction, however, and perhaps it was General Cárdenas, first as commander of the Pacific Military Region and later as minister of national defense, who best personified Mexico's cautious reaction to the embrace of the colossus of the North.

At the beginning of the war, the United States' main concern was to insure the coordination of the United States Command for the Western Region under the direction of General John De Witt, Jr., and his Mexican counterpart, General Cárdenas. The United States wanted to install a series of radar stations and airports in Baja California and to elaborate a joint plan of defense for use in case of an attack. Mexico accepted these demands in principle, but on condition that the personnel operating the radar stations and patroling the air zone be Mexicans, leaving the United States in charge of providing the equipment and the training.

Three radar stations were finally built, all operated by Mexicans, each with U.S. officers in charge only of transmitting pertinent information to the United States. The airports were never built. Mexico refused to allow the United States access to construct and operate them and, after 1943, the possibility of a Japanese attack on the coasts became so remote that the United States lost interest in installing them. Finally, an agreement was reached to develop joint operations in case of an attack. In January 1942, an important symbolic as well practical step was taken: the establishment of the already mentioned Mexican-American Joint Defense Commission, whose main but not exclusive task was to manage the military credits extended to Mexico by virtue of the Lend-Lease Act. These funds, originally $10 million and later increased to $40 million, provided Mexico with new aircraft for its air force and with its first mechanized ground division.

Mexico's military participation in the war was small. After 1943, the Mexican army volunteered to be present in an active theater, and in 1944 an agreement was reached by which Mexico sent an air-force squadron with three hundred men to be trained in the United States and transferred to the Pacific. In February 1945, the 201st Squadron, armed with P-47 fighters, was ready for service and the next month was transferred to the Philippines, where it remained in action until the end of the war. An agreement between the Mexican and U.S. governments made it possible for Mexican citizens who were resident in the United States to be recruited into the U.S. Army with the

promise of citizenship at the end of their service. By the end of
the war, fifteen thousand Mexican expatriates had seen combat in the
U.S. ranks and had suffered casualties of about 10 percent.

From the beginning, however, it was clear to all that Mexico's
substantive contribution to the war would not be military, but
economic, a contribution to the U.S. productive apparatus. In 1941,
Mexico and the United States signed a provisional agreement to buy
all Mexican production of copper, lead, zinc, graphite, and other
metals, as well as various hard fibers. By December 1942, after long
and difficult negotiations, the two countries subscribed to a formal
trade agreement which fully reopened the U.S. market to Mexican
oil. Besides hydrocarbons, the treaty encouraged Mexican export
of minerals, cattle, silver, beer, and agricultural products. Several
secondary agreements enabled the United States to acquire, at fixed
prices, Mexico's surpluses of rubber, guayule, henequen, istle, chick-
pea, chicle, salt, fish, and bananas. (Since the fixing did not apply to
goods imported from the United States, it was criticized as one-sided,
but it was maintained.) By 1943, 90 percent of Mexico's foreign trade
was with the United States; the European market, for all practical
purposes, had been lost because of the war.

Differences with the United States surfaced not so much in the
negotiation of the various trade agreements as with carrying them out
in daily practice. Mexican entrepreneurs complained, throughout the
war, that the United States did not provide them with raw materials
and manufactured goods required by Mexico's growing industries and
the U.S. exporters argued that the priorities imposed by the war did
not enable them to provide always or everything that Mexico demanded. The Mexican-American Economic Cooperation Commission was established in 1943 to minimize this conflict of interests.

Economic cooperation between the two countries extended beyond
the trade agreement. In order for Mexico to cope with the U.S.
demand for raw materials, it was necessary to improve its internal
transportation and to open lines of credit so Mexico could buy
equipment in the United States. In November 1941, the United
States authorized a credit of $40 million to stabilize the peso and
another credit of $30 million for communication routes. Although its
increasing foreign revenue enabled Mexico to use only part of these
credits at first, during the last year of the war and at the beginning of
the postwar period the country's commercial deficits grew and yet
new loans were required. At the end of Avila Camacho's administration, Mexico had obtained a total line of credit from the United States

of $90 million, of which it had used $60 million. From 1913 to 1941, Mexico had been excluded from the international loan market, but the war and the agreements on the payment of its foreign debt reopened the international credit system.

The development of the Mexican domestic market, the gradual vanishing of the fear of new expropriations, and the government's policy of industrialization contributed to the growth of confidence. Foreign capital flowed into Mexico not only as loans, but also as direct investments of capital that had either fled from Europe and sought temporary refuge in Mexico or as more stable investments designed to exploit the new opportunities created by the war. The total sum of this investment capital surpassed that obtained through loans. In 1940, DFI amounted to $449 million and, in 1945, to $568 million. This capital was welcomed, although some of the new Mexican manufacturers who had succeeded in business during the war feared the competition and the new foreign investors had to accept some governmental control. To the constitutional prohibition against investing in oil and agriculture, new regulations were added.

By to the decree of 29 June 1944, designed to regulate new foreign investments, the Ministry of Foreign Affairs was charged with granting permits to foreigners to acquire stock or establish enterprises in Mexico. Foreign ownership was limited to 49 percent of the total capital of any given enterprise, but the Ministry of Foreign Relations could drop the requirement that 51 percent of the enterprise be Mexican whenever the government considered majority foreign participation indispensable to the establishment of new enterprises that were in the national interest.

Economic areas into which no foreign capital was allowed were specifically listed—and taken out of the control of the Ministry of Foreign Affairs—in a circular of 17 April 1945. Excluded sectors were not necessarily the most important from a financial or economic point of view, but they all were in fields the Mexicans were sensitive about, and some of them were of political and strategic importance: radio broadcasting, the movie industry, domestic air and land transportation, fishing, publishing, and—rather oddly—the bottling of minerals waters. The extensive fields of investment left open to foreign capital were precisely those the government wanted developed—virtually all manufacturing and trade. At the end of Avila Camacho's administration, DFI in manufacturing had increased, from 7 percent in 1940 to almost 25 percent in 1945.

Mexico's contribution to the war economy of the United States also included labor. The repatriation of Mexicans lessened, and U.S. farmers began to ask for Mexican workers. In 1941, when the United States entered the war, the increasing demand for labor was met by resistance from Mexican rural businesses which needed to keep their workers and which feared the consequences of a massive exit of braceros to the neighboring country: emigration of the more educated, a shortage of laborers for the harvest, and a rise in wages. In 1942, despite the opposition of some groups in both countries, an agreement was reached whereby the U.S. Administration of Agricultural Security would itself hire the Mexican laborers, offering them guarantees against discriminatory treatment, compensation in case of unemployment, free transportation, and so forth.

The Mexicans were to work exclusively on U.S. railroads and on farms. In time, however, they were offered more skilled work in industry and services. Even sooner, there was news of discriminatory treatment, particularly in Texas, and the U.S. government was forced to accept the presence of Mexican inspectors to verify the fulfillment of the agreement. It is estimated that almost three hundred thousand Mexican laborers were hired under the terms of this agreement before the end of the war, and that an even larger number crossed illegally into the United States with the U.S. authorities' tolerance. The bracero program did not disappear with the end of the war: the reasons for it were deeper than the temporary shortage of stoop labor in the United States.

Other problems also began to yield. When the northern borderlands of Mexico began to be populated and their agriculture began to develop, for example, the use of the water of the rivers that cross both countries—the Colorado, Tijuana, and Bravo (Rio Grande)—became the subject of disputes. The construction of dams on the U.S. side, such as the Hoover Dam, diminished the amount of water received by Mexico, and the problem became a matter of primary importance to Mexico. After a series of long and difficult negotiations, an international agreement to regulate the use of water and control the flows of these rivers was reached on 8 November 1945.

Between 1942 and 1945, then, a substantial change in Mexican–U.S. relations took place: confrontation was replaced by cooperation. Mexican exports increased in value from $177.8 million in 1940 to $262.3 million in 1945. The temporary disappearance of a number of consumer goods from the international market set the scene for Mexico's substitution of locally made products for former imports. This in turn promoted the development of capitalism, strengthened the national bourgeoisie, and stranded the social projects of Cardenism. Not all of these projects were favorably viewed by U.S. authorities and business circles, anyway; some felt that the emergence of industry in Mexico after the Second World War was artificial, utopian, and contrary to the kind of international division of labor suggested by the economic law of comparative advantage. Only after 1949, as new opportunities were opened to foreign capital and trade with Mexico burgeoned as a result of the beginnings of industrialization, did this point of view lose ground in the United States.

First Fissures in the Good Neighbor Policy

The alliance between Mexico and the United States during the Second World War, though it was not free of friction, was a period in which the national interests of both countries, as defined by their respective governments, coincided more closely than ever before. However, the shadow of a new divergence between U.S. interests and those of Latin America as a whole appeared on the eve of victory over the fascists, and it darkened at the end of the war. The similarity of aims lessened as normality was regained.

In the Inter-American Conference on War and Peace Problems held in Mexico in 1945, the Latin Americans tried to emphasize the growing economic character of continental concern, but the United States considered such a shift in policy unattractive and unnecessary. At the end of the war, the United States was the world's leading power, conscious that no European power could dispute its influence in Latin America. The main threat to U.S. world interests proceeded from the Soviet Union—in 1947 President Truman described the world as divided in two irreconcilable factions: the "free world," supported by the will of the majorities, and the "communist" one that subsisted thanks to terror and oppression. The U.S. government was interested in directing the combined political and military effort in the hemisphere against communist penetration; hence its great interest in having the Latin American governments subscribe to the Inter-American Reciprocal Assistance Treaty in Rio de Janeiro in 1947, in giving final shape to the Organization of American States in Bogota the following year, and its almost total indifference to any type of multilateral economic agreement.

The Marshall Plan was designed to aid Western Europe in its recovery partly in order to prevent communist expansion in that area, but the United States did not deem such aid necessary in Latin

America. If Latin America also needed foreign capital, it would have to obtain it from private sources. These, however, would be forthcoming only if the various governments created a favorable climate and only if they offered adequate assurances to U.S. enterprise. But in Latin America, the private sector was subject to government credits and government guidance. The view of the Truman administration that succeeded Roosevelt's in 1945 was that state interference with market forces was of little service to either the United States or the Latin American countries, for it weakened the capitalist essence of their various economies. Mexican and U.S. ideas about how to help Latin America achieve economic growth differed in significant aspects, but mainly in the proper role of the state. Mexico insisted on the importance of direct state intervention in the country's economy and the United States considered such intervention unnecessary, even self-defeating. The United States continued granting credits to the Latin American countries, but not to the extent or on the terms desired.

On 1 December 1946, General Avila Camacho handed over the presidency to the first civilian since Venustiano Carranza—Miguel Alemán Valdes—whose victory spelled the demise of what socialist programs still survived from Cardenism. The political leadership of the Alemán government was determined to accelerate the industrialization process, its first priority being the manufacture of goods that would serve as substitutes for imports. To achieve this, Alemán's regime gave its utmost support, to the extent compatible with social tranquility, to the private sector—national and foreign—using and refining the mechanisms of authoritarian political control to keep the demands of labor to a minimum. The ideological justification for this accumulation of capital at the expense of labor consisted in presenting the economic growth of the private sector as the sine qua non of political independence and in insisting that true social justice was achieved by creating wealth first, so that in some later, unspecified period it could be distributed more equitably.

Alemán's policy was welcomed by the United States, though for some time the U.S. government objected to the policy of industrialization because it implied Mexican tariffs on imported goods to protect the nascent industries. In March 1947, the first visit of a U.S. president to the Mexican capital took place, a visit replete with symbolism, during which Truman handed over to the Mexican government some of the banners captured during the U.S. invasion one hundred years earlier.

The following month, Alemán visited Washington. Alemán supported the idea of a common defense of Western democracy along the lines of the so-called Truman Doctrine, and the reception he received had very few precedents in the history of that city. In the final joint communiqué, Mexico's support for the Good Neighbor policy and for hemispheric security was reiterated, and the United States agreed to extend two credits of $50 million each: the first to support the peso, whose stability was suffering owing to a growing deficit in the trade balance, and the other to finance projects to improve Mexico's infrastructure. In the following years, the Alemán administration received additional, albeit smaller, loans from the U.S. government.

During these years, the U.S. government abandoned its policy of refusing loans to PEMEX unless Mexico allowed the old expropriated enterprises to reenter the country and, in 1948, PEMEX was able to negotiate its first private foreign loan in the United States—$30 million. The oil companies whose property had been expropriated in 1938 had not given up the idea of returning to Mexico, but they expected PEMEX's financial difficulties to provide the opportunity for negotiating their reentrance. The situation developed differently: as PEMEX's financial difficulties persisted, Alemán's government signed in 1949 the first of a series of so-called risk contracts with smaller U.S. oil enterprises to complement Mexican oil exploration. The risk contracts were not a real success; little oil was found and the financial resources and equipment that Mexico so badly needed were not brought in by the small companies. Alemán came under sharp attack for allowing foreign, particularly U.S. capital directly into an area of the economy particularly sensitive to the influence of Mexican nationalism, and eventually, in the late sixties, these contracts were cancelled by the government.

The cold war that swept the world at the end of the forties as a result of the global U.S.–U.S.S.R. confrontation affected Mexico as well. During the Second World War, a pro-Allied propaganda apparatus had been set up in Mexico, and its activities did not cease when the war ended. Its channels were merely used for new objectives, and Mexican public opinion, as well as that of the rest of the continent, was bombarded with anticommunist views. This situation was exploited by Alemán's government, which denigrated its critics by accusing them of being communists and agents of the Soviet Union.

Nevertheless, the political support Mexico gave the United States had certain limits. Although Mexico's vote in the United Nations did follow the lead of the United States in its key confrontations with the

U.S.S.R., Mexico did not break diplomatic relations with the Soviet Union nor did it send any military contingents to participate with the U.N. forces in the Korean War, as other Latin American countries did. Perhaps the most significant limit to Mexico's anticommunism was that, although Mexico was a signatory of the Inter-American Reciprocal Aid Treaty, it did not sign—as did the rest of the Latin American countries—a bilateral military aid treaty with the United States. In February 1952, a delegation headed by General Edward M. Jones was sent to Mexico for two weeks of fruitless discussion of a possible agreement for military cooperation. The key disagreement arose because military aid was governed by a U.S. law which required Mexico, to "defend democracy." The Mexican representatives considered that such a clause could one day oblige their country to contribute troops to conflicts outside its borders, an eventuality which would perhaps serve U.S. global interests but hardly Mexican ones. Besides, since this obligation might conflict with the first precept of Mexico's foreign policy—nonintervention in the internal affairs of other nations—the rejection of U.S. military aid was supported by most national political groups. Some limited military cooperation between Mexico and the United States did continue after the war, however; an increasing number of Mexican officers received training in U.S. institutions.

Although the mass media in Mexico were anticommunist and pro-United States, the public did not discard its distrust of the United States. This distrust flared up in 1947, for example, when both governments cooperated to put an end to outbreaks of aphthous fever, which was afflicting Mexican cattle at the time. The effort to eliminate the disease as well as to stop its spread to the north and to prevent Mexican meat from losing foreign markets required, among other things, U.S. expenditures of several million dollars and the slaughtering of 168,000 head of cattle. The action was a compromise because the Mexican government favored the slow but politically safe process of vaccination, while U.S. authorities pressed for the slaughter of a million cows. Many Mexicans perceived the campaign as a U.S. conspiracy to destroy the national supply of cattle and to eliminate a competitor, and they mounted armed attacks on the teams of veterinarians and soldiers in charge of eliminating the infected cattle. The campaign had to be called off and Mexico proceeded alone toward the final eradication of the disease. From time to time similar stories of U.S. "plots" spread among the Mexican public.

The migration of Mexican workers to the United States created yet another problem. The demand for Mexican labor decreased at the end of the war (but it did not disappear), and pressure from U.S. unions, which feared that the continued presence of a large group of Mexican workers would lower salaries, forced the immigration authorities to take a hard line against illegal Mexican immigrants. In 1950, there were close to six hundred thousand arrests and deportations of undocumented Mexican workers. In March of the following year, the *New York Times* estimated that approximately a million Mexicans entered the United States illegally each year in search of work. They accepted very low salaries, lived in unsanitary conditions, competed with the local labor force, and provided the farmers of the Southwest with cheap labor and extraordinary profits. This image of discrimination against and exploitation of Mexicans was disseminated into the reservoir of Mexican public opinion and became an integral part of the way the Mexicans viewed the United States, in the same way as the image of the poor, dirty, uneducated Mexican of low social status became a stereotype in the United States.

In August 1951, the governments of Mexico and the United States signed a new agreement on the hiring of braceros, but the signature was preceeded by months of difficult negotiations. From the Mexican point of view, the U.S. farmers preferred to hire illegal workers because they paid them lower salaries and gave them no social benefits. Mexico therefore requested that employers who hired the so-called wetbacks be fined and that braceros should be hired only by contract and through Mexican agencies. This would have permitted Mexico to select the kind of worker best fitted for jobs in the United States and to give priority to the most depressed regions of the country, but it was not in the interest of U.S. farmers, and the problem remained unsolved.

As already mentioned, the U.S. government believed that Mexico and other Latin American countries should not stimulate their industrialization artificially by setting up protective tariff barriers. From the U.S. point of view, the less that governments interfered with the natural currents of international markets, the better. But to Mexicans, acceptance of the U.S. point of view meant to be condemned to remain a mining, agricultural, and cattle-raising country. The new Mexican bourgeoisie, which had already tasted the benefits of industrialization, pressed for all types of incentives and government protection to continue on that course; besides, the fall in the prices of raw materials that followed the war neutralized any sympathy for the so-called comparative advantage. There was no advantage in con-

tinuing to produce minerals or agricultural products if they were
constantly decreasing in value. In 1951, Mexico cancelled the commercial treaty signed with the United States during the war, so that
no commitment could prevent it from closing its doors to imports
that would compete with the manufactured products that Mexico
desired and could produce itself. The road toward Mexican "import
substitution industrialization"—a strategy recommended by the Economic Commission for Latin America to the governments of the
region—was wide open.

Industrialization became the dominant note in the social and
economic transformations of Mexico during the forties, and Alemán's
administration (1946–52) turned this process into an irreversible
fact. Since Europe was engaged in its own reconstruction, the only
foreign investors that could take full advantage of these new opportunities were U.S. investors and so they did. During Alemán's term of
six years, DFI went from $575.5 million to $728.6 million; in 1946,
25 percent of DFI was concentrated in manufacturing, and six years
later it reached 30 percent. That foreign investors became responsive
to the new reality and were ready to occupy a predominant place in the
manufacturing sector—the most dynamic of the postwar Mexican
economy—created fears in nationalist circles and in the many entrepreneurs who did not welcome competition.

Adolfo Ruiz Cortines was inaugurated in on December 1952. The
so-called cheerful years of Alemán, with their aura of corruption, gave
way to relative austerity and respectability in public office, but
actually there were no profound changes. The political, economic,
and social changes that had originated in previous years continued on
their preestablished course. Perhaps the only important innovation
consisted in the initiation of a monetary and economic strategy that
became known as "stabilizing development," and which remained in
force until the early seventies. Essentially, this policy consisted of
striking a budgetary balance (to a certain extent through the use
of foreign credits) through close control over public expenditures, of
maintaining the peso's value vis-à-vis the dollar (12.50 pesos to a
dollar in April 1954 and for many years after), and of encouraging
private investment. All of this put to an end to the inflationary spiral
associated in the United States with the Korean War and exported to
Mexico by the United States. This policy turned Mexico into an
model of stable prices and free exchange for Latin America. The
disappearance of inflation was rightly considered to be important,

since it made possible the maintenance of official control over the labor movement and provided the underpinning of social and political stability that was prerequisite to economic growth.

During this period, relations between Mexico and the United States were not affected by any crisis, but there were some difficult moments. The cold war was at its peak and it eventually surfaced in Latin America. That the Mexicans would not follow U.S. cold-war policy every step of the way became clear in the differences between the U.S. and Mexican positions in the inter-American meetings in Rio de Janeiro in 1947 and Bogota the following year; however, the most dramatic evidence of these differences arose during the discussion of the Guatemalan situation in 1954.

After the fall of the dictator in that neighboring country in 1944, a group of young officers anxious to introduce their own reforms began to transform the old political and social structures under the leadership of Juan José Arévalo. Their work conflicted with the U.S. banana interests when, in 1952, the Guatemalan government headed by Jacobo Arbenz tried to initiate an agrarian reform that affected the powerful United Fruit Company. The tactic of peasant mobilization and action initiated by Arbenz, and the expropriation of United Fruit latifundia were viewed by Washington as the beginning of a communist take-over. In the Inter-American Conference in Caracas, the Mexican delegation—defending the principle of nonintervention—clashed with the U.S. demand for open condemnation of the Guatemalan regime for having become an instrument for "communist intervention" in the hemisphere. Its most solid proof was a shipload of small-calibre weapons sent by Czechoslovakia to the Guatemalan government. Only Mexico, Guatemala, and Perón's Argentina—the last had been in conflict with Washington for some time—opposed, without much success, the U.S. project of condemning a Latin American government for its conduct in its own country.

In the end, the United States took radical action to resolve what it considered to be a hemispheric problem affecting inter-American institutions: it supported a counterrevolutionary movement which, in October 1954, overthrew Arbenz's government and ended social reform in Guatemala. Mexican nationalist and leftist groups protested in vain against Washington's clandestine action, but their government in Mexico City remained discreetly silent, considering that it had already defended nonintervention up to the point which was possible and desirable. If intervention had nevertheless taken place, Mexico had not given it legitimacy and did not have the power to prevent it. Besides, it was not prudent to deepen its differences with the United States.

Given the dangers of the international environment, Ruiz Cortines's administration decided to concentrate on trying to solve some aspects of the bilateral trade relationship with the United States and the problems stemming from the signing of a new *bracero* agreement in 1954. With the end of the Korean War, Mexican exports had declined: in 1956, the total value of exports was $807 million, but it decreased by almost $100 million in each of the two subsequent years.

Cotton was one of the principal products whose price fell, mainly because the U.S. government could now sell its cotton surplus in the world market. This policy was designed to help U.S. agriculture, not to create difficulties with Mexico, but all the same, it did. And in 1958, the U.S. Congress imposed quotas on the import of lead and zinc, minerals which were important Mexican exports. Mexico's efforts to ward off these blows to its export trade were not successful, and it was not until 1962 that the total value of Mexican exports recovered to the level of 1956.

The foreign currency needed to continue the industrialization program came not only from exported goods but also from money remitted by Mexican laborers in the United States, on direct and indirect foreign investments, and increasingly on tourism. The number of workers who entered the United States illegally (the wetbacks) was still higher than the braceros recruited through the officially established channels. In 1954, during the renegotiation of the bracero agreement, the situation reached a crucial point: the Mexican government, anxious to obtain more advantages than the U.S. government was willing to grant, brought negotiations to a standstill and Washington then proceeded to hire Mexican workers unilaterally. Ruiz Cortines' government tried to prevent workers from going to the United States, but the chief result was the civil disorder that ensued when the police tried to prevent the aspiring braceros from leaving the country. One month later, Mexico modified its negotiating position and, in March 1954, both governments signed a new agreement on seasonal Mexican laborers. This agreement, like the previous one, did not provide for all the Mexican laborers who sought jobs in the United States. The magnitude of the problem was pointed up when the U.S. government embarked on "operation wetback" and deported, in 1954 alone, more than one million people who had entered without documentation. In the following years, the number of those deported decreased.

In areas aside from trade and migrant workers, the situation was more encouraging, allowing the governments to maintain a tone of normality in their relations. Between 1952 and 1958, DFI—almost entirely from the United States—increased 60 percent, and during 1958 almost half of it ($497 million) was placed in industry. This spectacular growth in DFI encouraged economic development; it also created uneasiness among the small and medium-sized business owners who were grouped in the Cámara Nacional de la Industria de la Transformación (CANACINTRA, or National Chamber of Manufacturing Industry). The Cámara struck a nationalistic pose and demanded that the government regulate foreign investments more strictly. From their point of view, DFI was only a complement to local investment and should never finance competition with already existing companies; it should not exploit nonrenewable resources nor be lodged in strategic economic spheres. The stronger industrialists, who were not afraid of competition but instead sought an association with foreign capital and acted to facilitate its rapid entrance into the country, deemed such legislation unnecessary: they believed it would endanger the smooth and beneficial entry of foreign investment and slow the country's modernization. Official circles listened to both groups and decided not to interfere with the almost free flow of foreign investment. They merely granted incentives for Mexican investments in mining—an area that foreigners were abandoning anyway owing to its lack of dynamism—and prohibited the participation of foreign capital in investment banking.

An important element in the policy of stabilizing development was the systematic subsidy of the private economy through the sale, at artificially low prices, of services and goods from state-owned enterprises, even though this reduced the income of the public treasury. Since it was against policy to resort to large deficit spending—that would have undermined the basis of the anti-inflationary model itself—the government managed to finance part of the state's investments by loans contracted abroad, particularly in the United States. Alemán's administration did not raise much money this way, but the government of Ruiz Cortines found relatively new institutions, such as the Export-Import Bank and the International Reconstruction and Development Bank, that were willing to accept Mexican paper.

At the same time, Mexico and other Latin American countries

pressed for the creation of the Interamerican Development Bank. The
United States finally accepted the idea, and a new source of international capital was created. Mexico's long-term foreign debts, those
maturing in a year or longer, grew from $156 million in 1952 to
$603 million in 1958. Mexico's foreign credit, destroyed by the
Revolution but reestablished by the Second World War, was spectac-
ularly reaffirmed during this period.

A "Special Relationship"?

From the Second World War until the beginning of Adolfo López
Mateo's administration in December 1958, Mexico's foreign relations
had been almost exclusively with the United States, and those in
responsible positions had not seriously considered the convenience
and possibility of an alternative policy. Ever since the agreements of
1942 and the Mexican–U.S. collaboration in the struggle against the
Axis, Mexican goverments had seemed willing to believe that past
antagonism between Mexico and the United States had given way to a
closer and more positive relationship and that, without being entirely
free of contradictions, it was so different from that of the past that it
could be viewed as a "special relationship" between the two countries.
The assumption was that it could be maintained despite the extraordinary differences between Mexico and the United States in history,
power, levels of development, and international interests.

The United States was beginning to come around to the view that,
after all, the Mexican Revolution had been positive and that Mexico
could become one of the best examples of democratic change in an
underdeveloped country. In Mexico, a few advised caution; they
wanted to know the boundaries of the "limited concord" between the
two countries, in the prudent phrase used by Daniel Cosío Villegas in
1947.

This situation began to change in the sixties. At the beginning of
his administration, López Mateos had to face serious labor disturbances that, for a moment, seemed to endanger official control over
the labor movement. The rural areas—particularly in the north—
were also shaken by those who demanded a revitalization of the
agrarian reform. The government faced these problems with a mixture of reformism and repression which had already begun to characterize Mexican politics. López Mateos promoted a series of measures
aimed at increasing the real income of the workers and accelerating
agrarian reform. This, together with the use of left-wing rhetoric,

alarmed the rightists, especially the business community, which took advantage of a controversy stirred up by the introduction of free textbooks into the elementary schools—conservatives viewed these books as too radical in their view of Mexican history and society—and mobilized large contingents of their sympathizers in the streets of various cities. To these internal stresses we must add the undeniable impact on public opinion of the Cuban Revolution of 1959 and of its rapid transformation into a socialist revolution that presented itself as an alternative mode of development in Latin America. Thus, the cold war was heightened in the Western Hemisphere just when the United States and the Soviet Union had initiated a détente. The Mexican nationalist and leftist groups, so sluggish in previous years, began to gain strength, especially after Lázaro Cárdenas lent them his support. In reaction, the anticommunist forces—the Catholic church and business—expressed their militancy as well, and another former president came to the forefront: Miguel Alemán. López Mateos had to maneuver skillfully to maintain himself in the political center, the government's natural space after 1940.

This increase in the political awareness of Mexican society took place in an atmosphere of economic change. A debate began about whether the stage of substitution of Mexican goods for imports was coming to an end. An affirmative response required a search for new internal and foreign markets in order to advance toward real industrialization, i.e., local manufacture of intermediate and capital goods. According to the well-known sociologist, Pablo González Casanova, in 1963 the way to achieve this was to legislate the redistribution of wealth so that the Mexicans who had been left out of the bonanza—and they were numerous—could participate in and revitalize industrialization, at the same time broadening the internal market. Others, who adhered to the theories of the Economic Commission for Latin America, believed that the best approach was to create a Latin American zone of free trade that would eventually become—following Western Europe's footsteps—a common market of the whole region.

The search for new markets and political relations with other countries that might help to diversify an excessively confining relationship with the United States led López Mateos to visit and receive an unprecedented number of chiefs of state from all over the world, and in 1960 to support the creation of the Latin American Free Trade Association (ALALC). Establishing a pattern, a series of meetings was held between the presidents of Mexico and the United States—this time, between López Mateos and Dwight Eisenhower. To Mexico, the most important issues in 1959 were stabilizing the prices of cotton and minerals and the construction of a dam that would supplement the Falcon Dam on the Rio Grande. In 1961, López Mateos had another meeting with his U.S. counterpart, President John F. Kennedy, and this time solutions were announced to two old problems. El Chamizal, which had been on the Mexican side of the Rio Grande when the border was drawn but which was transferred to the U.S. side when the river changed its course in 1864, was returned to Mexico. And Kennedy assured Mexico that the water from the Colorado River would flow into Mexico with less salinity. Until then, the desalination carried out in Arizona had made those waters unfit for irrigation in the formerly rich Mexicali valley.

In regard to Latin America, the main subject was the newly created Alliance for Progress. Through this program, the U.S. government tried to provide some of the political and economic resources needed to promote the development of the Latin American countries and to counter the influence of the Cuban Revolution. Mexico was not particularly enthusiastic about the Alliance for Progress and received only marginal aid through it.

In 1964, just before the end of his term, López Mateos again met with a new president of the United States—Lyndon B. Johnson—and this time Washington reaffirmed its decision to lessen the salinity of the Colorado River, still plaguing Mexico in spite of the earlier commitment.

None of the exchanges between the chief executives of Mexico and the United States diverged from the formal scenario: to reaffirm the friendship between the two countries, to support continental solidarity, and to raise only those bilateral problems with seemingly feasible solutions. But as mentioned before, López Mateos's initiatives took place in conjunction with the establishment or strengthening of relations with other countries.

In 1959, for example, López Mateos visited Canada as well as the United States. The following year, he left on an international tour which included six Latin American countries, and in 1962 he visited some of the most important leaders of the newly formed nonaligned movement. On that occasion, López Mateos visited Asia, and his tour included India and Indonesia, whose leaders were the founders of the movement which sought independence from both the United States and the U.S.S.R. Finally in 1963, the Mexican president went to Europe, the region with which Mexico had traditionally attempted to balance its close ties with the United States. His visit to five countries of that continent included France, and his meeting with Charles de Gaulle was particularly significant, since the French general was the leading proponent in Europe of a policy relatively free of U.S. influence. Equally significant were López Mateos's visits to Poland— the first by a Mexican president to a country close to the Soviet Union—and to Marshall Tito's socialist and nonaligned Yugoslavia.

Mexico's efforts to diversify its international trade, and the fact that Europe and Japan were still recuperating from the ravages of the war, produced some modest but significant results. In 1955, the United States accounted for 78 percent of Mexico's total foreign trade; by 1963, that level had dropped to 69 percent. Although trade with Latin America increased, it did not reach the expected levels. ALALC never could surmount its internal divisions; the Latin American economies were more competitive than complementary and the ALALC did not develop into the common market that had been sought.

More important than the presidential tours, and more revealing of Mexico's possibilities and limitations in following a relatively independent foreign policy vis-à-vis the United States, was the Mexican reaction to the crisis that the inter-American system faced owing to Cuba's revolutionary transformation. In 1961, Mexico's dilemma consisted, on the one hand, in the necessity to defend the two pillars of its foreign policy, nonintervention and self-determination. The actions and declarations of the United States, and of some other members of the inter-American system regarding Cuba, were abhorrent to Mexico. On the other hand, Mexico knew that it was advisable to avoid a direct confrontation with the United States. The solution at that moment was to avoid linking the defense of Mexico's traditional principles to the defense of communism in Latin America and, even less, to the defense of the Soviet Union's policies in the Western Hemisphere. Had Mexico developed an intimate relationship with the Cuban revolutionaries, the United States would have applied economic and political pressure, as it had in the past. This would have wrecked López Mateos's efforts to promote economic development; besides, it would have awakened powerful conservative and reactionary internal forces. Also, and ultimately, the Mexican government was committed to the preservation of capitalism.

Still, to accept Washington's anti-Cuban policy would have meant accepting the leadership of the Organization of American States (OAS), which had turned its back on Cuba and urged Mexico to do the same. Did the OAS have the power to judge what the member countries could or could not do in their internal and foreign affairs? If so, this implied a threat to Mexico's own sovereignty; it also meant abandoning a whole nationalist tradition that had been created as a result of the struggle against U.S. hegemony. The ground over which the Mexican government had to move was, therefore, treacherous. The government gained legitimacy by preserving the basic shape of the nationalist tradition in foreign policy, an element of particular importance given its poor relationship with the left after the violence unleashed in 1958 against the independent labor movement. And it stayed on excellent terms with the Cubans, with the minimum antagonism from Washington. Let us analyze the main aspects of this policy.

In 1960, the revolutionary Cuban government announced its plans to apply the agrarian reform laws to a number of U.S. properties on the island; later, it expropriated U.S.-owned oil refineries for refusing to refine crude oil imported from the U.S.S.R. In reprisal, Washington closed its market to the main and almost sole Cuban export: sugar. Indirectly, this measure made it possible for Mexico to increase its foreign trade, since Mexican exports became part of the substantial U.S. sugar quota that Cuba had previously held; at the same time, the Mexican government was concerned about the open use of the kind of economic pressure that had adversely affected its own country in the past and that it did not want used again anywhere. In order to avoid appearing to make common cause with this type of action, López Mateos invited the president of Cuba to come to Mexico during a visit to Venezuela and Brazil. During President Osvaldo Dortico's visit in June 1960, the Cuban revolutionary process was ceremonially joined to the one that began in Mexico in 1910. A Mexican legislator condemned the U.S. sanctions against the Cuban government, triggering a gratifyingly annoyed official reaction from Washington. Cuba had not yet declared itself other than simply nationalistic, which facilitated the Mexican gesture.

The Cuban revolutionary process rapidly became more radical, and the Cuban–U.S. conflict heightened, particularly in April 1961, after an invasion by U.S.-backed Cuban counterrevolutionaries. It culminated in Fidel Castro's famous declaration in December 1961, wherein he announced to the world the project of organizing a political party that would lead his country toward socialism. This development allowed Mexico's leaders to regard the Cuban problem as no longer simply a matter of Latin American nationalism, but rather as part of the larger and more complex East-West confrontation. After 1961, Mexican officials stopped emphasizing the similarities between the Mexican Revolution and what was happening in Cuba; nevertheless, Mexican public opinion and political tradition impelled the government to reject any action that would encourage intervention in the inter-American system. Mexico adopted a line of policy and action very different from the legal and political posture struck not just by the United States, but eventually by the rest of Latin America as well. Not for the first time, Mexico isolated itself in the field of foreign policy.

At first, the Mexican position was to try to conciliate the irreconcilable. Thus, during the Seventh Consultation Meeting of Foreign Relations Secretaries—inaugurated in San José, Costa Rica, in August 1960 within the OAS framework—the Mexican delegation joined those who condemned an intervention or a threat of intervention in the hemisphere by an "extra-continental power," a clear reference to the growing closeness of the Cuban government to the Soviet Union. At the same time, Mexico warned against a repetition, in Cuba, of the pressures contrary to self-determination that several countries of the continent had brought to bear upon Mexico itself in 1915. In any event, according to Mexico, the 1960 declaration of San José was not a condemnation of Cuba's government, which is precisely what the United States was seeking. The Mexican posture became more difficult in April 1961, when a counterrevolutionary invasion occurred at Playa Girón, since its objective was to establish a provisional anti-Castro government that would immediately receive recognition and support from the United States. The news of the invasion provoked in Mexico, as it did in other countries, public demonstrations in favor of the Cubans and against the United States. Mexican representatives at the United Nations condemned this U.S. action and insisted that the problem should be discussed in the U.N. rather than in the OAS (the United States had less influence in the world organization than in the inter-American institution). The Mexican representative, speaking before the United Nations, by implication condemned the United States as well as certain Central American countries, particularly Nicaragua, when he insisted on the responsibility of those members of the international community who did not prevent invasions from being organized in their territories.

At the beginning of 1962, the Eighth Consultation Meeting of the OAS was convened in Punta del Este, Uruguay. On this occasion, the U.S. delegation was committed to bringing about a general diplomatic isolation of Cuba as well as a blockade of the island. Mexico tried to work out a compromise. The Mexican foreign relations secretary stated that "there is an incompatibility between belonging to the OAS and to a Marxist-Leninist profession." At the same time, and without admitting any inconsistency, Mexico rejected the possibility of expelling Cuba from the regional organization, arguing that the OAS charter did not contemplate that possibility.

By the end of 1962, Cuban–U.S. relations were again at a critical point, since the Soviet Union had just installed nuclear missiles in the Caribbean island. Cuba considered this a precaution against another invasion, but the United States viewed it as an intolerable threat and President John Kennedy imposed a naval and maritime blockade on the island in order to force the Soviet Union to withdraw its atomic weapons. The possibility of a direct conflict between the United States and the Soviet Union thus became very real; and the crisis in the Caribbean acquired global proportions. President López Mateos, returning from a trip to the Far East, was notified of this U.S. decision, which could be escalated into a world war, and he was subjected to extraordinary pressures. Finally, he publicly supported the U.S. measure and instructed his representative to the OAS to vote in favor of a resolution that demanded the dismantling and withdrawal of all armed installations in Cuba that had any "offensive capacity." Mexican support for the United States was still conditional: the crisis was not to be used as a justification for the invasion of Cuba.

A year after the so-called missile crisis, in October 1963, the government of Venezuela requested a ninth consultation of the OAS to denounce Cuban aggression. According to the Venezuelans, the Cubans were supporting the actions of various Venezuelan insurgent groups. Mexico opposed this summons to convene, but most of the members agreed to meet, and did in July 1964, almost at the end of López Mateos's term. Anticipating what was coming, Mexico warned that if the majority of the OAS members demanded that sanctions be imposed on the Cuban government—such as suspending diplomatic, airline, or trade relations—because it supported guerrilla wars in Latin America, Mexico would not observe them. According to Mexico, the Cuban action did not constitute a violation of Venezuelan sovereignty nor of its territorial integrity within the terms of the Inter-American Reciprocal Aid Treaty invoked by Venezuela. What Mexico feared did happen: the majority of the OAS voted in favor of diplomatic sanctions against Cuba. Bolivia, Chile, and Uruguay broke relations with Cuba; Mexico, the fourth country which still had diplomatic relations with Cuba, rejected the resolution and maintained its diplomatic ties and airline connection.

Bilateral relations between Mexico and the United States were not greatly impaired by Mexico's adoption of an independent political stand on to the Cuban issue, however. By this time, decisions of President Nasser of Egypt, and some other events, had demonstrated to the United States that not all nationalism in the underdeveloped world was the product of the Soviet Union's machinations. The U.S. ambassador to Mexico declared that the different points of view of the two governments did not alter their bilateral relations because the government in Washington understood that Mexico was defending a principle—nonintervention—and not Fidel Castro's regime. The ambassador knew what he was talking about: in practice, the existence of diplomatic relations between Mexico and Havana did not reflect any real warmth. The air flights between Havana and Mexico, for example, were controlled by the Mexican authorities, who systematically put all travelers on a blacklist and confiscated all material of a political nature proceeding from the island. That is, Mexico did maintain a disguised but effective blockade against the Cuban revolution. Finally, the United States' main interest in Mexico was, more than ever, the preservation of social and political stability. A Mexican foreign policy of relative independence was a way of maintaining the internal legitimacy of a system essentially acceptable to U.S. politicians and business. Furthermore, the United States could present Mexico's independent behavior as objective evidence that it had friends, not satellites.

It appears that, following the differences over Cuba, the U.S. government accepted the idea that internal stability in Mexico required the airing of differences about matters that were not of central importance for the United States but vital to Mexico. Direct U.S. investment in Mexico is a good indicator of this situation: despite all the differences between Mexico and the United States in regard to Castro's Cuba, such investment increased from $922 million in 1959 to almost $1,300 million at the end of López Mateos's term in 1964. On the other hand, direct U.S. financial and economic aid to Mexico was minimal, perhaps one of the prices that Mexico had to pay for its independent policy in the hemisphere. Nor was Mexico's access to foreign capital markets affected by the Cuban affair.

Gustavo Díaz Ordaz's administration (1964–70) also characterized by a conservative tone in domestic affairs, coincided with a decrease in the importance of the Cuban model of development in Latin America. The guerrilla movements that with great enthusiasm tried to repeat the Sierra Maestra experience in other countries of the region were supressed by Latin American armies (frequently aided by U.S. advisors) which more than once profitted from the occasion to grasp political power. The death of the legendary commander Ernesto Guevara in the Bolivian mountains, in October 1967, became a symbol of the defeat of the strategy followed by several Latin American leftist movements in those years and in Chile, power was grasped by electoral means. To a great extent, the model offered by the guerrillas was replaced by the electoral mobilization of the masses and by the creation of popular fronts in Latin America. In this context, Mexican foreign policy appeared normal and differences with the United States became less acute. If Díaz Ordaz was interested at all in the world outside Mexico, it was mainly for commercial reasons. He did not travel much except for visits to the United States and Central America, where he promoted foreign trade.

In January 1965, it was announced that representatives of Mexico and the United States had finally drawn up a concrete plan to reduce the salinity of the Colorado River's waters. In January 1968, a five-year agreement on reciprocal fishing rights to boats of both countries in an area covering between 9 and 12 nautical miles along the coasts of the two countries was signed. In April 1970, President Díaz Ordaz and President Richard Nixon made public a formal agreement to solve old border problems created by change in the course of the Rio Grande; the treaty was duly ratified by the respective congresses in 1971. Vested U.S. interests in Mexico exhibited little concern over official efforts to force enteprises to accept Mexican participation. General Electric of Mexico put 10 percent of its stock up for sale in the local market. (This example was not followed by any of the other big enterprises; Ford and General Motors, for example, remained 100 percent foreign.) In a basically symbolic act in 1969, PEMEX cancelled the so-called risk contracts of production undertaken between 1949 and 1951 with four independent U.S. oil companies; the cost of Mexico was modest: $18 million and no protests from the United States. And, during the Mexican political crisis of 1968 that hurled thousands of middle-class youngsters into the streets to protest against the regime's authoritarianism and that culminated in the violent repression of 2 October, the government in Washington followed events closely and attentively without passing judgment and quietly accepted the use of force by Díaz Ordaz.

The United States spent the second half of the sixties in the search for a solution to the problems created by its intervention in Southeast Asia, while Cuba and Latin America resumed their traditional place in the background. For a brief moment, the Caribbean regained importance to the United States: this time, the problem occurred in the Dominican Republic. In February 1963, right after the assassination of dictator Rafael Leónides Trujillo, Juan Bosch assumed power in the first free elections since 1924. Less than a year later, the army decided it perceived a threat from the communists, seized power, and ended the democratic experiment in the country. However, this action was taken in the absence of a consensus in the armed forces, and a group of young officers tried to reinstall Juan Bosch. Conservative elements in the army resisted, and a civil war began to develop in April 1965.

Fearing that the instability in the Dominican Republic might find a radical solution, perhaps one following the Cuban example, President Lyndon Johnson ordered the occupation of the Dominican capital by a force of U.S. Marines. This resulted, not surprisingly, in a political tilt toward the conservative side. Mexico was again faced with a violation of the principle of nonintervention on the American continent and reacted accordingly. While the majority in the OAS went through the motions of trying to legitimize what really was a unilateral decision by the United States to create an inter-American force—which included the United States—to restore order in the Dominican Republic, Mexico and four other Latin American countries refused to acknowledge this fig leaf. President Gustavo Díaz Ordaz, in his annual report to Congress, condemned the U.S. action for its unilateral character.

Of more significance to Mexican–U.S. relations, however, were those measures that directly affected the day-to-day conduct of affairs between the two countries. When Díaz Ordaz officially visited Washington, the main subject of his speeches was the need to halt the constant deterioration of the international prices of raw materials vis-à-vis the manufactures of the developed world. There were also more specific problems, such as the so-called interception operation carried out by the U.S. authorities, which took place during a three-week period between 21 September and 10 October 1969. All travelers entering the United States from Mexico, regardless of their nationality, were subjected to careful inspection by U.S. customs officials instead of being quickly waved through after a cursory check, the former practice. The delays at the customs sheds interfered with normal border traffic and, as the days went by, also with the trans-border commercial transactions vital to the economic health of the whole area.

The ostensible reason for this operation was the constant leakage of drugs from Mexico into the United States, but the real reasons, while related, were more complex. The U.S. authorities felt that the Mexicans could do far more about the drugs than they were bothering to do and believed that a brief show of strength would be a salutory reminder to the Mexicans that their cooperation in limiting drug traffic would make life generally easier for them on the frontier. Even more important was the desire of Washington to project to the U.S. public an image of active antidrug policies. Four-and-a-half million persons were searched at the border towns during the three weeks of the operation, both to put pressure on Mexico and to demonstrate to the public that its government was acting effectively to put an end to the illegal traffic in marijuana, cocaine, heroin, and other drugs. The operation, which cost the U.S. government $30 million, intercepted only 3,202 pounds of marijuana, 60 pounds of peyote, 1.5 kilos of heroin, and insignificant amounts of other drugs and barbiturates. Sales of goods to U.S. citizens in Mexican border towns fell by half, and sales in U.S. stores to Mexican visitors also decreased. Such direct pressure, exerted on Mexico without any previous warning, did lead the Mexican government to organize an effective and permanent campaign against the traffic in narcotics, but it also generated a great deal of resentment. Díaz Ordaz, knowing full well that it had originated in President Richard Nixon's office, publicly called it a "bureaucratic mistake." He also stated that it had built "a wall of suspicion among our peoples." Whatever remained of the idea that there was a special relationship between Mexico and the United States almost vanished.

10

New Problems Join the
Old Ones: 1971–1985

The Effort to Redefine Foreign Policy

When the administration of Gustavo Díaz Ordaz came to an end in
December 1970, a long series of unsolved problems began to take its
toll on the political system. The repression of the student movement
of 1968 had shown the worst face of Mexican authoritarianism to the
public, and there was a dangerous lack of commitment to the system
among important segments of the middle classes and to a lesser
extent, among urban workers and even peasants. Abroad, the "special
relationship" with the United States was almost empty of content,
but there was nothing about the Mexican–U.S. relationship to keep
lights in Washington burning late at night. The most obvious
economic problems were a maldistribution of wealth and income,
unemployment and underemployment, the deficit in the balance of
payments, and the sluggishness of the agricultural sector.

When he assumed the presidency in December 1970, Luis
Echeverría Alvarez, the previous secretary of the interior, was aware of
the damage that the crisis of 1968 had inflicted on the public
acceptability of both the regime and the single-party system itself.
The full police power of the state had been employed in Mexico City
against striking and demonstrating students and other members of
the middle class. A large part of his task as chief executive was to
regain the trust of the middle class, members of which were beginning to question the legitimacy of the ruling party—the Party of the
Institutionalized Revolution (PRI).

At first, Echeverría scorned the pursuit of a more adventurous
foreign policy, either as a means of distracting public attention from
domestic troubles or of reaping some positive and beneficial concessions from other countries. He turned to the United States, but its

government proved unsympathetic to his problems, and would not, for instance, exempt Mexican goods from its 10 percent surtax on imports, designed to alleviate the deficit in the U.S. balance of payments. This occurred in August 1971, during Echeverría's first year in office, and was his initiation into the cruel world of international relations.

Frustrated abroad, Echeverría attempted to use populist policies at home to revitalize the political legitimacy of the system, but his attempt to use the increasingly important independent labor movement as an additional basis of power failed.

Echeverría then decided on a foreign policy similar to that of López Mateos, although even more ambitious. While remaining on reasonably good terms with the United States and without abandoning his efforts to improve bilateral trade relations, Echeverría tried to widen Mexico's economic and political horizons by traveling to thirty-six countries, holding talks with sixty-four heads of state and exchanging diplomatic representatives with sixty-seven countries in all. The aim of this extraordinary diplomatic effort was not new: to diversify Mexico's commercial and political partners in order to stimulate its industry and lessen its dependency on the United States.

Together with Carlos Andrés Pérez, president of Venezuela, Echeverría managed to obtain support from many of the Latin American countries, including Cuba, to create the Latin American Economic System (SELA). He also signed an agreement with the European Economic Community; he negotiated a commercial, scientific, and cultural agreement with Eastern Europe through the COMECON; and he backed the creation of the Empresa Naviera del Caribe to promote direct trade between the countries of the Caribbean zone. One result of all of this effort was his presentation, before the United Nations, of the Charter of Economic Rights and Duties of States. This document was finally approved by the U.N. General Assembly, although it was disregarded by the United States and other major industrialized countries that were not willing to grant underdeveloped countries the economic concessions they were demanding and that Echeverría felt they should have. The government presided over by Echeverría was involved in a total of 160 treaties and international agreements designed to expand Mexico's economic, technological, and cultural exchanges with the rest of the world.

The result of this effort did not correspond at all to expectations. Mexico under Echeverría was making an effort to orient itself diplomatically and, especially economically, away from the United States, and to be perceived as doing so. True, a certain amount of progress was made—66.3 percent of Mexico's trade was with the United States in 1969 and by 1974 this proportion had declined to 59.4 percent—but the trend was not maintained. By 1980, 70 percent of Mexico's trade was with the United States, an actual increase.

Although Mexico was the United States' main customer in Latin America and its fifth largest in the world, its relative economic importance, from a global standpoint, was less impressive, since commercial exchanges between the two countries represented less than 5 percent of the United States' total foreign trade. Nor did Mexico's commercial dependency change, except for the worse: its trade with the United States showed a deficit of a little more than $1 billion by 1975. Moreover, while the actual purchasing power of the peso was diminishing, the Echeverría administration persisted overlong in its efforts to maintain its traditional value relative to the dollar.

This persistence led to an economic crisis in 1976, the last year of Echeverría's administration, and to a 50 percent devaluation of the peso. Deficits piled up as a result of the protectionist policies of the large industrial powers, the lack of competitiveness of Mexican industry, and the rapid increase in imported food (to almost $11 billion in 1974). Foreign debt became a serious and chronic problem. In 1971, the foreign debt of the Mexican public sector amounted to $4,543 million; when Echeverría left the presidency, it had reached the sum of $19,600 million, much of it owed to U.S. or U.S.-controlled institutions. In 1970, direct foreign investment (DFI) amounted to $2.822 million, of which 62 percent was in U.S. hands; by 1976, the sum had reached $4,262 million, and more or less the same proportion was controlled by U.S. interests.

The economy of the border region—traditionally linked to the U.S. market—became even more dependent on foreigners. By the end of the seventies there were about sixty million border crossings from the United States annually. Totally foreign-owned industries were created all along the Mexican border: in these, Mexican workers assembled products with parts imported from the United States and made finished products which were exported to the United States, subject only to duty on the value added. This so-called in-bond plant program was established in 1965 to mitigate the unemployment created by the termination of the bracero program. By 1980, the program comprised 583 plants which employed more than 118,000 Mexican workers—and it was under attack from U.S. labor unions.

The growth in population and the desire for better-paid jobs in Mexico and the demand for cheap labor in some sectors of the U.S. economy created such an increase in emigration to the United States that it became a major issue in the relations between the two countries. There is no exact count of the magnitude of this migration but, in 1976, 773,000 Mexican citizens who had entered the United States illegally were deported, and it was estimated that a million-and-a-half more were able to enter without being caught. Mexican governments have always maintained that the drift of Mexican laborers to the United States is largely balanced by voluntary return. That is, Mexicans who have entered illegally typically work for a relatively brief period in the United States—until a particular crop is harvested, for example—and then take themselves and the money they have saved back to their families and villages. The United States, while granting that there is indeed a certain amount of voluntary return, has not agreed about its magnitude. From the U.S. perspective, the illegal presence of Mexican workers was a central problem in the relationship with Mexico at the end of the seventies, a time of economic recession. The Mexican point of view was different. The migration of Mexicans to the United States was seen as a kind of natural phenomenon, extremely difficult to terminate given the great disparity between the two economies and the persistent U.S. demand for the services of the Mexicans.

All the indicators clearly show that the disparity between the two neighboring economies increased during the seventies. At the end of the decade, Mexico's gross national product was only 3.7 percent of that of the United States, and the bases for widening or simply maintaining Mexico's relative economic independence were weakened. Nevertheless, Echeverría missed no opportunity to publicize the quest for independence.

To begin with, the president linked Mexico strongly to the political positions of the Third World. Mexican representatives took stands in various forums on subjects which had been tactfully avoided in the past. The results were mixed. Mexico became an important actor in the policies of the Third World and thus began to play a role in a movement that was questioning some key U.S. policies regarding the underdeveloped countries. This movement became particularly important after 1973, when the oil embargo demonstrated that the nonindustrial nations could affect some very important interests of the United States and its allies.

On the other hand, Mexico's bargaining vis-à-vis the industrialized nations did not improve perceptibly, and unforeseen problems sometimes emerged. In 1975, for example, Mexico voted, along with many other countries in the United Nations, in favor of an Arab resolution which defined Zionism as a form of racism. Jewish organizations worldwide swiftly organized a tourist boycott of Mexico which had an immediate effect. Mexico had to retract its vote and its statements in Jerusalem itself and replace its foreign minister—but Echeverría's condemnations of "imperialisms of one side or the other" did not abate.

Within the context of Mexican–U.S. relations, even more important than the attempt to link Mexico to Third World positions was the growing warmth of its relations with Cuba—for the first time a Mexican president visited that country—and the political and even material support that Mexico gave to Chile's leftist and nationalist government, the *Unidad Popular* (Popular Unity) headed by Salvador Allende. In 1973, after a spectacular political crisis, Allende was overthrown in a military coup in which the United States seems to have been involved. Mexico broke diplomatic relations with the military junta that assumed power, denounced its dictatorial nature, and gave asylum to a goodly number of Allende's supporters.

Economic relations between the United States and Mexico were adversely affected by a new law regulating foreign investment, a piece of legislation not particularly welcomed by the State Department or by U.S. companies in Mexico. At the beginning of Echeverría's administration, DFI in Mexico was more than double its value ten years earlier. Later, for political as well as economic reasons, DFI lost this dynamism and began to slow down. Just after Echeverría left office, the book value of DFI in Mexico was $4.6 billion, but at 1960 prices this amounted to only $1.2 billion, a real increase of only 11 percent in seventeen years. The U.S. share of DFI fell from 79 percent in 1970 to a little less than 70 percent in 1977; four-fifths of this investment was in manufacturing.

The relative loss of importance of DFI in the Mexican economy can be partially explained by the terms of the Law to Promote Mexican Investment and Regulate Foreign Investment, enacted 9 February 1973. The law was a compilation of existing legislation plus some innovations, two of which were significant: the creation of a National Registry for Foreign Investment and a National Commission on Foreign Investments. The commission was an interagency regulatory body and the highest authority on foreign investments.

The new legislation facilitated the participation of Mexican capital in foreign-owned enterprises and gave the government an instrument with which to guide new investment into the areas it considered important and to declare others off limits to DFI. In May 1979, the commission produced a document entitled *Policies Regarding Direct Foreign Investment*, a set of guidelines, but by then, DFI had lost some of its attractiveness to Mexican authorities. The eagerness of foreign banks and other institutions to lend money to the Mexican government—indirect foreign investment—was a more attractive alternative. At the end of 1981, DFI accounted for only about 20 percent of Mexico's foreign debt.

The Crisis of 1976

By 1976, Mexico's economy was in crisis and its political relations with the United States had deteriorated badly. That year a group of U.S. congressmen, mainly from the border states, sent an open letter to President Gerald Ford in which they questioned some of the central policies of Echeverría's administration and warned against the leftist tendencies of the Mexican government. Some large U.S. newspapers gave wide circulation to the rumors of a possible coup d'etat in Mexico. Nothing came of this, however.

In December 1976, Echeverría's finance secretary, José López Portillo, assumed the presidency. His main concern was to restore the confidence of investors (both national and foreign) so as to pull the country out of its economic morass. During his first presidential visit to the United States, López Portillo declared that his administration was going to be characterized by austerity and discipline, precisely what those who could support Mexico from the outside were asking for. Actually, three months before he assumed office, the Mexican government signed an agreement with the International Monetary Fund (IMF), valid for three years as of January 1977 (and therefore with López Portillo's consent), in which it promised to limit new international loans to no more than $3 billion per year as well as to control the budgetary deficit (46 billion pesos in 1976). The Mexican left accused the new administration of submitting the country, under pressure from the United States, to a monetarist economic model very popular among military dictatorships in South America.

Monetarism, according to these critics, emphasized a market economy and private enterprise instead of jobs and social security. López Portillo defended his policies, reminding his critics that Mexico had joined the IMF as an act of free will, fully aware of the influential role that the United States played in that international organization as well as of the obligations and privileges of joining it.

Oil and International Activisim

As emergency measures began to produce results, and as a part of them, the new administration decided to alter Mexico's traditional oil policies, particularly in view of the rising price of crude oil in the world market. Despite the shortage of money, the new administration increased its expenditures for the exploration and production of oil in order to bring onto the market the gas and oil reserves known to be available. Its purpose was to make Mexico once again an exporter of petroleum.

Oil would supply the financial resources necessary to close the increasing gap between imports and exports and, at the same time, would constitute collateral that would reopen Mexico's doors to international credit without the restrictions and discipline of the IMF. The oil market was then dominated by the sellers and prices were on the rise; thus the government could afford to drill to depths unthought of only a few years earlier and to use improved methods of extraction. The verified reserves increased from 6 billion barrels in 1976 to more than 72 billion at the beginning of 1981.

The left and the nationalists, however, continued to advocate a moderate policy that would leave much of the available oil and gas in the ground for the future, and demanded that much of what was pumped be processed into finished or partially finished manufactures instead of shipping it out as crude. They were worried about mortgaging the energy resources of Mexico by making commitments to export large amounts of crude over a long period instead of using the oil and gas to help resolve some of the structural problems of the economy such as its relative incapacity to export manufactured goods and the loss of dynamism in its production of food for its own people. While the government did not alter its policies, it did promise not to export more gas or oil than was actually needed to generate sufficient cash to keep the country running on its new and improved standard. Eventually, in response to pressure, it set a maximum "production platform" of 2.2 million barrels a day. The maximum was raised to 2.7 barrels per day by the end of 1980; half of that was destined for the international market and half for the domestic market. That policy was still in force at the end of 1984.

Washington liked the oil policies of López Portillo's administration. It regarded the increased availability of hydrocarbons in the Western Hemisphere as a good thing in itself, and the decision by the Mexicans to stay free of extraneous obligations or commitments to OPEC even though it followed the organization's guidelines for prices. In view of López Portillo's policies and a further declaration that Mexico did not aspire to any sort of leadership within the Third World, Washington felt fairly comfortable.

Harmonious bilateral relations did not last long. Once again, certain U.S. actions were perceived as unilateral and even arrogant. This happened when the cash flow from the newly marketed oil had restored to López Portillo a certain freedom of action. The Mexican economy had had a powerful shot in the arm, the credit windows at every bank in the world were wide open to Mexico, and the news from the fields in Campeche was of more reserves being located and confirmed. At this moment, the U.S. government—specifically, the Department of Energy in President Jimmy Carter's administration—handled relations with Mexico very ruthlessly indeed.

In 1977, the Mexican oil monopoly Petróleos Mexicanos (PEMEX) reached an agreement with six U.S. gas enterprises by which they were to acquire 2,000 million cubic feet of Mexican natural gas daily. The price of the gas was fixed at $2.60 per thousand cubic feet, high at the time in comparison with the $2.16 that the United States was paying to Canada, but the world price of the fuel was expected to rise and it was thought that fairly soon $2.60 would be in line with it. PEMEX, with the president's consent, immediately embarked on a costly ($1,500 million) enterprise: the construction of a gas pipeline 48 inches in diameter with a length of 1,350 kilometers to connect the production field in the Mexican southeast with the U.S. border. The pipe was not manufactured locally at the time and had to be imported, worsening Mexico's balance of payments in the short run.

In December 1977, when the gigantic Mexican project had already begun, President Carter's administration abruptly decided to cancel the contract if Mexico did not lower its price. The Mexican government, its internal prestige already at stake because it had accepted such a close economic link with the United States—oil was the concrete symbol of Mexican nationalism in the twentieth Century—reacted sharply in an attempt to recover the ground lost in the eyes of the Mexican public. First, it announced that it would not sell the gas at the price demanded by the United States even if that meant having to waste it; second, from that moment on, gas would be substituted for oil in Mexico's industrial plants. This would still give the gas pipeline a reason to exist—although not its dimensions or the extra cost of rapid building—for it would provide the north of the country with gas, thus freeing additional oil for export. Finally, Mexico would seek to diversify its oil market so as not to depend ever again on any one buyer, even though this meant losing the advantage in transport costs that the U.S. market offered. Mexico's 1980 Energy Plan specified that it would not, in the future, sell more than 50 percent of its exported fuel to a single client. In February 1979, during a reception in honor of President Carter, López Portillo surprised his guests by denouncing the United States: he declared that "between permanent and not occasional neighbors, unexpected measures or a sudden swindle or abuse are poisonous fruits that sooner or later have reversible effects."

The quick recovery of the Mexican economy, plus the fact that Mexico had the sixth most important world reserves of hydrocarbons, enabled the Mexican government to take a stronger and more independent stand with the United States by that time. In 1978, for example, Mexico even dared to explore the possibility of shipping crude oil to Cuba, with the U.S.S.R. sending, in exchange, a similar amount to Spain, Mexico's proper client, in order to lessen crosshauling. The plan was never carried out but, the following year, López Portillo felt confident enough to receive Dr. Fidel Castro with great cordiality on the small Mexican island of Cozumel. At about the same time, Mexico's secretary of foreign affairs announced that the deposed shah of Iran would not be allowed to reenter Mexico, where he had previously been received in response to an informal request from the United States.

Finally, that same year, Mexico broke diplomatic relations with the Nicaraguan government of dictator Anastasio Somoza, an act that was correctly interpreted as support for the rebel forces that were successfully contending for control in that country. The United States, fearful of the leftist and nationalistic character of the anti-Somoza guerrillas, attempted to neutralize their success through the intervention of the Organization of American States (OAS), but Mexico, along with other Latin American countries, blocked the U.S. plan, giving the revolutionaries time to gain power unconditionally. After the triumph of the Nicaraguan Revolution, Mexico offered the new government its full support, adopting a very active role in a territory that up to then had been dominated by the United States. Mexico's economic, technical, and political presence in Nicaragua had a double objective; first, to support what was viewed as a thorough-going reformist and modernizing nationalism in the area (whereas the United States supported only minimum reforms); and second, to provide an alternative to the radical influence of Cuba.

Finally, Mexico gave some support to the rebel Salvadorean coalition—already defined by President Ronald Reagan's administration as the executing arm of Cuban and U.S.S.R. designs in Central America—by considering it a valid interlocutor within that country's political structure. Mexico accused the Salvadorean government of violating human rights and, in August 1981, joined France in a comuniqué asking for negotiations between the insurgents and the government in El Salvador.

The Mexican government believed that the solution in El Salvador required those groups that had traditionally exercised and retained authority in the country to negotiate with the opposition in order to reduce polarization and give the moderates of both the right and the left a chance. The object of negotiations would be the reallocation of power within the society so that a new political structure that would correspond more closely to the transformations in the material environment of Central America with its nationalist and anti-imperialist overtones, could be created. Mexico viewed the ongoing revolution in Central America as unavoidable. The sooner it was accepted by the outside world—particularly by the United States—the better, for otherwise the most radical and orthodox elements of the left would advocate closer links to Cuba and the Soviet Union as the only way to counter the attack from the national and international right, an outcome that would not be in the Mexican government's interest. Mexico was guided, at the time, by the possibility of changing the region's status from that of a subordinate of the United States to a more independent group of loosely confederated countries.

Mexico's self-appointed role of champion of nationalism and moderation in Central America inevitably led to a series of disagreements with the United States. In 1981, President López Portillo warned the United States against any invasion of Cuba or Nicaragua. The following year, Mexican officials denied the importance of the U.S.-backed elections in El Salvador as a way of solving the real problems of that nation and exhibited no enthusiasm for President Reagan's Caribbean Basin Initiative of July 1982. This initiative was intended to draw up a plan of economic cooperation between the United States, Canada, Venezuela, and Mexico, on the one hand, and Caribbean and Central American nations on the other. It was unacceptable to Mexico because it excluded Cuba and Nicaragua. At the beginning of 1982,

López Portillo had paid a well-publicized visit to Nicaragua during which he declared that the Sandinista Revolution was the continuation of a process started by the Mexican Revolution and did not represent a threat to U.S. security. He asked for a nonagression pact among all the countries of the region and, specifically from the United States, for a declaration against the use of force against Nicaragua. The U.S. government ignored both Mexico's plea and its efforts to mediate in the region's conflicts.

Mexico's policy in Central America was not confined to declarations and other symbolic gestures. In 1980, Mexico and Venezuela decided to use their best international instrument—oil—to influence developments in Central America. The so-called San José Agreement was a commitment between Mexico and Venezuela (although the policies of both countries in Central America did not always coincide) to provide the normal oil needs of the Caribbean and Central American countries at 70 percent of the world prices, designating the other 30 percent as loans, at a very low rate of interest, for the creation of a fund for the economic development of the region and for finding alternative sources of energy, principally hydroelectric power.

Mexico's emergence as an oil power at the beginning of the eighties, one far from the war-torn Middle East, led some private groups in the United States to propose the formation of a common market consisting of Mexico, the United States, and Canada. Mexico was to provide the hydrocarbons and the labor power. To Mexico, the plan meant that it must abandon further industrial development and renounce the possibility of an independent economic and political future. The proposal aroused no enthusiasm at that time: the nationalistic sectors emphasized the danger to the national sovereignty; furthermore, most Mexican manufacturers dreaded the disappearance of protectionist barriers and said so immediately. In 1980, Mexico had refused to sign the General Agreements of Tariffs and Trade (GATT) recommended by U.S. and by some Mexican officials interested in liberalizing trade between the two countries, and GATT was no threat at all compared to this common-market idea.

The project for the economic integration of North America once again raised one of the basic issues in the relationship between Mexico and the United States: the persistent massive emigration of Mexican workers to the United States. At the time, the rate of unemployment in the United States was high and large sectors of U.S. society saw in the illegal migration a threat to the national identity of the United States. In mid-1981, President Reagan submitted legislation to

Congress which would legalize the then-unauthorized stay of Mexicans who could prove they had entered the country before 1980 and which would allow them to become permanent residents after ten years. The measure included an increase from twenty thousand to forty thousand in the number of annual visas issued to Mexicans for legal residency. On the other hand, Reagan asked for increased funds for the Border Patrol and for penalties against U.S. employers who engaged workers who lacked the proper documents. He advocated a two-year pilot program that would allow the annual admission of fifty thousand Mexican "guest workers," who would be permitted to stay in the United States for one year.

The U.S. Congress took the matter into its own hands. In March 1982, Senator Alan K. Simpson and Representative Romano L. Mazzoli introduced a bipartisan bill for the reform of the immigration law. On the one hand, it would have legalized the status of an important group of aliens; on the other, it called for fines and other penalties for those who employed them. The Simpson-Mazzoli bill opened a long, and at times passionate, debate in the United States as well as in Mexico about the cause and effect of migrant Mexican workers in the United States. The debate involved the unions as well as the Hispanic community, the churches, agricultural interests and academicians. At the end of 1984, Congress adjourned without enacting the law because the various and often contradictory interests could not reach an acceptable compromise. The issue remained a very lively one.

Any immigration policy of the United States affects Mexico's vital interests because every year millions of Mexican workers lacking permits cross the border into the United States looking for temporary jobs. Although these are low-paid jobs with few or no legal rights, they were an improvement over conditions in Mexico, especially since 1982, when the peso was devalued and Mexico entered a deep economic recession. By 1970, U.S. authorities were deporting about a quarter-million Mexicans yearly. By 1980, the figure reached the million mark. Even though about seven out of eight undocumented workers returned to Mexico after some months in the United States, the problem remained a grave one.

Some in the United States viewed the large number of undocumented workers as one of the main problems of foreign policy and labelled it a "silent invasion" that threatened the social and cultural fabric of the country. Others argued that this labor filled a real need in the U.S. economy because many of the jobs performed by

Mexicans were considered unacceptable even to unemployed U.S. citizens. The Mexican government, while very concerned about the outcome of the debate, could do very little. The U.S. immigration law was a domestic problem. Furthermore, it was impossible for Mexico to provide all the employment opportunities that a young and expanding labor force required: about eight hundred thousand new jobs were needed annually, in the mid-1980s, just to keep unemployment from growing.

Problems without Simple Solutions

At the very beginning of the 1980s, oil and gas appeared to offer Mexico the opportunity to make the leap from an undeveloped to a developed country, fulfilling a very old desire of Mexican society and an equally old committment of its leadership. This promise vanished. A surplus world supply of fuel began to change the sellers' market into a buyers' market and, in 1981, the price of oil began to drop. The deficit in Mexico's balance of payments reached $12.9 billion.

Hoping against hope, Mexican authorities decided to continue their costly plan of development almost without alteration. Instead of devaluing the peso drastically and cutting governmental expenditures, they added $22 billion to an already staggering foreign debt. Toward the end of the short-lived oil boom, a flight of capital—mostly to the United States—occured: $16 billion between 1981 and 1982. Oil prices did not improve. In August 1982, Mexico announced to the world that it was bankrupt and could not make the current payments on its foreign debt of $83 billion.

The possible default on the second largest foreign debt in the world was viewed with alarm in international financial circles, especially in the United States. Mexico owed money to 1,400 banks (mostly in the United States), loans which were supported by its oil exports (around 1.5 million barrels a day in 1982). The U.S. government acted rapidly to support the Mexican government and avoid a total collapse of Mexico's economic international position which could have triggered a series of defaults in Latin America. The Federal Reserve and other U.S. agencies provided an emergency loan of $1.9 billion and worked closely with Mexican officials and international financial agencies—mainly the IMF—to renegotiate the Mexican debt. The other side of the coin was the acceptance, by Mexico's new administration (López Portillo's presidential term ended the last day of November 1982 and Miguel de la Madrid assumed office), of an austerity plan negotiated with the IMF and indirectly supported by the United States. The arrangement meant new foreign-exchange controls, devaluation, an abrupt cut in governmental expenditures, and salary controls. As a result, Mexico's economy did not grow at all in 1982 and, in 1983, it shrank by about 5 percent. All observers agreed that Mexico was experiencing its worst economic crisis in a half-century.

One of the results of the policy of economic austerity was a decline of 68 percent in Mexico's imports between 1981 and 1983. This gave Mexico its first favorable balance of trade in many years—$5.5 billion in 1983—but at very heavy social cost. By the end of that year, the average income of Mexicans had shrunk by 25 percent. Mexicans were not the only ones affected: U.S. exports to Mexico dropped by 41 percent, and much more in the border areas. Texan exports to Mexico, for example, were, in 1983, one-tenth of what they were in 1981. Almost three hundred thousand jobs were lost in the United States as a result of the economic crisis suffered by the third-largest buyer of U.S. goods and services in the world.

By 1984, Mexico was exporting about $16 billion worth of oil, gas, and petrochemicals, but not enough agricultural and industrial products to enable it to pay its debt and renew its economic growth. Moreover, in the absence of a commercial treaty with the United States and membership in GATT, Mexican companies able to compete in the international market confronted many obstacles. The U.S. steel and textile industries, for example, resented Mexican competition and asked the government to limit the entry of these and other products. It was a matter of great importance for both countries to overcome this conflict of interests. For economic as well as for security reasons, the United States wanted a relatively healthy and stable society south of the border, and an increase in Mexico's foreign trade was necessary to the achievement of this mutually desirable goal.

During the 1970s, indirect investment—loans—became the most important source of foreign capital for Mexico, but after the 1982 crisis, foreign banks were unwilling to lend Mexico more than what was strictly necessary to overcome the danger of default. This meant that DFI could regain its relative importance in Mexico's foreign economic policy. In 1984, there were almost three thousand U.S. companies in Mexico, but little fresh money was being made available for new investments and the substantial remittances abroad by foreign enterprises were a drain on Mexico's sparse foreign-exchange reserves. That year, when the Mexican government tried to curb a $200-

million trade imbalance in the drug industry, dominated by seventy-five foreign concerns, the U.S. government objected to the way Mexico chose to reach its goal: by requiring pharmaceutical firms to make their products locally while offering no patent protection. Pharmaceuticals became a test case between the Mexican and U.S. approach to the control of DFI. At the end of 1984, this still-unresolved problem was the chief obstacle to the signing of a commercial agreement between the two countries. The pharmaceutical situation was modified and a trade agreement finally signed in April 1985.

While the differences regarding migration, trade, investment, fishing rights, and similar economic matters were at the heart of U.S.–Mexican relations in the mid-1980s, the most dramatic disagreement was of a political nature: the proper policy toward revolutionary change in Central America and the Caribbean. Mexico's economic crisis and the change of government in 1982, when De la Madrid became president, combined to reduce Mexico's political activism in the region. The open and direct diplomacy of López Portillo's administration was replaced by multilateral and less conspicuous diplomacy. The result was the Contadora group, named after the Panamanian island where the representatives of Venezuela, Colombia, Panama, and Mexico met at the beginning to 1983 to promote a negotiated settlement of the area's political problems through nonagression pacts, disarmament, and cutbacks in foreign advisors. Formally, the U.S. government welcomed the efforts of the Contadora group, but in reality it gave then very little support to the plan. The invasion of Grenada by U.S. troops in October 1983, the construction of U.S. military bases in Honduras, and President Reagan's support of counterrevolutionary forces operating in Honduras against the government of Nicaragua placed Mexico and the United States at almost opposite poles of the problems of Central America. Nevertheless, in 1984 the State Department accepted Mexico's offer to mediate direct talks between U.S. and Nicaraguan officials on Mexican soil. The results were not encouraging. A peaceful solution to the Central American crisis seemed to have eluded Latin America.

Some of the issues between Mexico and the United States in 1985 were different than those of the past, but others persisted and their background had not changed very much, at least from the Mexican standpoint. Mexico's position vis-à-vis the United States was still basically defensive: given the enormous difference in the power of the two nations and Mexico's growing dependency on its northern neighbor, it could not have been otherwise. Underlying the serious differences between Mexico and the United States still lay the search for and the defense of sufficient independence to allow Mexican nationalism—nurtured through more than a century-and-a-half of conflict—to survive alongside of the overwhelming presence of the United States.

Bibliography

Alcaraz, Ramón, et al. *Apuntes para la historia de la guerra entre México y los Estados Unidos.* Mexico City: 1848.

Alessio Robles, Vito. *Coahuila y Texas desde la consumación de la independencia hasta el Tratado de Guadalupe Hidalgo.* Mexico City: Robredo, 1945–46.

Almonte, Juan N. *Noticias estadísticas sobre Texas.* México City: Imprenta de Ignacio Cumplido, 1835.

American Assembly. *Mexico and the United States.* Englewood Cliffs. N.J.: Prentice-Hall, 1981.

Bancroft, Hubert H. *History of North Mexican States and Texas.* 2 vols. San Francisco: 1884–1889.

Barker, Eugene Campbell. *Mexico and Texas, 1821–1835.* Dallas: P. L. Turner Co., 1928.

Bauer, Karl Jack. *The Mexican War, 1846–1848.* New York: Macmillan, 1974.

Bazant, Jan. *Historia de la deuda exterior de México, 1823–1946.* Mexico City: El Colegio de México, 1968.

Binkley, William C. *The Expansionist Movement in Texas, 1836–1850.* Berkeley and Los Angeles: University of California Press, 1925.

Bosch García, Carlos. *Historia de las relaciones entre México y los Estados Unidos, 1819–1848.* Mexico City: UNAM, 1961.

————. *Material para la Historia Diplomática de México: México y los Estados Unidos, 1829–1848.* Mexico City: UNAM, 1957.

————. *Problemas diplomáticos del México independiente.* Mexico City: El Colegio de México, Fondo de Cultura Económica, 1947.

Brooks, Philip C. *Diplomacy and the Borderlands: The Adams-Onís Treaty of 1819.* Berkeley and Los Angeles: University of California Press, 1939.

Calderón, Francisco. "La Vida Económica." In *Historia Moderna de México,* edited by Daniel Cosío Villegas. Vol. 3, *La República Restaurada.* Mexico City: Hermes, 1958.

Callahan, James Morton. *American Foreign Policy in Mexican Relations.* New York: Cooper Square Publishers, 1967.

———. *The Diplomatic History of the Southern Confederacy*. Baltimore: Johns Hopkins University Press, 1901.

Calvert, Peter. *The Mexican Revolution, 1910–1914: The Diplomacy of Anglo-American Conflict*. Cambridge: Cambridge University Press, 1968.

Carreño, Alberto Ma. *La diplomacia extraordinaria entre México y Estados Unidos, 1789–1947*. México City: Editorial Jus, 1951.

———. *México y E.U. de América: Apuntaciones para la historia del acrecentamiento territorial de los E.U. a costa de México, desde la época colonial*. Mexico City: Editorial Jus, 1962.

Casasús, Joaquín D. *Demanda, réplica, alegato e informe presentados por el Lic. Joaquín D. Casasús ante el Tribunal de Arbitraje y Sentencia, pronunciada por el mismo tribunal*. Mexico City: E. Gómez de la Puente, 1911.

Castañeda, Carlos E. "Relations of General Scott with Santa Anna." *Hispanic American Historical Review* 29, no. 4 (1949): 455–73.

Castañeda, Jorge. *México y el orden internacional*. Mexico City: El Colegio de México, 1956.

Ceceña, José Luis. *México en la órbita imperial*. Mexico City: El Caballito, 1979.

Centro de Estudios Internacionales. *Continuidad y cambio en la política exterior de México*. Mexico City: El Colegio de México, 1977.

———. *Indocumentados: Mitos y realidades*. Mexico City: El Colegio de México, 1979.

———. *La política exterior de México realidad y perspectivas*. Mexico City: El Colegio de México, 1972.

Chamberlin, Eugene Keith. "Baja California after Walker: The Zerman Enterprise." *Hispanic American Historical Review* 34, no. 2 (1954): 175–89.

Chidsey, Donald Barr. *The War with Mexico*. New York: Crown Publishers, 1968.

Clendenen, Clarence Clemens. *Blood on the Border: The U.S. Army and the Mexican Irregulars*. New York: Macmillan, 1969.

———. *The United States and Pancho Villa: A Study in Unconventional Diplomacy*. Ithaca, N.Y.: Cornell University Press, 1961.

Cline, Howard F. *The United States and Mexico*. Cambridge: Harvard University Press, 1958.

Coerver, Don M., and Linda B. Hall. *Texas and the Mexican Revolution: A Study in State and National Border Policy, 1910–1920*. San Antonio: Trinity University Press, 1984.

Connor, Seymour V., and Odie B. Faulk. *North America Divided: The Mexican War, 1846–1848*. New York: Oxford University Press, 1971.

Cornelius, Wayne A. *Building the Cactus Curtain: Mexican Migration and U.S. Reponse from Wilson to Carter*. Berkeley and Los Angeles: University of California Press, 1980.

Cosío Villegas, Daniel. *Extremos de América*. Mexico City: Fondo de Cultura Económica, 1949.

————. *United States versus Porfirio Díaz*. Lincoln: University of Nebraska Press, 1963.

————, ed. *Historia Moderna de México*. Vol. 3, *El Porfiriato: La Vida Política Exterior*. Mexico City, Hermes, 1963.

Daniels, Josephus. *Shirt-Sleeve Diplomat*. Westport, Conn.: Greenwood Press, 1973.

Davis, Jules. *American Political and Economic Penetration of Mexico, 1877–1920*. New York: Arno Press, 1976.

Erb, Richard D., and Stanley R. Ross, eds. *United States Relations with Mexico: Context and Content*. Washington, D.C.: American Enterprise Institute for Public Policy Research, 1981.

Estrada, Genaro. *La Doctrina de Monroe y el fracaso de una conferencia panamericana en México*. Mexico City: Secretaría de Relaciones Exteriores, 1959.

Fagen, Richard R., and Olga Pellicer, eds. *The Future of Central America: Policy Choices for the U.S. and Mexico*. Stanford, Calif.: Stanford University Press, 1983.

Fajnzylber, Fernando, and Trinidad Martínez Tarragó. *Las empresas Transnacionales: Expansión a nivel mundial y proyección en la industria mexicana*. Mexico City: Fondo de Cultura Económica, 1976.

Fernández Mac Gregor, Genaro. *El Istmo de Tehuantepec y los Estados Unidos*. Mexico City: Elede, 1954.

Filadelfia, S., ed. *Correspondencia que ha mediado entre la legación extraordinaria de México y el Departamento de Estado de los Estados Unidos sobre el paso del Sabina por tropas que mandaba el general Gaines*. 1836.

Filisola, Vicente. *Memorias para la historia de la guerra de Tejas*. Mexico City: Imprenta de Ignacio Cumplido, 1849.

————. *México y la Independencia de Centro America*. In Genero Gardia, ed., *Documentos inéditos o muy raros para la historia de México*. 2d ed. Mexico City: Biblioteca Porrúa, 1974.

Fincher, Ernest Barksdale. *Mexico and the United States: Their Linked Destinies*. New York: Thomas Y Crowell, 1983.

Flaccus, Elmer W. "Commodore David Porter and the Mexican Navy." *Hispanic American Historical Review* 34, no. 3 (1954): 365–73.

Foster, John W. *Trade with Mexico: Correspondence between the Manufacturers Association of the Northwest Chicago and the Hon. John W. Foster, Minister Plenipotentiary of the U.S. to Mexico*. Chicago: 1878.

Fuentes Mares, Jose. *Juárez y los Estados Unidos*. Mexico City: Libro Mex, 1960.

————. "La misión de Mr. Pickett." *Historia Mexicana* 11, no. 4 (April–June 1962): 387–518.

Fuller, John O. *The Movement for the Acquisition of All Mexico*. New York: Da Capo Press, 1969.

Galindo, Ignacio. *Breves apuntes sobre la debatida cuestión de reclamaciones de indemnización a los mexicanos perjudicados por depredaciones de los indios*. Monterrey, Mexico: Tipografía del Comercio, 1875.

Garber, Paul M. *The Gadsden Treaty*. Gloucester, Mass.: Peter Smith, 1959.

Gobierno de México. *Caso Benjamín Weil contra México*. Mexico City: Imprenta del Gobierno Federal, 1877.

————. *Cayo Armas y otras islas Guananeras en los Mares de Campeche y Yucatán: Correspondencia entre los gobiernos de México y los Estados Unidos de América acerca del dominio de dichas Islas*. Mexico City: Imprenta del Gobierno Federal, 1895.

————. *Correspondencia de la Legación Mexicana en Washington durante la Intervención Extranjera, 1860–1868: Colección de documentos para formar la historia de la Intervención*. Mexico City: Imprenta del Gobierno, 1870.

————. *Correspondencia Diplomática relativa a las invasiones del Territorio Mexicano por fuerzas de los Estados Unidos, 1873–1877*. Mexico City: Imprenta de Ignacio Cumplido, 1878.

————. *Informe general de la comisión pesquisidora de la frontera del noroeste al ejecutivo de la Unión en cumplimento del artículo 3 de la ley del 30 de septiembre de 1872*. Mexico City: Imprenta Eco de Ambos Mundos, 1875.

————. *Memoria instructiva de los derechos y justas causas que tiene el gobierno de los Estados Unidos Mexicanos para no reconocer . . . : La subsistencia del privilegio concedido a Don José Garay para abrir una vía de comunicación entre los océanos Atlántico y Pacífico por el Istmo de Tehuantepec*. Mexico City: Rea, 1852.

————. *Opinión del comisionado mexicano M. M. Zamacona en el caso 213 de Samuel S. Dennison contra México, uno de los relativos a la expedición de Zerman*. Mexico City: Comisión de Reclamaciones de México y Estados Unidos de América, n.d.

————. *Plan para la Defensa de los Estados invadidos por los Bárbaros propuestos por la Junta de Representantes creada porla Ley del 24 de abril del presente año*. Mexico City: Imprenta de Ignacio Cumplido, 1849.

————. *Reclamaciones a México por los fondos de California*. Mexico City: Tipografía de El Tiempo, 1902.

————. *Reclamaciones de indemnización por depredaciones de los indios: Dictamen del señor D. Francisco Gómez Palacio*. Mexico City: Imprenta del Gobierno en Palacio, 1872.

————. *Reclamaciones del Gob. de Estados Unidos de América contra México respecto del Fondo Piadoso de las Californias: Documentos principales relativos mexicanos*. Mexico City: Imprenta de Francisco Díaz de León, 1903.

————. *Reclamaciones Internacionales de México y contra México sometidas a arbitraje*. Mexico City: Imprenta de Francisco Díaz de León, 1873.

————. *Report of the Committee of Investigation Sent in 1873 by the Mexican Government to the Frontier of Texas*. New York: 1875.

————. *Sinopsis Histórica de la Comisión Mixta de Reclamaciones entre México y los Estados Unidos de América*. Mexico City: Imprenta Políglota de C. Ramírez Ponce de León, 1876.

————. *Tratados ratificados y convenios ejecutivos celebrados por México*. Mexico City: Senado de la República, 1973–74.

————. *Tratados y Convenciones concluidos y ratificados por la República: Mexicana desde su Independencia hasta el año de 1878*. Mexico City: Edición oficial, Imprenta de G. A. Esteva, 1878.

————. *Ultimas comunicaciones entre el gobierno mexicano y el enviado extraordinario y ministro plenipotenciario nombrado por el de los Estados Unidos sobre la cuestión de Texas y admisión de dicho agente*. Mexico City: Imprenta de Cumplido, 1846.

Gorostiza, Manuel Edouardo de. *Don M. E. de Gorostiza y la questión de Texas*. Mexico City: Porrua, 1971.

Grayson, George W. *The United States and Mexico: Patterns of Influence*. New York: Praeger Publishers, 1984.

Green, Rosario. *El endeudamiento público externo de México: 1940–1973*. Mexico City: El Colegio de México, 1973.

Grieb, Kenneth. *The United States and Huerta*. Lincoln: University of Nebraska Press, 1964.

Gutiérrez Zamora, Renato. *Nuevo aspecto del incidente de Antón Lizardo*. Mexico City: Citlaltepetl, 1967.

Herrera, René, and Mario Ojeda. *La política de México hacia Centro América, 1979–1982*. Mexico City: El Colegio de México, 1983.

Hill, Larry D. *Emissaries to a Revolution: Woodrow Wilson's Executive Agents in Mexico*. Baton Rouge: Louisiana State University Press, 1973.

Iglesias Calderón, Fernando. *El egoismo Norte-americano durante la intervención francesca*. Mexico City: Imprenta Económica, 1905.

————. *Las supuestas traiciones de Juárez: Cesión de territorio, Generalísimo Americano, Antón Lizardo, El Tratado McLane*. Mexico City: Tipográfica Económica, 1907.

Jay, William. *A Review of the Causes and Consequences of the Mexican War*. Boston: Benjamin B. Mussey and Co., 1849.

Jeffrey-Jones, Rhodri, ed. *Eagle against Empire: American Opposition to European Imperialism*. Oix-en-Provence: Université de Provence, 1983.

Jones, Robert V. *Drawing the Mexican Boundary*. New Haven and London: Yale University Press, 1968.

Katz, Friederich. *The Secret War in Mexico: Europe, the United States and Mexican Revolution*. Chicago: University of Chicago Press, 1981.

Kaufman Purcell, Susan, ed. *Mexico–United States Relations*. New York: Academy of Political Science, 1981.

La cuestión de Tehuantepec: Notas del enviado extraordinario y ministro plenipotenciario de la República Mexicana en Washington y algunos artículos que sobre esta materia se han publicado. New York: Impreso por Juan F. Trow, 1852.

Liss, Sheldon B. *Century of Disagreement: The Chamizal Conflict, 1864–1964*. Seattle: University of Washingotn Press, 1967.

MacCorkle, Stuart A. *American Policy of Recognition towards Mexico*. New York: AMS Press, 1933.

Manning, William Ray. *Early Diplomatic Relations between United States & Mexico*. Westport, Conn.: Greenwood Press, 1968.

McBride, Robert H., ed. *Mexico and the United States*. Englewood Cliffs, N.J.: Prentice-Hall, 1981.

McCornack, Richard Blaine. "Los Estados Confederados y México." *Historia Mexicana* 4, no. 3 (February–March 1957): 337–52.

———. "Porfirio Díaz en la frontera texana 1875–1877." *Historia Mexicana* 5, no. 3 (February–March 1958): 337–72.

Mecham, John Lloyd. *A Survey of U.S. Latin American Relations*. Dallas: Houghton Mifflin, 1965.

Message of the President of the United States, with the Correspondence Therewith Communicated between the Secretary of War and Other Officers of the Government on the Subject of the Mexican War. Washington, D.C.: Wendel and Van Benthiusen, Printer, 1848.

Meyer, Lorenzo. *México y los Estados Unidos en el conflicto petrolero, 1917–1942*. Mexico City: El Colegio de México, 1972.

Meyer Michel. *Huerta: A Political Portrait*. Lincoln: University of Nebraska Press, 1977.

Miller, Robert Ryan. *Arms across the Border: U.S. Aid to Juarez during the French Intervention in Mexico*. Philadelphia: American Philosophical Society, 1973.

———. "Matías Romero: Mexican Minister to the United States during the Juárez-Maximilian Era." *Hispanic American Review* 45, no. 2 (1965): 228–45.

Nance, Joseph Milton. *After San Jacinto: The Texas-Mexican Frontier, 1842*. Austin: University of Texas Press, 1963.

———. *Attack and Counterattack: The Texas-Mexican Frontier, 1842*. Austin: University of Texas Press. 1962.

Nicolau d'Olwer, Luis. "Las inversiones extrajeras." In *Historia Moderna de Mexico*. Vol. 2, *El Porfiriato: La Vida Económica*, edited by Daniel Cosío Villegas. Mexico City: Hermes, 1965.

Ojeda, Mario. *Alcances y límites de la política exterior de México*. Mexico City: El Colegio de México, 1976.

Olliff, Jonathan, C. *Reforma Mexico and the U.S.: A Search for Alternatives to Annexation, 1854–1861*. Birmingham: University of Alabama Press, 1981.

Pellicer, Olga, and Esteban Mancilla. *Historia de la Revolución Mexicana, Periodo 1952–1960: El entendimiento con los Estados Unidos y el desarrollo estabilizador*. Mexico City: El Colegio de México, 1978.

Peña Reyes, Antonio de la. *Algunos Documentos sobre el Tratado de Guadalupe y la situación de México durante la invasión*. Mexico City: Secretaría de Relaciones Exteriores, 1930.

Pletcher, D. M. *Rails, Mines and Progress: Seven American Promoters in Mexico, 1867–1911*. Ithaca, N.Y.: Cornell University Press, 1958.

———. *The Awkward Years of American Foreign Relations under Garfield and Arthur*. Columbia: University of Missouri Press, 1962.

————. *The Diplomacy of Annexation: Texas, Oregon and the Mexican War.* Columbia: University of Missouri Press, 1973.

————. "México: Campo de inversiones nortemaericanas, 1867–1880." *Historia Mexicana* 2, no. 4 (April–June 1953): 564–74.

————. "The Building of the Mexican Railways." *Hispanic American Review* 30, no. 1 (1950): 26–62.

————. "The Fall of Silver in Mexico, 1870–1910, and Its Effects on American Investments." *Journal of Economic History* 18 (1958): 33–35.

Poinsett, Joel Roberts. *Notes on Mexico: Made in the Autumn of 1822.* New York: Praeger Publishers, 1969.

Polk, James K. *The Diary of a President, 1845–1849.* New York: Longmans, Green and Co., 1952.

Price, Glen W. *Origins of the War with Mexico: The Polk-Stockton Intrigue.* Austin: University of Texas Press, 1967.

Quirk, Robert E. *An Affair of Honor: Woodrow Wilson and the Occupation of Veracruz.* Louisville: University of Kentucky Press, 1962.

Ramírez, José Fernando. *Memoria: Negociaciones y documentos para servir a la Historia de la Comunicación Inter-Oceánica por el Istmo del Tehuantepec.* Mexico City: Imprenta de Ignacio Cumplido, 1853.

————. *México durante su guerra con los Estados Unidos.* Mexico City: Bouret, 1905.

————. *Reciprocidad comercial entre México y los E.U.,* Mexico City: Oficina Tipográfica de la Secretaría de Fomento, 1890.

Reeves, Jesse Slidell. *American Diplomacy under Tyler and Polk.* Baltimore: John Hopkins University Press, 1907.

Richmond, Douglas W. *Venustiano Carranza's Nationalist Struggle, 1893–1920.* Lincoln: University of Nebraska Press, 1983.

Rippy, J. Fred. *Joel Roberts Poinsett, Versatile American.* Durham: University of North Carolina Press, 1935.

————. *The United States and Mexico.* New York: F. S. Crofts and Co., 1931.

Rittenhouse, Jack. *Disturnell's Treaty Map: The Map That Was Part of the Guadalupe Hidalgo Treaty on Southern Boundaries, 1848.* Sante Fe: Stagecoach Press, 1965.

Rives, George Lockhart. *The U.S. and Mexico, 1821–1848.* New York: Charles Scribner's Sons, 1913.

Roa Bárcena, José Ma. *Recuerdos de la invasión norteamericana, 1846–1848.* Reprint. Mexico City: Porrúa, 1947.

Roenfeldt, David, et al. *Mexico: Petroleum and U.S. Policy Implications for the 1980s.* Santa Monica, Calif.: Rand Corporation, 1980.

Romero, Matías. *Artículos sobre Mexico: Publicados en los Estados Unidos de América en 1891–1892.* Mexico City: Oficina Impresora de Estampillas, 1892.

————. *Mexico and the United States.* New York: G. Putnam, 1898.

————. *Mexico and the United States: A study of Subjects Affecting Their Political, Commerical and Social Relations, Made with a View to Their Promotion.* New York: G. P. Putnam's Sons, 1898.

————. *Report of the Secretary of Finance of the United States of Mexico, Rectifying the Report of the Hon. John Foster.* New York: G. Putnam, 1880.

Rosenzweig, Fernando. "El Comercio Exterior." In *Historia Moderna de México.* Vol. 2, *El Porfiriato: Vida Económica,* edited by Daniel Cosío Villegas. Mexico City: Hermes, 1965.

————. "Las exportaciones mexicanas de 1877 a 1911." *Historia Mexicana* 95, no. 3 (1960): 394–413.

Ross, Stanley R., ed. *Views across the Border: The United States and Mexico.* Albuquerque: University of New Mexico Press, 1978.

Rydjord, John. *Foreign Interest in the Independence of New Spain.* Durham, N.C.: Duke University Press, 1935.

Santa Anna, Antonio López de. *Guerra con Tejas y los Estados Unidos.* In Genaro García, ed., *Documentos inéditos o muy raros para la historia de México.* 2d ed. Mexico City: Biblioteca Porrúa, 1974.

————. *Historia militar y politica, 1810–1874.* In Genero García, ed., *Documentos inéditos o muy raros para la historia de México.* 2d ed. Mexico City: Biblioteca Porrúa, 1974.

————. *Memoria del Corl. Manuel Ma. Giménez, 1798–1878.* In Genaro García, ed., *Documentos inéditos o muy raros para la historia de México.* 2d ed. Mexico City: Biblioteca Porrúa, 1974.

Schmitt, Karl M. *Mexico and the United States, 1821–1973.* 1922. Reprint. New York: John Wiley and Sons, 1974.

Scholes, Walter V. *Mexican Politics during the Juárez Regime, 1855–1872.* Columbia: University of Missouri Press, 1969.

Schoonover, Thomas D. *Dollars over Dominion: The Triumph of Liberalism in Mexican–United States Relations, 1861–1867.* Baton Rouge: Louisiana State University Press, 1978.

Scott, Florence J. *Royal Land Grants North of the Rio Grande, 1777–1821.* Rio Grand City, Texas: La Retama Press, 1969.

Scroggs, William O. *Filibusters and Financiers: The Story of William Walker and His Associates.* New York: Macmillan, 1916.

Secretaría de Fomento. *Dictámenes sobre el Abuso de las Aguas de los Ríos Bravo, Colorado y sus afluentes.* Mexico City: Oficina Tipográfica de la Secretaría de Fomento, 1892.

Secretaría de Relaciones Exteriores. *Correspondencia de la Legación Mexicana en Washington con el Ministerio de Relaciones de la República Mexicana y el Departamento de Estado de los Estados Unidos, sobre la captura, juicio y ejecución de don Maximiliano de Habsburgo.* Mexico City: Imprenta del Gobierno, 1868.

————. *Exposición dirigida al Supremo Gobierno por los Comisionados que firmaron el Tratado de Paz con los Estados Unidos.* Querétaro, Mexico: Imprenta de José M. Lara, 1848.

————. *La labor diplomática de don Ignacio Vallarta como Secretario de Relaciones Exteriores.* Mexico City: Secretaría de Relaciones Exteriores, 1961.

————. *La labor diplomática de Manuel María Zamacona.* Mexico City: Secretaría de Relaciones Exteriores, 1928.

Sepúlveda, Bernardo, et al. *Las empresas transnacionales en México.* Mexico City: El Colegio de México, 1974.

Sepúlveda, César. *Las relaciones diplomáticas entre México y los Estados Unidos en el siglo XX.* Monterrey, Mexico: Universidad de Nuevo León, 1953.

————. "El Chamizal y algunas cuestiones diplomáticas pendiente entre México y los E.U." *Revista de la Facultad de Derecho de México* 11, no. 47 (1962): 487–99.

Smith, Justin H. *The Annexation of Texas.* New York: Barnes and Noble, 1941.

————. *The War with Mexico.* New York: Macmillan Co., 1919.

Smith, Peter H. *Mexico: The Quest for a U.S. Policy.* New York: Foreign Policy Association, 1980.

Smith, Robert F. *The United States and Revolutionary Nationalism in Mexico.* Chicago: University of Chicago Press, 1977.

Teiltelbaum, Louis M. *Woodrow Wilson and the Mexican Revolution.* New York: Exposition Press, 1967.

Tello, Carlos, and Clark Reynolds, eds. *Las relaciones México–Estados Unidos.* Mexico City: Fondo de Cultura Económica, 1981.

Tello, Manuel. *México: Una posición internacional.* Mexico City: Joaquín Mortiz, 1972.

Tornel y Mendivil, José Ma. *Tejas y los E.U. en sus relaciones con la República Mexicana.* Mexico City: Imprenta de Ignacio Cumplido, 1837.

Torres, Blanca. *Historia de la Revolución Mexicana, Periodo 1940–1952: México en la Segunda Guerra Mundial.* Mexico City: El Colegio de México, 1979.

Tyler, Ronnie Curtis. *Santiago Vidaurri and the Southern Confederacy.* Austin: University of Texas Press, 1973.

Ulloa, Berta. *La revolución intervenida: Relaciones diplomáticas entre México y Estados Unidos, 1910–1914.* Mexico City: El Colegio de México, 1976.

Valadés, José C. *Breve historia de la guerra con los E.U.* Mexico City: Editorial Patria, 1947.

Weber, Francis J. "The Pious Fund of the Californias." *Hispanic American Historical Review* 43, no. 1 (1963): 78–94.

Whitaker, Arthur P. *The United States and the Independence of Latin America 1809–1830.* Baltimore: Johns Hopkins University Press, 1941.

Zamacona, Manuel M. *Opinión en el caso de la Compañia Minera "La Abra" contra México, num. 489.* Washington, D.C.: R. Beresford, 1875.

Zorrilla, Luis G. *Historia de las relaciones entre México y los Estados Unidos de América, 1800–1958.* 2 vols. Mexico City: Porrúa, 1977.

Index

Maximilian of Habsburg, 70, 71,
72
Mayo, Henry, 112
Mazatlán, 44
Mazzoli, Romano L., 194
Mesilla: cession 61; valley, 59,
67; territory, 60, 61; Treaty
61, 74
Mexican: army, 40, 41, 52, 65,
96, 101, 105, 139; army reserves, 43, citizens, 48, 159,
186; Columbian plans, 26;
courts, 30, 85; economy, 97,
111, 112, 153, 160, 161, 168,
175, 184, 189, 191, 196; exports 2, 89, *Herald*, 106, 107;
immigration, 90; nationalism,
6, 7; Packing Co., 106; Petroleum Company, 92; repatriation, 58; Telegraph Company
92; territory, 25, 36, 38 46,
48, 51, 52, 61, 62, 67, 68;
trade, 90; tribunals, 38; wetbacks, 167, 170; workers, 3,
97, 99, 141, 153, 145–48,
162, 166, 167, 170, 183, 185,
186, 194
Mexican-American Joint Defense
Commission, 157, 159, 160
Mexican–U.S. War, 2, 4, 38, 52,
69
Mexico: border, 26, 56, 81–82,
98–99, 101–2, 105, 116, 141–
42, 154, 174, 180, 185, 190,
194, 196; border crossing, 56,
81, 82; border troubles, 53–54,
62, 73, 75–78, 80–81, 85;
braceros, 162, 167, 170, 185;
City, 1, 21, 23, 28, 34, 35,
39, 45, 46, 52, 59, 63, 65,
66, 68–70, 78, 83, 85, 98,
108, 129, 131, 137, 145; College of Mining, 21; claims, 56,
57, 61, 74–76; colonization

law, 33, 90; compensation to
U.S. oil companies, 156, 157;
Congress, 46, 49, 76, 79, 81,
83, 102, 111, 118, 123, 124,
133, 147, 181; 1824 Constitution, 21; 1857 Constitution,
63, 64; 1917 Constitution, 17,
118, 119, 128, 129, 132;
debt, 97, 129, 130, 134, 139,
140, 145, 156, 157, 161, 172,
185, 186, 195, 196; devaluation of the peso, 46, 185, 194,
195; duty-free border zone, 76,
82, 87; Empire, 5, 20, 22, 23,
70, 71, 87; Federal Republic,
32, 33; foreign investment, 91,
92, 96, 120, 123, 196; foreign
trade, 144, 160, 162, 168,
170, 173, 174; foreign policy,
166, 176, 177, 179, 183, 184;
independence, 22; invasion, 50,
52, 102; U.S. investments, 5,
73, 74, 85, 87, 90, 92, 97,
101–2, 124, 127, 152, 179,
180, 187–88, 196–97; loans,
165, 188, 195, 196; migration
141, 162; military occupation,
112, 113, 117, 124, 136;
mines, 97, 149, 171; Mining
Code, 90; Mining Law, 92;
nationalization of oil, 147–52;
northern states, 23, 29, 34, 53,
67, 68, 77, 84, 90; oil, 90,
92, 97, 99, 119, 120, 123,
124, 127, 131, 133–36, 139,
140, 143, 160, 165, 186,
190–93, 195, 196; population
33, 97, 186; U.S. recognition,
23, 80, 82, 83, 85; Revolution, 5, 98, 100, 103, 143,
152, 172, 177, 193; Senate,
28; social classes, 96, 141,
167, 183; southern border, 86,
87, 88; "stabilizing develop-